Indigenous Intermediaries

NEW PERSPECTIVES ON EXPLORATION ARCHIVES

Aboriginal History Incorporated

Aboriginal History Inc. is a part of the Australian Centre for Indigenous History, Research School of Social Sciences, The Australian National University, and gratefully acknowledges the support of the School of History and the National Centre for Indigenous Studies, The Australian National University. Aboriginal History Inc. is administered by an Editorial Board which is responsible for all unsigned material. Views and opinions expressed by the author are not necessarily shared by Board members.

Contacting Aboriginal History

All correspondence should be addressed to the Editors, Aboriginal History Inc., ACIH, School of History, RSSS, 9 Fellows Road (Coombs Building), Acton, ANU, 2601, or aboriginal.history@anu.edu.au.

WARNING: Readers are notified that this publication may contain names or images of deceased persons.

Indigenous Intermediaries

NEW PERSPECTIVES ON EXPLORATION ARCHIVES

Edited by Shino Konishi,
Maria Nugent and Tiffany Shellam

Australian
National
University

PRESS

Published by ANU Press and Aboriginal History Inc.
The Australian National University
Acton ACT 2601, Australia
Email: anupress@anu.edu.au
This title is also available online at http://press.anu.edu.au

National Library of Australia Cataloguing-in-Publication entry

Title: Indigenous intermediaries : new perspectives on exploration
                   archives / edited by Shino Konishi,
                   Maria Nugent, Tiffany Shellam.

ISBN: 9781925022766 (paperback) 9781925022773 (ebook)

Subjects: First contact of aboriginal peoples with
                   Westerners--Australia.
                   Aboriginal Australians--Australia.
                   Discoveries in geography.

Other Creators/Contributors:
                   Konishi, Shino, editor.
                   Nugent, Maria, editor.
                   Shellam, Tiffany Sophie Bryden, 1979- editor.

Dewey Number: 994.01

Cover design and layout by ANU Press.

Cover image: Sir Thomas Mitchell, explorer and government surveyor, studying a portrait of Piper, an Aboriginal guide who accompanied him on his third expedition through inland NSW. W.H. Fernyhough, [Album of portraits, mainly of New South Wales officials, c. 1836], PXA 617, Mitchell Library, State Library of New South Wales, published with permission.

Back cover image: W.H. Fernyhough, 'Piper. The Native who accompanied Major Mitchell in His Expedition to the Interior', c. 1836. [Album of portraits, mainly of New South Wales officials, c. 1836], PXA 617, Mitchell Library, State Library of New South Wales, published with permission.

Contents

List of illustrations

List of contributors

Catherine Bishop is a historian at the Australian Catholic University and the University of Sydney. She graduated with an MA ('A Woman Missionary Living Amongst Naked Blacks: Annie Lock, 1876–1943') in 1991 and a PhD ('Commerce Was a Woman: Women in Business in Colonial Sydney and Wellington') in 2012 from The Australian National University. She is the author of *Minding Her Own Business: Colonial Businesswomen in Sydney* (NewSouth, 2015) and has also published articles on Australian mission history, gender and heritage, and women in business, including in *History Australia* and *Law and History Review*.

Len Collard is Professor with the School of Indigenous Studies at the University of Western Australia. He is a Whadjuk Noongar and a Traditional Owner of the Perth Metropolitan area, its surrounding lands, rivers, swamps and ocean, and its culture. He has a background in literature and communications and his research interests are in the area of Aboriginal Studies, including Noongar interpretive histories and Noongar theoretical and practical research models. Len has conducted research funded by the Australian Research Council, the National Trust of Western Australia, the Western Australian Catholic Schools, the Swan River Trust and many other organisations. Len's research has allowed the broadening of the understanding of the many unique characteristics of Australia's Aboriginal people and has contributed enormously to improving the appreciation of Aboriginal culture and heritage of the south-west of Australia. Len's groundbreaking theoretical work has put Noongar cultural research on the local, national and international stages.

Bronwen Douglas was a Fellow and Senior Fellow in Pacific and Asian History at The Australian National University for 16 years and is an Adjunct Associate Professor in 'retirement'. She is a historian of the interplay of race, geography, and practical encounters with people and places in Oceania. Her research interests include the identification of traces of Indigenous agency and the power of place in colonial and elite representations and the use of visual materials and maps as ethnohistorical texts. She is author of *Across the Great Divide* (Harwood Academic Publishers, 1998) and *Science, Voyages, and Encounters in Oceania 1511–1850* (Palgrave Macmillan, 2014). She is co-editor of *Foreign Bodies: Oceania and the Science of Race 1750–1940* (with Chris Ballard, ANU E Press, 2008). Her paper 'Naming Places: Voyagers, Toponyms, and Local Presence in the Fifth Part of the World, 1500–1700' was awarded the prize for the best article published in the *Journal of Historical Geography* in 2014 and is included in *Virtual Special Issue: Celebrating the Journal of Historical Geography at 40*.

Felix Driver is Professor of Human Geography at Royal Holloway, University of London. He has written on the history of geography, exploration and empire, including his book *Geography Militant* (Blackwell, 2001). In recent years he has worked on the visual cultures of exploration and travel. He curated an exhibition, *Hidden Histories of Exploration*, at the Royal Geographical Society. He has also worked on collections in collaboration with major heritage institutions in the United Kingdom, including the Royal Botanic Gardens Kew, the Science Museum and the V&A Museum. He is currently writing a history of the *Geographical Magazine* founded by Michael Huxley in 1935.

John Gascoigne was educated at Sydney, Princeton and Cambridge universities and has taught at the University of New South Wales since 1980, where he is now a Scientia Professor of History. His publications have focused on the impact of the Scientific Revolution and Enlightenment, particularly in relation to exploration of the Pacific. His two most recent books are *Captain Cook: Voyager between worlds* (Continuum, 2007), winner of the Frank Broeze prize of the Australian Association for Maritime History, and *Encountering the Pacific in the age of the Enlightenment* (Cambridge, 2014), winner of the New South Wales Premier's Prize for General History. He is a fellow of the Australian Academy of the Humanities, and in 2016–17 is holder of the Gough Whitlam and Malcolm Fraser Chair of Australian Studies at Harvard University.

Shino Konishi is Senior Lecturer in History and Indigenous Studies at the University of Western Australia. She is the author of *The Aboriginal Male in the Enlightenment World* (Pickering and Chatto, 2012), and a number of essays on cross-cultural encounters between Aboriginal people and European explorers. She is Aboriginal and identifies with the Yawuru people of Broome, Western Australia.

Antje Lübcke is a PhD student in the School of Culture, History and Language in the College of Asia and the Pacific at The Australian National University. She received an MA in 2009 from the University of Otago on the photograph albums of the New Zealand Presbyterian Mission to the New Hebrides.

Her current research is on the visual conception of British New Guinea and, in particular, the ways in which Reverend William G. Lawes and John W. Lindt defined the visual grammar for representing this region of the world through their photography.

Maria Nugent is a Fellow in the Australian Centre for Indigenous History, School of History at The Australian National University. She is the author of *Botany Bay: Where Histories Meet* (Allen & Unwin, 2005) and *Captain Cook was Here* (Cambridge, 2009). She publishes in the fields of memory studies and Indigenous history. In 2015–16, she is Visiting Professor of Australian Studies at the University of Tokyo.

Dave Palmer lives on *Noongar boodjar* (Noongar country) with his family. He is responsible for the Community Development Programme, Murdoch University, in Perth, Western Australia. Most of his research and writing has focused on relationships between Aboriginal and non-Aboriginal Australians in the past and present. He also spends much time in regional and remote parts of Western Australia working with community groups who are seeking cultural solutions to contemporary challenges.

Harriet Parsons is a PhD candidate in the School of Culture and Communication, Melbourne University. Her thesis, 'Collaborative Art Practices on Captain Cook's *Endeavour* Voyage, 1768–1771', re-examines the visual archive of the voyage through the creative processes of its artists, looking particularly at the Polynesian Tupaia who joined the voyage in Tahiti. Her investigation into the art of the *Endeavour* began in research for her Master's degree in 2010 at the Victorian College of the Arts. After graduating in 2012, she began her PhD in art history in 2013. She is currently on exchange to the School of History, Classics and Archaeology at Edinburgh University, which has been made possible by the generous support of her department and faculty and the Alma Hansen and Eugenie la Gerche scholarships.

Tiffany Shellam is Senior Lecturer in History at Deakin University. She publishes on the history of encounters between Aboriginal people and Europeans in the contexts of exploration, early settlement and mission stations in the nineteenth century. Her book *Shaking Hands on the Fringe: Negotiating the Aboriginal world at King George's Sound* was published by UWA Publishing in 2009.

Richard White retired as Associate Professor at the University of Sydney in 2013, where he had taught Australian history and the history of travel and tourism since 1989. His publications include *Inventing Australia*; *The Oxford Book of Australian Travel Writing*; *Cultural History in Australia*; *On Holidays: A History of Getting Away in Australia*; *Symbols of Australia* and *Playing in* *the Bush: recreation and national parks in New South Wales.* He has held an ARC Discovery Grant and a Harold White Fellowship at the National Library of Australia for a project exploring the history of tourism to the past in Australia. Other current research includes work on the history of Australian tourism to Britain and a history of the cooee. He was co-editor of the journal *History Australia* from 2009 to 2013.

Preface

This collection arises from a conference called 'Local Intermediaries in International Exploration', which was held at The Australian National University in July 2013. Over two days we had 30 speakers present their research on intermediaries of different kinds, who acted as guides, informants, and brokers between local people and the Western explorers and travellers who visited foreign lands in Australia, New Guinea, the Pacific, Asia and Africa.

Our interest, as both conference organisers and the editors of this collection, was to gain new insights into the role and perspectives of Aboriginal people who acted as guides and intermediaries in the exploration of Australia. The diversity of geographies, temporalities, and the cultural backgrounds of the intermediaries and explorers alike, combined with the innovative approaches taken by the conference participants, offered myriad viewpoints, and richly informed our own project on Australian Aboriginal history. This collection follows an important thread that weaves through many papers: the question of how to recover the histories of local intermediaries whose experiences and contributions have long been excluded from the histories and even effaced in the original accounts. The chapters in this collection are primarily concerned with questions exploring how we recover these 'hidden histories' from the archives, how we can interpret these fragmentary histories, and how such histories of Indigenous intermediaries can serve new purposes in the present.

We would like to thank all of the participants who generously contributed rich insights to the conference conversation, especially our keynotes speakers, Felix Driver, John Gascoigne, Len Collard and Dave Palmer, who have all contributed chapters to this collection. We also thank the Australian Centre for Indigenous History who hosted the conference, The Australian National University's College of Arts and Social Sciences, which provided financial support, as well as the Australian Research Council, for funding the two projects from which the conference stemmed (DI100100145 and DP110100931). We also thank Allison Cadzow who provided excellent assistance in organising the conference.

For this collection in particular, we thank Rani Kerin, the Aboriginal History Inc. monographs editor, as well as the two manuscript reviewers who provided valuable advice. And finally we are indebted to all of the contributors whose thoughtful and engaging chapters provide wonderful new insights on the history of Indigenous intermediaries and the exploration archive.

1

Exploration archives and indigenous histories: An introduction

Shino Konishi, Maria Nugent and Tiffany Shellam

Since the 1990s, a number of scholars have sought to uncover 'hidden histories' of exploration, as Felix Driver and Lowri Jones have referred to it.[1] Working against a conventional emphasis on the exploits and achievements of the singular heroic explorer, imperial and colonial exploration is recast as a collective enterprise involving a diverse labour force and upon which expeditions were dependent for their progress and success.[2] Various approaches are pursued for writing a more representative history of exploration, such as recuperating from the archives the stories of little- or lesser-known participants; rewriting histories of particular expeditions through the lens of their encounters and interactions with indigenous people; or giving greater prominence to the work of intermediaries of many kinds, including interpreters, brokers, guides, porters and other labourers.[3] The result is a more complex and multivocal account of the practices and politics of European exploration, the social and historical contexts in which it occurred, and the relationships, networks and institutions it created and on which it depended.

---

1   Driver and Jones 2009.
2   Thomas 2014.
3   Kennedy 2013; Maddison 2014.

This book contributes to these reinterpretations of exploration history by turning our attention to the 'indigenous intermediaries', such as professional guides or other labourers who accompanied expeditions.[4] They, as Dane Kennedy has recently argued, 'helped to make expeditions much more complex and culturally hybrid enterprises than conventional accounts suggest'.[5] In taking this focus, we seek to build not only on Kennedy's comparative work on British exploration in Australia and Africa, but also on the earlier histories by Henry Reynolds and Don Baker, among others, which identified the crucial contribution made by Aboriginal people to Australian exploration.[6] But our project goes beyond historical recuperation and belated recognition. We are interested in understanding the historically situated processes and practices of 'mediation', particularly within cross-cultural encounters and exchanges. In this respect, this volume of essays articulates with other contemporary scholarly interest in the go-betweens, brokers, agents, diplomats, negotiators or other intermediaries who operated in diverse imperial and colonial contexts in different parts of the globe and at different points in time.[7]

In their introduction to *The Brokered World: Go-Betweens and Global Intelligence, 1770–1820*, Simon Schaffer, Lissa Roberts, Kapil Raj and James Delbourgo define the 'go-between' as 'not just a passer-by, or a simple agent of cross-cultural diffusion, but someone who articulates relationships between disparate worlds or cultures by being able to translate between them'.[8] They observe that histories of trade and commerce, of international relations and diplomacy, of religious contact and conversion, and of scientific travellers and knowledge production have all contributed to teasing out the crucial role that such intermediaries played in 'making sustained encounter and interaction across different cultures possible throughout history'.[9] In their aim to go beyond Western representations of the 'other' and to investigate interactions between 'mobile figures', they recognise that the 'go-between' is key. Intermediaries of many kinds were, they insist, instrumental in creating new kinds of 'knowledge spaces', even though the vital work of translation and mediation they performed has 'become strangely obscured'.[10]

---

4   A companion volume, Shellam et al. (eds), *Brokers and Boundaries: Colonial Exploration in Indigenous Territory*, is forthcoming.
5   Kennedy 2013: 193.
6   Reynolds 1990; Baker 1998.
7   See: Metcalfe 2005; Schaffer et al. 2009; Ballantyne 2013, 2015; Merrell 1999; White 1991; Murphy 2003; McDonnell 2009; Kennedy 2013.
8   Schaffer et al. 2009: xiv.
9   Schaffer et al. 2009: xi.
10   Schaffer et al. 2009: xv.

This work on 'go-betweens and global intelligence' articulates with other historical studies that are more focused on the part intermediaries played in forging new relationships between indigenous people and newcomers within the borderlands of imperial and colonial frontiers. North American studies have been particularly influential here, notably the work of Richard White (not to be confused with the Australian historian by the same name who co-authored Chapter 3 in this volume) and his now widely applied concept of the 'middle ground', as well as James Merrell's studies on the people and places involved in brokering relations between 'natives and newcomers' on the Pennsylvania frontier from the 1680s to the mid-eighteenth century.[11] White has memorably described the 'middle ground' as both a process and a space where different peoples come together and 'adjust their differences through what amounts to a process of creative, and often expedient, misunderstandings'.[12] These are the 'spaces' where intermediaries are typically found. As Merrell observes, 'wherever and whenever different peoples have met, there one finds a go-between'[13] – or 'go-betweens', plural, because, as White emphasises, the role can be assumed by groups as much as individuals. The focus on intermediaries and the work they do to articulate across different cultures and to forge new communities and alliances has been fruitfully extended into later historical studies of the United States of America. Studies by Michael McDonnell and Lucy Eldersveld Murphy are two notable examples. Each gives particular attention to the role that women played. McDonnell, for instance, identifies women's mobility as key to their work as cultural brokers, while Murphy suggests that Metis women were able to exploit 'overlapping ideals of womanhood common to both Anglos and Native-descended people' as they sought to create new alliances, families and communities.[14]

The North American scholarship is matched by a growing scholarship on southern hemisphere colonies, such as Alida Metcalfe's important study of go-betweens in the colonisation of Brazil in the sixteenth century. Her study examines a diverse range of 'go-betweens' and the different kinds of brokering they performed. She disaggregates the go-between on Brazil's colonial frontiers into three types,[15] but it is her second category, which covers the 'transactional' work of translation, negotiation and cultural brokerage, that is closest to our own interests. Likewise, Tony Ballantyne's recent study of early colonial New Zealand, *Entanglements of Empire*, gives particular attention to processes of cross-cultural translation and knowledge production and exchange. He highlights what he calls 'strategic intimacies' cultivated by male colonial agents with 'elite

---

11   White 2011 [1991]; Merrell 1999. See also Connell Szasz 1994.
12   White 2011: xii.
13   Merrell 1999: 19.
14   McDonnell 2009; Murphy 2003: 142.
15   Metcalf 2005: 9–11.

colonised men' as crucial to the knowledge economy upon which colonial states depended 'as they worked to extend their sovereignty, map colonised terrains, know their subject peoples and consolidate their authority'.[16]

Exploration was a key site of imperial and colonial knowledge production. How indigenous intermediaries engaged in exploration shaped 'the production and circulation of knowledge' is a question that Dane Kennedy explores in the chapter he devotes to them in his *The Last Blank Spaces: Exploring Africa and Australia*.[17] A comparative approach allows him to delineate the knowledge and skills for which local indigenous guides and other labourers were valued in each context. In Australia, a guide's ability to read and navigate terrain was paramount, but less important in African contexts where expeditions followed established roads and trade routes, for instance. He argues that their superior knowledge and skills made Aboriginal guides highly valued by explorers in Australia.[18] But he offers a more circumspect assessment of their value as intermediaries, when he writes that 'the contributions these intermediaries made as cultural brokers usually elicited a more ambivalent response', not least because in the absence of shared language and deep knowledge of cultural practices and protocols explorers were 'rarely certain they were speaking and acting on their behalf'.[19]

Not surprising then, the matter of an intermediary's own identity – and of the nature and politics of their allegiances and alliances – can not be taken as given or fixed. As Felix Driver notes in his chapter in this volume, it is 'apparent that the people explorers often relied most upon for "local knowledge" were strictly speaking neither "local" nor "indigenous"'. The themes of allegiance and identity are also discussed in chapters by Maria Nugent and Tiffany Shellam. Thrown into doubt, then, are questions of who was leading whom. As D. Graham Burnett reveals in his study of Royal Geographical Society expeditions in British Guiana, these expeditions were typically accompanied by large numbers of Amerindian guides, translators, political intermediaries and porters, even though they were rarely mentioned in published accounts. Moreover, it was most likely that rather than accompanying the explorers, the explorers were adjuncts to the regular, seasonal Amerindian journeys.[20]

Important as a focus on intermediaries is for revising histories of imperial and colonial exploration, it is not without its methodological and interpretive challenges. A characteristic of current scholarship is, then, methodological

---

16   Ballantyne 2013: 7.
17   Kennedy 2013: 163.
18   Kennedy 2013: 177–178. For different conclusions drawn from a comparison between expeditions in Australia and the United States of America, see Baker 1995.
19   Kennedy 2013: 164.
20   Burnett 2002.

innovation, aimed at addressing difficulties in detecting, recovering and interpreting the lives, histories and contributions of indigenous intermediaries and other 'marginal' participants whose presence and contribution have been 'strangely obscured'. These challenges are almost universally noted, for most scholars now recognise that indigenous people were not simply overlooked by historians of exploration, but were often deliberately effaced in published explorer accounts.[21] Even when the presence of others was admitted, their contributions to the exploration enterprise and its outcomes would invariably be obscured by their being reduced to 'mere servants' or 'unnamed assistants'.[22] Alternatively, there was little or no acknowledgement of 'native' and 'local' knowledge in the natural histories, geographic studies and cartography produced by Europeans, as John Gascoigne's, Hilary Parsons's and Bronwen Douglas's chapters in this volume all illustrate. Moreover, colonial textual practices typically obscured the fragility of the European explorer and their deep dependence on indigenous intermediaries by depicting the 'natives' as fragile, immature, ignorant, and in need of European civilisation, as Burnett and others have observed.[23] Gascoigne illuminates explorers' reliance on Aboriginal intermediaries – such as Moowattin, Calgood, Bungaree,[24] Bagra and Nanbaree – who assisted in the collection of knowledge about indigenous botany. His chapter reminds us how colonial knowledge – ethnographic, cartographic or botanical information – was generated, being 'co-produced' by explorers and local indigenous people who shared and brokered information.[25] In this way, his work articulates with a much broader scholarship which traces the circuits of imperial intelligence and knowledge production across the eighteenth and nineteenth centuries.[26] Re-reading exploration archives with and alongside indigenous knowledge of country can work to correct such projections and misrepresentations, as the chapter by Len Collard and Dave Palmer demonstrates.

The contributions to this volume share a concern with questions of how to recover and interpret the experiences, histories, biographies and legacies of indigenous people involved in exploration in Australia and further afield using Western/imperial-authored sources and repositories. A number of approaches are canvassed, all engaging in different ways with the limits and possibilities of what Driver refers to in his chapter as 'the archives of exploration'. Aware of the challenges of interpreting indigenous people's presence, agency, autonomy, authority and experience, often in the absence of their own accounts or with

---

21 Driver and Jones 2009.

22 Fritsch 2009.

23 Burnett 2002.

24 Bungaree is the mostly widely used spelling of his name, but it has other variants. Shellam in her chapter in this volume uses an alternative spelling: Boongaree.

25 Schaffer et al. 2009; Clark 2008.

26 Bayly 1996; Schaffer et al. 2009; Roque and Wagner 2011.

only fragmentary evidence to work with, the authors in this collection ask new questions of existing archival materials, suggest new interpretive approaches and present innovative ways to enhance sources so as to generate new stories. All contributors are engaged with the nature and processes of knowledge production, and with the politics of recognition, both past and present, a theme that is at the heart of the chapter by Catherine Bishop and Richard White.

For his chapter, Driver uses examples from a range of imperial and colonial settings, including Nepal and North America, to introduce themes and issues that are explored by other contributors whose studies focus mainly on Australia and Oceania. Driver reminds us that evidence of indigenous intermediaries appears unevenly in the archives, ranging from rich biographical details to little more than shadowy hints. He makes the important point that intermediaries' agency, authority and power are not indexed in any straightforward way to their archival imprint. As always, attention must be given to the contexts and conditions that structure relationships and which contribute to recognition of local people's labour and legacies. Following this is a trio of chapters that focus on Aboriginal guides who contributed to land and maritime exploration in nineteenth-century Australia. The politics and nature of the public recognition accorded to Aboriginal guides is a theme that Bishop and White examine in their contribution. Correcting a common misapprehension that Aboriginal guides received little or no acknowledgement, their study provides a useful typology of notice and reward that Aboriginal guides received. The phenomenon of 'hidden histories' they identify is less a consequence of the practices and prejudices of the explorers at the time than a result of the later habits of settler history-making, particularly the emergence of national history that denied Aboriginal people any part in the story of Australia's 'foundations'. But even here Bishop and White caution against an overly simplistic account of historical invisibility, by showing that while national histories might erase or minimise the contribution of Aboriginal guides to colonial exploration, they remained persistently popular subjects for local commemorations and histories.

Whereas Bishop and White discuss a number of Aboriginal guides, in their respective chapters Maria Nugent and Tiffany Shellam provide detailed studies of one or two. In her chapter, Nugent addresses questions about recognition, reputation and representation through a discussion of one of the most famous Aboriginal guides, Jacky Jacky. The archive is central to her analysis as she considers the ways in which the making of Jacky's testimony about the expedition in which he participated contributed to the construction of his public persona and reputation as the archetypal faithful guide. Shellam provides a study of Boongaree (known more commonly as Bungaree), another well-known Aboriginal guide, and Miago, who each accompanied maritime expeditions in the early nineteenth century. Her focus is on the mediating role they played in brokering relations between expeditions and local people. In a perceptive reading of descriptions of their actions and responses, she prioritises the agency of local intermediaries, recasting exploration encounters in a triangular relationship in which intermediaries were frequently in the middle.

A further collection of chapters moves beyond Australia to focus on Oceania and engage with the issue of the co-production of knowledge and the ways in which 'local' contributions become increasingly invisible over time as texts circulated beyond the places and times of their original production. Positioning local people as active shapers and co-producers in the formulation and recording of knowledge about Oceania is the focus of Douglas's chapter. She highlights the influence of local people in written and visual representations, locating 'textual residues' of indigenous interlocutors in exploration texts. Her methodological approach of searching for indigenous 'countersigns' makes visible indigenous knowledge and agency that was crucial to exploration and otherwise obscured in marginalia, word lists and cartography. Gascoigne's chapter is centrally concerned with epistemologies as he considers the ways in which European science incorporated indigenous people's knowledge acquired through encounters that occurred in the course of maritime exploration in the Pacific, but obscured or disavowed its sources through processes of generalisation and abstraction. In tracing this global history of science, Gascoigne performs a great service because as he charts it he retrieves details of the indigenous intermediaries – the collectors, the pilots, the navigators and others – who were the original if unacknowledged sources for the information on which many maps, collections and taxonomies were based. Parsons's contribution complements Gascoigne's chapter as she takes as her focus some of the maps that he mentions, in particular Tupaia's maps, to explore the collaborative methods by which they were originally produced. Parsons studies these 'texts' within the context of their production, highlighting the creative and collaborative negotiations between indigenous people and British naval men that were involved. Employing an approach to art history that understands drawing as a method of problem-solving rather than as representation, Parsons points us yet again to the collective nature of exploration and to the idea that knowledge was frequently a 'co-production' between expedition leaders and local intermediaries, while also reminding us how easy it is to forget or overlook this as historical interpretations continually fall back on ideas of independent, autonomous and self-realising action and retain a commitment to single authorship and individual authority. In another chapter focused on visual culture, Antje Lübcke examines photography and the role of the camera as a mediator in encounters in British New Guinea in the late nineteenth century. She reads the photographic archive for evidence of local people's agency and recognises their imprint in shaping the visual record through their active participation in composing photographs.

The final chapter in the volume demonstrates an innovative approach to the archives of exploration involving contemporary and creative engagements. Collard and Palmer go beyond the textual colonial archive, utilising a Noongar and non-Noongar history practice in order to place Noongar people at the 'centre' of historical encounters between Aboriginal people and newcomers. Explorers' journals are interpreted by 'talking back' to the 'old people', adopting a Noongar hermeneutic method that is inspired by Collard's Noongar knowledge and the ways in which the 'old people' read the country and interpret the past. This chapter provides a model for engaging in creative and ethical ways with Aboriginal people and communities as collaborators and partners in the research process, and in ways that open up exploration archives to recursive readings. Along with the earlier chapters, it returns us to questions of 'the archive' itself – to histories of the making of collections and institutional repositories of the vast materials of imperial and colonial exploration, as well as to the metaphors we use to describe our approaches to them.[27] As Driver reminds us in his chapter, in the archives of exploration

> there is not so much a hidden layer of meaning waiting to be uncovered through the application of the scholarly equivalent of a trowel than multiple pits and channels to be worked across such materials: indeed, new layers of interpretation and new kinds of evidence (notably oral history or creative practice) may need to be added before they can be made to generate new stories, suggesting a programme of construction as much as archaeology.

The chapters included in this volume might be thought about as just some of the 'multiple pits and channels' currently being worked on across the archives of exploration, and through which new stories are being generated and by which the archives themselves are being expanded, enhanced and reconstructed. With their attention to teasing out the presence, agency and contribution of indigenous people, and to reading the archival imprints and traces of them, all of the chapters contribute in different ways to a broader scholarly project to draw indigenous history and exploration history closer together. This includes continuing to experiment with ways to write new kinds of histories of exploration, ones that do not reproduce the politics of visibility and recognition that characterises the archives of exploration, but that instead make it a central conceptual issue with which to engage.

---

27   Burton 2006; Steedman 2001; Roque and Wagner 2011.

References

Baker, Don 1995, 'Wanderers in Eden: Thomas Mitchell compared with Lewis and Clark', *Aboriginal History* 19(1): 3–20.

——1998, 'Exploring with Aborigines: Thomas Mitchell and his Aboriginal guides', *Aboriginal History* 22: 36–50.

Ballantyne, Tony 2013, 'Strategic intimacies: knowledge and colonization in southern New Zealand', *Journal of New Zealand Studies* NS14: 4–18.

——2015, *Entanglements of Empire: Missionaries, Maori, and the Question of the Body*, Auckland University Press, Auckland.

Bayly, Christopher A. 1996, *Empire and Information: Intelligence Gathering and Social Communication in India, 1780–1870*, Cambridge University Press, Cambridge.

Burnett, D. Graham 2002, '"It is impossible to make a step without the Indians": nineteenth-century geographical exploration and the Amerindians of British Guiana', *Ethnohistory* 49(1): 3–40.

Burton, Antoinette (ed.) 2006, *Archive Stories: Facts, Fictions and the Writing of History*, Duke University Press, Durham, NC.

Clark, Philip A. 2008, *Aboriginal Plant Collectors: Botanists and Australian Aboriginal People in the Nineteenth Century*, Rosenberg Publishing, Dural.

Connell Szasz, Margaret (ed.) 1994, *Between Indian and White Worlds: The Cultural Broker*, University of Oklahoma Press, Norman.

Driver, Felix and Lowri Jones 2009, *Hidden Histories of Exploration: Researching the RGS-IBG Collections*, Royal Holloway, University of London, and Royal Geographical Society (with IBG), London.

Fritsch, Kathrin 2009, '"You have everything confused and mixed up …!" Georg Schweinfurth, knowledge and cartography of Africa in the 19th century', *History in Africa* 36(1): 87–101.

Kennedy, Dane 2013, *The Last Blank Spaces: Exploring Africa and Australia*, Harvard University Press, Cambridge, MA.

Maddison, Ben 2014, *Class and Colonialism in Antarctic Exploration, 1750–1920*, Pickering & Chatto, London.

McDonnell, Michael 2009, '"Il a Epousé une Sauvagesse": Indian and Métis persistence across imperial and national borders', *Moving Subjects: Gender, Mobility and Intimacy in an Age of Global Empire,* Tony Ballantyne and Antoinette Burton (eds), University of Illinois Press, Urbana: 149–171.

Metcalf, Alida C. 2005, *Go-Betweens and the Colonization of Brazil, 1500–1600,* University of Texas Press, Austin.

Merrell, James H. 1999, *Into the American Woods: Negotiators on the Pennsylvania Frontier,* W.W. Norton, New York.

Murphy, Lucy 2003, 'Public mothers: Native American Metis women as Creole mediators in the nineteenth-century Midwest', *Journal of Women's History* 14(4), Winter: 142–166.

Roque, Ricardo and Wagner, Kim (eds) 2011, *Engaging Colonial Knowledge: Reading European Archives in World History,* Palgrave, London.

Schaffer, Simon, Lissa Roberts, Kapil Raj and James Delbourgo (eds) 2009, *The Brokered World: Go-Betweens and Global Intelligence, 1770–1820,* Science History Publications, Sagamore Beach, MA.

Shellam, Tiffany, Maria Nugent, Shino Konishi and Allison Cadzow (eds) (forthcoming), *Brokers and Boundaries: Colonial Exploration in Indigenous Territory,* ANU Press, Canberra.

Steedman, Carolyn 2001, *Dust,* Manchester University Press, Manchester.

Thomas, Martin (ed.) 2014, *Expedition into Empire: Exploratory Journeys and the Making of the Modern World,* Routledge, London.

White, Richard 2011 [1991], *The Middle Ground: Indians, Empires and Republics in the Great Lakes Region, 1650–1850,* Cambridge University Press, Cambridge.

2

Intermediaries and the archive of exploration

Felix Driver

The work of exploration

In 1861, the Schlagintweit brothers published the first of a multi-volume account of their large-scale scientific explorations in India between 1854 and 1858.[1] Dedicated to the Royal Society, the book was co-published in London (by Trübner) and Leipzig (by Brockhaus), an arrangement reflecting the transnational nature of their expedition, which had been sponsored jointly by the East India Company and the King of Prussia. The bulk of the first volume was devoted to reported calculations of latitude and longitude, together with tables of magnetic observations. This was prefaced by, amongst other things, a narrative of the violent death of the youngest brother Adolph (who was beheaded in Kashgar) and an account of the expedition's 'establishment', or staff.

Unusually, the three surviving Schlagintweit brothers took the trouble to name all the key members of what they called their 'establishment', made up of numerous observers, interpreters and collectors, in addition to a constantly changing

1   Schlagintweit 1861. Subsequent quotes come from this volume (pp. 36–42). Of the projected nine volumes of scientific publications, only four were published. The Schlagintweits' expedition was recently the subject of a major exhibition at the Alpine museum in Munich: see Brescius et al. 2015.

retinue of servants. The 'observers' included a Mr (subsequently Lieutenant) Adams, a soldier in the British army; a Muslim named Abdul, appointed as a draughtsman and assistant surveyor in the Madras presidency; a Brahman doctor, Harkishen, who oversaw the work of the plant collectors and undertook surveying work; a so-called Eurasian, Mr Daniel, from Calcutta; Eleazar and Salmonji, so-called 'black Jews' or Jews of mixed race from Bombay, who acted as guides; Ramchand, a Hindu munshi from Peshawar; and Mohammad Hassan, also from Peshawar, fluent in English, Hindustani and Persian. Then there were the 'interpreters', including Mani Singh, described as a 'member of an influential and wealthy family from Johar' in the Kumaon Himalaya, who had previously served the East India Company in an administrative capacity; two of his cousins, Dolpa and Nain Singh, who could read and write Tibetan and who travelled with the Schlagintweits to Ladakh; Mohammad Amin, from Yarkand, who assisted in their expedition to Turkistan, as did Makshut, a Muslim from Delhi; and Cheji, a Lepcha, who interpreted in Sikkim and Bhutan. The 'collectors' meanwhile included long-serving staff such as Mr Monteiro, an Indo-Portuguese zoologist from the Asiatic Society in Calcutta; Dablong, a Bhutia who had travelled with Joseph Hooker in the Himalayas; and Chagi, a Lepcha; Luri, Joha, Khrishna and Mohon Singh, from the Kumaon Himalaya; and a man named as Sukha, from Gwalior. Finally, concerning the personal servants, the Schlagintweits said it was impossible to do with less than eight or 10 at any time, due to what they described as 'the Indian mode of travelling'. Any substantial expedition needed a large workforce 'such as Kalassis (or Laskars), for tent pitching; Bhistis, for fetching water; Ghasvalas, for cutting grass; Saises, for attending to the horses; Chaprassis (or Piuns), for procuring supplies; Chaukedars, for guarding the camp at night; Dhobis, for washing, etc'. Only one of these ordinary servants was actually named – Dhamji, a Parsi, who was employed from start to finish.

The Schlagintweits' roll-call of the names of these key intermediaries amongst their employees is relatively unusual in the literature of exploration during this period. While nineteenth-century exploration narratives often highlighted the role of individual guides and interpreters in enabling European explorers to negotiate unfamiliar landscapes, these were often presented as exceptional or eccentric characters rather than as an integral part of an expedition workforce. In this context, of course, naming was not necessarily acknowledging anything like indigenous agency: to the contrary, it was intended to make transparent the nature of the instruments on which European scientific explorers relied.[2] Like experimenters faithfully describing their apparatus at the start of a laboratory report, the Schlagintweits were presenting for inspection the moral, racial and intellectual characteristics of their employees in the field. At one

---

2   The Schlagintweits' calibration of their 'instruments' was to be much further developed by the British in their training of 'native surveyors' for the Survey of India, including Nain Singh: see Raj 2002.

point they described their camp as a sort of 'ethnographical museum of living specimens', a turn of phrase that was anything but fanciful. Drawing attention to the diverse ethnic and linguistic composition of their establishment was intended to inspire confidence in the reliability of their evidence, dependent as it was on the exploitation of local knowledge and local labour. Furthermore, as became clear in later publications from their expedition, several members of the 'ethnographical museum' contributed their own bodies to the service of science (together with those of hundreds of others) by having plaster casts taken of their hands, heads and feet. Yet it was in their capacity as instruments that these intermediaries were most valued. Like any equipment, they had to be tested, and any weaknesses examined, before an account was given of the data they had collected. As far as the Schlagintweits' readers were concerned, the critical factor was the degree of trustworthiness of the 'native observer', especially when that observer could converse in languages unknown to the explorer, and might travel where the explorer could not.

What the Schlagintweits' account also makes clear is something so obvious, so banal, that it is easy to pass over: scientific exploration was a job of work, and major expeditions required large labour forces. Their three and a half years' work on the subcontinent was devoted to the measurement and collection of just about everything under the sun: places (in the form of latitudes, longitudes and elevations), landscapes (in the form of Humboldtian views and panoramas), natural materials (in the form of rocks, soils, animals, plants, even water itself, sampled and bottled for chemical analysis), physiognomies (in the form of anthropometry), religious artefacts and manuscripts, and so-called 'technical products' (including specimens of textile and paper design from across South Asia).[3] All this cost a great deal of money and effort. By enumerating the extent and characteristics of their labour force, the Schlagintweits were also accounting for their own expenditure, as well as calibrating their instruments. In the process they mapped a division of labour that remained invisible in many other expedition accounts.

The Schlagintweits figure only very marginally in British histories of survey and exploration. Perhaps they achieved little in the way of genuine scientific discovery; perhaps, as has recently been suggested, their nationality was a hindrance to a more generous endorsement. Certainly the death of the celebrated geographer Alexander von Humboldt in 1859 removed their most influential patron, and influential voices in the London geographical community

---

3   On the collections, see Armitage 1992; on the urge to collect, see Finkelstein 2000.

subsequently moved against them.[4] A particularly scathing review of their work was published in the *Athenaeum* in the summer of 1861, singling out the above account of the expedition establishment for stinging criticism: 'there are actually biographical sketches, written in the most matter-of-fact style, of all the observers, interpreters, collectors and servants, filling seven quarto pages'.[5] These were compared, with a racist colonial sneer, to 'the dirty pieces of paper which on our arrival at the Indian ports natives force into our hands, recommending their services as washermen, valets or something worse'. It is difficult to judge what offended the *Athenaeum* reviewer the most: the fact that substantial funds had been provided to Germans who could never really know India, their unembarrassed enthusiasm for data accumulation rather than analysis, or their failure to follow colonial convention in the way the labour of non-Europeans was described. By 'giving the poor natives a character when they have none', in the unceremonious words of this reviewer, the Schlagintweits had shown themselves naïve at best, dupes at worst. Of course it is possible to read this today as an imperial, specifically British, voice railing imperiously against the Germans. But the nub of the issue, I think, is not simply national chauvinism; rather, it lies in the Schlagintweits' presentation of the expedition as a collective project of work, deserving recognition as such. Historians who look for evidence of the labour of locals and intermediaries in the history of exploration and natural history – and many now are doing so – will find much evidence of the contributions of individual headmen, guides, collectors or interpreters, but I can think of few exploration narratives that so systematically delineate the skilled labour requirements of an expedition. Read today, admittedly with a healthy dose of anachronism, it is as if a confession was being made: whisper it quietly, but Europeans were not at all the masters of all they surveyed. Most of the surveying here, it turns out, was done by those others in the Schlagintweits' 'ethnographical museum': Muslims, Hindus, Buddhists, Turks, Jews, Parsi, speakers of Hindustani, Bengali, Gujerati, Maharati, Punjabi, Kashmiri, Persian, Tibetan, Turkish and Portuguese.

Hidden histories of exploration

For historians, understanding exploration as a collective project of work remains a challenge.[6] Much of the literature on the subject, scholarly as well as popular, remains resolutely fixated on the individual explorer, whether as

---

4   Opinion at the Royal Geographical Society (RGS) was particularly sensitive. The Council declined the offer of a dedication of the third Schlagintweit volume (on trans-Himalayan routes and a geographical glossary): Schlagintweit to Murchison, 9 November 1861, Everest to Norton Shaw, 29 November 1861, RGS-IBG archives, Fellows correspondence.

5   *Athenaeum*, 17 August 1861: 216.

6   For a notable recent response to this challenge, see Thomas 2015.

hero or villain, and rarely do we hear about the work done by others. This state of affairs provided the impetus for an exhibition on 'Hidden histories of exploration', which I curated with Lowri Jones in London in 2009.[7] Using the collections of the Royal Geographical Society (RGS) as our base of operations, we wanted to carry out an experiment: was it possible to make the labours of those others more visible, using the very materials stored up by the explorers and their supporters in one of the metropoles of empire?

The exhibition explicitly presented exploration as a form of work, largely the work of non-Europeans, on which the Europeans depended for their lives as well as for their reputations. After all, explorers did not usually find their own way into the bush, across savannah, swamp, ice or sea; they were almost always guided, piloted and portered through the landscape. Who was leader and who was led in this context is a matter for debate. This emphasis on exploration as work reflected a wider conception of exploration knowledge as co-produced. Once you looked for it, we argued, there was plenty of evidence of the contribution of indigenous peoples to the making of new knowledge – including but not confined to maps and mapping, as in the case of the charts brought back by early nineteenth-century Arctic explorers based in part on Inuit testimony and sometimes their drawings.[8] This was presented in one section of the exhibition through the language of 'uneasy partnerships', which was a shorthand way of saying that while explorers and locals worked together, they were not always (in fact rarely) after the same thing.

The notion of bringing 'hidden histories' to the surface, of highlighting and celebrating the labours of 'forgotten heroes' in exploration, undoubtedly had, and still has, a popular appeal. In the process of planning the exhibition, however, it soon became evident that a more nuanced approach was necessary. The opposition between 'the explorer' and 'the local', for example, had its own limitations as a way of capturing the dynamics of human relations in the course of an expedition; indeed, it was a polarity which in some respects could be argued to be a product of colonialism itself. Our initial goal of reversing the terms in which the history of exploration is normally understood, and emphasising the dependence of Europeans on local peoples (for food, shelter, protection, company, information, knowledge), was itself flawed, for it quickly became apparent that the people explorers often relied most upon for 'local knowledge' were strictly speaking neither 'local' nor 'indigenous'. And more often than not, these people were also explorers themselves, like the Africans who led Europeans across the continent or the Amerindians who guided successive expeditions through the river systems of Amazonia. It was in this context that

---

7   Driver and Jones 2009. Exhibition images may be viewed at: www.hiddenhistories.rgs.org.
8   On a celebrated lithograph depicting the work two Netsilik Inuit 'hydrographers', see Driver and Jones 2009: 14–15; Craciun 2013: 183–186.

the figure of the intermediary – or the 'go-between' – seemed to offer a fruitful way of investigating the ways in which knowledge of geography, natural history and ethnography actually gets translated in the process of exploration.[9]

Working across the archives of exploration held at the RGS, it was possible to identify several distinct types of intermediary, including guides and pilots, interpreters, merchants and traders, local rulers and other elites (or those with direct access to them), and individuals regarded as possessing, or capable of acquiring, other kinds of specialist knowledge useful to explorers.[10] What all these different figures had in common, at least in principle, was access to unusual or privileged forms of knowledge and mobility. Drawing up such a typology is only a starting point, of course, and it is clear from this and other work that there is much more work to do on the term 'intermediary'. To take one example, following Tiffany Shellam's painstaking work on the archives of encounter at King George's Sound,[11] we need to think more carefully about the extent to which intermediary figures were valued by explorers and colonists precisely because they mediated between various different indigenous groups as well as between locals and newcomers.

A further issue posed by the very title of the 2009 Hidden Histories exhibition, with its seductive promise of whole realms of historical experience waiting to be uncovered, concerned the relationship between archival visibility and what counts as authoritative historical knowledge. Implicit in the rhetoric of 'hidden histories', a term remarkably prevalent in contemporary heritage practice in the United Kingdom, was the imperative of what might be called rescue archaeology. This suggests that in order to retrieve experiences which have been undervalued, or simply forgotten, all that is necessary is a certain amount of digging beneath the visible surface. At one level, this analogy is innocuous enough: digging, after all, requires physical effort, often teamwork, and to that extent provides a workable metaphor for a shared scholarly endeavour. But in the context of the archive of exploration, indeed the colonial archive as a whole, such a metaphor is problematic. On the one hand, it risks minimising the difficulties in engaging with metropolitan archives in which, as postcolonial scholars have long argued, evidence is constructed in very particular and partial ways.[12] In this perspective, there is not so much a hidden layer of meaning waiting to be uncovered through the application of the scholarly equivalent of a trowel than multiple pits and channels to be worked across such materials; indeed, new layers of interpretation and new kinds of evidence (notably oral history

---

9   On the role of intermediaries in exploration, survey and natural history, see Raj 2006; Schaffer et al. 2009; Jones 2010; Kennedy 2013; Smith 2013.
10   Jones 2010.
11   Shellam 2009.
12   Pandey 2000.

or creative practice) may need to be added before they can be made to generate new stories, suggesting a programme of construction as much as archaeology. On the other hand, easy assumptions about the 'hidden' presence of certain kinds of agency tends to distract attention from the ways in which indigenous presence, as well as the labour of intermediaries, could in some circumstances be all too visible in the archive of exploration.

Like any archive, the collections of the RGS – its books, manuscripts, maps, photographs, artefacts and films – structure the evidence they may yield in certain ways, and it is important to be reflective about that. But this archive does not altogether erase the presence or contribution of locals and intermediaries to the work of exploration, as might be assumed: a more plausible interpretation is that it often makes them *partially visible*. I do not offer this model of 'partial visibility' as a universal principle, equally valid in different settings and for different archives. Rather it is intended as a challenge to researchers to consider ways of deciphering even the most unpromising of materials to release the residue of their meaning beyond that which explorers themselves, and more especially the guardians of the received narratives of exploration, have so often ascribed to them. There are many inspirations for this approach, not least in Australia – I am thinking of the anthropological writings of Greg Dening, the historical narratives of Inga Clendinnen, and the visual re-readings of Bronwen Douglas, to name a few of the more prominent examples.[13] The notion of partial visibility also encourages us to challenge simplistic ways of thinking about colonial texts and colonial image-making, and to consider in particular what happens, or might happen, when such texts and images travel through space and time. In the context of the RGS, for most of its history an institution closely associated with the 'heroic' narrative of exploration, these are important moves to make.

This argument can be briefly illustrated with a single image from the RGS collections (Figure 2.1). Originally captioned 'Capt Noel kinematographing the ascent of Mt Everest from the Chang La', this iconic photograph was reproduced in the official account of the 1922 Everest expedition.[14] It speaks volumes about the heroisation of British mountaineering as another form of adventurous colonial exploration. Here what is celebrated is not only the attempted ascent by a British expedition, but also the technological achievement represented by the specially adapted Newman Sinclair camera, with its zoom lens, fully operational at 23,000 feet. Look closely, however, and you will see something

---

13 Dening 1996; Clendinnen 2003; Douglas 2009. For work which teases out aspects of indigenous history from colonial archives of exploration in Australia, see Nugent 2008; Shellam 2009; Davis 2013; Veth et al. 2008. For examples of related cross-cultural archival work in a variety of other contexts, see Burnett 2002; Fogel-Chance 2002; Govor 2010; Mueggler 2011; Newell 2010.

14 Bruce 1923.

else: a partially visible Sherpa holding up the tripod, one of eight men deputed to carry the equipment all the way up the mountain. The Sherpa is indisputably there, helping to make the image what it is, but strangely enough he is not usually seen: most captions to this much-reproduced photograph have simply ignored his presence entirely. We may also wonder who took the photograph – not Noel himself, I think, though he is usually credited with it. And here there is some telling indirect evidence buried within the RGS archives: a catalogue to a 1923 exhibition of Everest photographs taken by British climbers (held at the Alpine Club to raise funds for the next expedition in 1924) in which this photograph was included.[15] Of the hundreds of exhibits, by Noel and the other British climbers, this was the only one not attributed, an authorial absence that surely speaks volumes. On this occasion, even if Noel set up the shot, it must have been one of the Sherpas who operated the camera.

Figure 2.1 'Captain Noel and kinematograph camera with large telephoto lens established on the Chang La [North Col] at 23,000 feet'.
Unknown photographer, 1922, 8 x 10 cm.
Source: Photographic print, MEE22/0602, RGS-IBG Collections.

---

15 *Catalogue of the exhibition of photographs and paintings from the Mount Everest expedition, January 21 to February 6, 1923*, RGS-IBG Everest Expedition Archives, EE 6/6/3.

In trawling the archive of exploration for evidence of those who made exploration possible but were rarely out of the shadows – the carriers and guides, the interpreters and fixers – we often find these kinds of traces. In such circumstances, instead of making good an erasure, conjuring into presence the lost stories of those silenced by the archive, we have to deal with conditions of *partial visibility*: usually fragmentary and often distorted, these are nonetheless signs of another kind of presence. Several issues then arise: under what conditions were these others recognised by contemporaries? When and how, for example, were these individuals actually named? In what ways was their work and its relationship to the project of exploration presented? By what means might we seek to recognise their contributions to the history of exploration and travel today?

Intermediary lives

In what follows, using selected materials from the RGS collections taken from the period between c. 1850 and 1914, I want to show by example how we might begin to tackle such questions. My first example is the subject of a small pen and ink portrait entitled 'King Freezy' in an album compiled by a naval surgeon named John Linton Palmer (Figure 2.2).[16] The album was compiled in the 1870s, but the portrait was one of several said to be 'sketched in canoes alongside HMS Portland in 1851 when coming alongside Vancouver's Island (Victoria), N. America'.[17] Each of the images of people and their material culture on this page repays detailed study in its own right: the fishing tools, kayaks, hats and adornments, and women playing a dice game (possibly a unique picture of the game known as *smētalé* which was first described 40 years later, when it was remembered rather than played, by the anthropologist Franz Boas).[18] On other pages of this album, Linton Palmer carefully arranged further topographic sketches from his sketch books showing sites and settlement and a burial ground. As documents of First Nations material culture and settlement such materials have a value that goes beyond the antiquarian – similar kinds of materials have figured, for example, in multi-million dollar First Nations land claims.

---

16 This section draws on work in progress on the Linton Palmer albums that forms the basis of a forthcoming publication.
17 The page may be viewed in one of the galleries at: www.hiddenhistories.rgs.org.
18 Maranda 1984: 5–48.

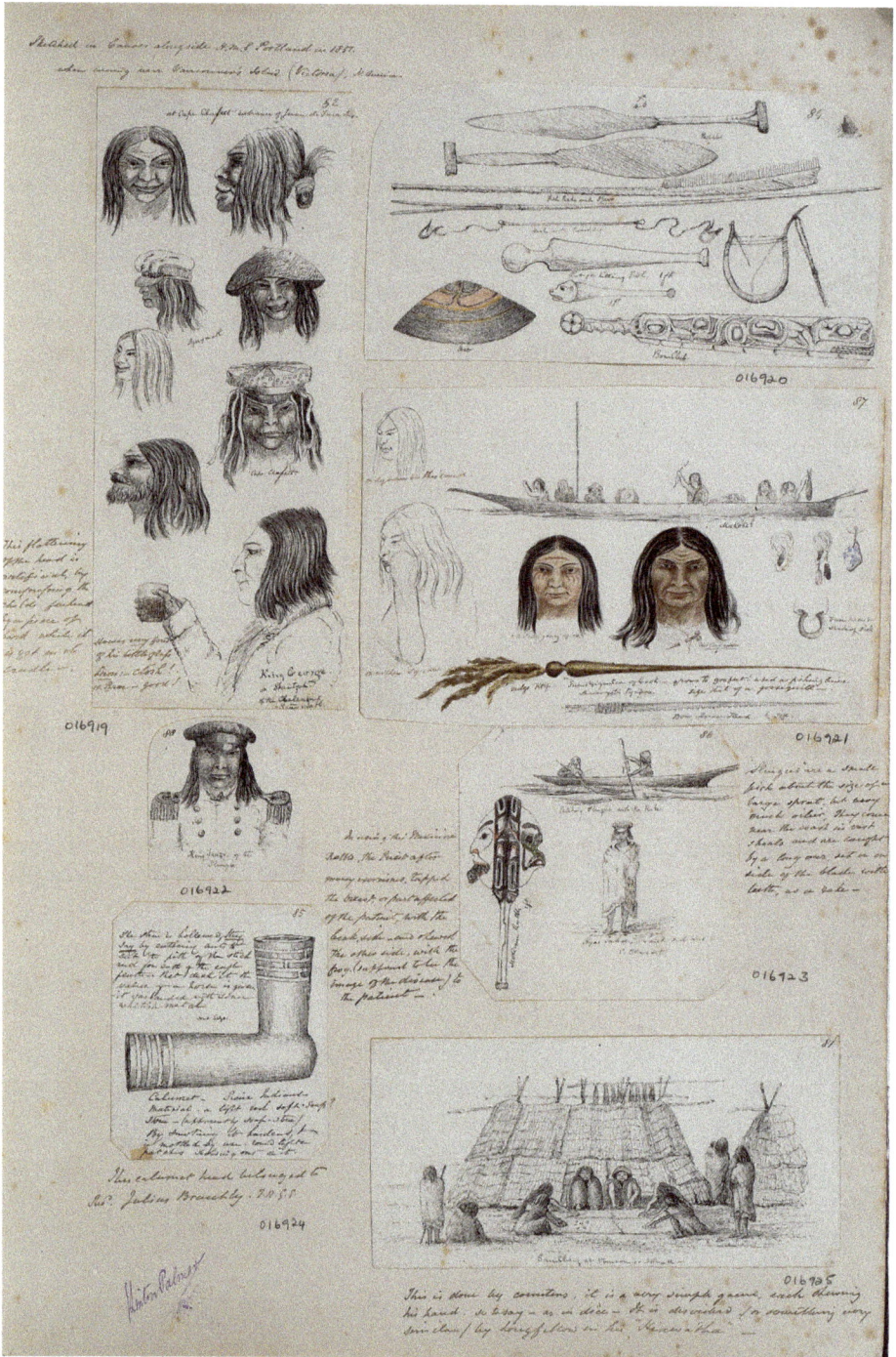

Figure 2.2 'Sketches from Vancouver Island', 1851.

Pencil, pen and ink with watercolour, 52 x 36 cm.

Source: John Linton Palmer, Album no. 4, 'From Chile to the Arctic', F30/4, RGS-IBG Collections.

The making of sketches by naval officers was an integral part of the practice of both naval survey and natural history, and had been at least since the days of Cook and Vancouver.[19] In this context, the sketch 'on the spot' was a memory device, a guardian against fickle memory, designed to record objectively what was seen, often fleetingly. However, in this case the album format presents a further order of memorialisation, re-contextualising the sketch as both a memory object and a form of evidence. In this context, Linton Palmer's albums might be seen as a personal appropriation of the grand atlases of earlier naval expeditions, mapping cultures through their artefacts depicted, as here, as specimens. So a genuinely historical reading of such images requires attention to both the epistemology of the sketch and the cultural meaning of the album. But it also requires something else – an awareness of the circumstances under which the sketches were made, and a knowledge of the key role in these transactions by intermediaries.

Such portraits of people and their material culture required a degree of negotiation and exchange, often in the form of barter. A naval vessel dropping anchor in Esquimalt Bay for little more than a week would allow the officers some opportunity for limited exploration, walking and sketching, a process mediated by interpreters, guides or other local authorities. It is in this context that 'King Freezy' makes his appearance. It is important to make careful note of the date of these sketches – July 1851, just a few years after the establishment of a regular British military presence on the north-west coast, including the construction of a palisaded fort at Victoria. The systematic colonisation of Vancouver Island was yet to come: at this point the island's indigenous population has been estimated as at about 17,000, compared to a few hundred white settlers. The establishment of the fort attracted several groups (including the Songhees, part of the Lekwungen peoples) to move their winter settlements to the north-west shore of the harbour (opposite the fort) in order to trade with the colonists.[20]

In the early 1850s, James Douglas, the chief factor and then governor of Fort Victoria, made the first treaties with the chiefs of a number of local tribes, exchanging blankets for land.[21] One of these chiefs who signed was King Freezy. Except that he was not called by that name in the treaty. The Songhees people themselves knew him as Cheealthluc. Four years earlier, the travelling artist Paul Kane had painted his portrait in oils, part of a series of portraits made on the model of George Catlin's gallery of North American Indian types.[22] A later *carte de visite* photograph (in the Royal BC Museum archives) shows

---

19   Smith 1985; Martins 1999; Greppi 2005.
20   On developments at Fort Victoria and the subsequent history of settler–indigenous relations in this part of Vancouver Island, see Mackie 1997, chapter 11; Lutz 2008, chapter 4; Edmonds 2010, chapter 4.
21   Duff 1969.
22   Keddie 2003; Lister 2010: 276–277; Pratt 2013.

him once again in naval uniform, prompting comparison with the army jacket of Aboriginal intermediary Bungaree recently discussed by Grace Karskens in *Aboriginal History*.[23] Such portraits of Freezy/Cheealthluc bear further examination precisely for their differences, because they provide hints of a different kind of history of image-making, in which indigenous peoples are not simply the subjects of views, but active in the making of their own images, differently in different contexts – as Freezy in naval uniform, as Cheealthluc in indigenous dress. It seems from the surviving evidence that he acted as the key intermediary figure between the Songhees and a variety of newcomers and visitors, including Linton Palmer.

This example highlights how intermediaries could, under some circumstances, become 'characters' in Western eyes, as they were engaged by successive explorers and travellers seeking access to local cultures. The same could be said of some of those employed on larger-scale exploring expeditions in many other parts of the world. Intermediaries such as Bungaree in Australia, Sidi Mubarak Bombay in East Africa or Pedro Caripoco in Amazonia assisted successive generations of explorers, sometimes becoming minor celebrities in the literature of travel and exploration.[24] Yet their work was liable to be presented to the readers of travel narratives in terms of fidelity rather than agency – these were often cast as more-or-less faithful followers and loyal servants, not recognised as initiators of exploration. In rare cases, as with the 'pandit' Nain Singh who was awarded the much-coveted RGS Gold medal for his contribution to the mapping of Tibet, Ladakh and Central Asia (much of it covertly undertaken in territory beyond British control), recognition of exceptional labours could be made. And yet this was a particular kind of agency, more akin to the role of the secret agent than the autonomy we usually associate with the term: Nain Singh, whose first experiences of expedition-making were learned with the Schlagintweits, was by the 1860s, quite literally, a subaltern. The story of the 'pandits' secret missions on behalf of the Survey of India – supposed to have been undertaken with the aid of prayer wheels (in which maps were secreted) and rosaries (whose beads were used to count paces) – was soon incorporated within imperial mythology. The literature of the Great Game has framed and limited the ways in which this story has been told: conceiving exploration as espionage may create a new kind of hero, but it does not pose a challenge to colonial ways of thinking about intermediaries as instruments of British power.[25]

In this context, the figure of the 'native' surveyor in British India might usefully be contrasted with that of the interpreter. (Interestingly, some of the pandits themselves employed interpreters on their travels – even the most celebrated

---

23   Savard 2010: 69–70; Karskens 2011.
24   Driver and Jones 2009.
25   Jones 2010; Raj 2006.

intermediaries sometimes needed their own intermediaries.) Karma Paul, who worked for the British on successive Everest expeditions between 1922 and 1938, provides a good example of the value placed on the role of the interpreter as a go-between. Born in Tibet and raised by missionaries in Darjeeling, Karma Paul – or Palden as he was born – became a master of many languages. His role as a broker between the British climbers and Tibetan authorities was undoubtedly important, and indeed was recorded for posterity in John Noel's 1922 film, *Climbing Mount Everest*, the earliest moving images of Tibet which survive. A key scene in the film shows the interpreter Karma Paul acting as a go-between, quite literally, between the monks of Rongbuk monastery and members of the British expedition team, at the foot of Everest.[26] Noel's intertitles present this moment as a vital rite of passage, with the Head Lama giving his blessing for the planned ascent. At this time, Nepal was closed to the British, and so the Northern route was the only way of reaching the mountain: the agreement of the Tibetan authorities was thus an essential precondition for any future expedition.

But there is more than one way of viewing this scene. On the basis of clues in the footage, including the gift of a bronze statue of a white Tara presented by the Head Lama (which we know was actually presented later) we can surmise that the footage was made after the climbers had returned from the mountain, following a disastrous accident in which eight Sherpas were killed in an avalanche.[27] Karma Paul's prominence in the scene reflects the importance attached to local negotiations, and yet elsewhere here is evidence that his performances also gave rise to suspicion. General Bruce, leader of the expedition, commented in the official expedition report on the ease with which he moved between British and Tibetan modes of behaviour, treating it not simply as a skilled accomplishment but rather as a source of amusement. Yet Karma Paul used the British climbers as much as they used him: by cornering the market as far as interwar British expeditions were concerned, he secured reliable and well-paid employment, and connections which otherwise would not have been available to him. It took decades of struggle and determination for the Sherpa climbers to achieve the same level of recognition.

The contexts in which exploration took place inevitably shaped the kinds of roles available to intermediaries. In some situations, explorers and travellers developed close personal relationships with intermediaries in the field, even to the extent of describing their role in terms of partnership. One compelling example is that of Juan Tepano, who worked as an assistant for the Quaker ethnologist Katherine Routledge during her archaeological fieldwork on Rapa

---

26   The footage may be viewed at: hiddenhistories.rgs.org/index.php/gallery.
27   Driver and Jones 2009: 40–41.

Nui, or Easter Island, in 1914–15.[28] Tepano was a respected and influential figure on the island who had previously served in the Chilean military. Routledge's reliance on him as her key intermediary is clear from the archives of her fieldwork, which survive at the RGS. He provided access to sites and, crucially, to people with stories to tell about the material culture and history of the island, notably his own mother, Victoria Veriamu, probably the oldest woman living on the island at the time. Routledge placed great value on the methods of what would now be called oral history, as a way of making sense of ethnographic materials gathered by previous travellers. She credited Tepano with primary responsibility for the success of the expedition. Interestingly, 20 years later he played a similar role for the Swiss ethnographer Alfred Metraux. As Jo Anne Van Tilburg has argued, Tepano used his role as intermediary to create a niche for himself as the guardian of the cultural history of the island; indeed, she concludes that 'he single-handedly identified, collected, recorded, influenced, shaped and reconstructed the quintessential data all researchers today regard as the ethnography of Rapa Nui'.[29]

Cheealthluc or Freezy, Sidi Mubarak Bombay, Pedro Caripoco, Nain Singh, Karma Paul, Juan Tepano: all intermediaries working in different ways and on very different kinds of expeditions. To their names may be added countless others more familiar in an Australian context, most famously Bungaree, and of course many more unnamed individuals. In most of the cases I have discussed, exploration was closely associated with the extension of colonial and military influence; and in the remainder, the imbalance of power was clearly evident. The role of the intermediary should not be romanticised: go-betweens were vulnerable to criticism for getting too close, or not getting close enough, to those who employed them. The language of partnership in this context is necessarily compromised by the wider inequalities that characterised the colonial era. Yet by working carefully and creatively across the archives of exploration, we can begin to tease out aspects of the history of such relationships which may exceed and even defy colonial definition.

Conclusions

Recovering the historical agency of intermediaries requires new ways of thinking about exploration, involving a wider variety of actors and relationships than have usually been considered. It also requires sensitivity to the politics of language, especially of names and naming, which is an essential part of the

---

28 Van Tilburg 2003: 182–184.
29 Jo Anne Van Tilburg, 'Easter Island's ethnographic triangle', Easter Island Statue Project, 4 May 2009, www.eisp.org/1853/.

story. In this context, the biographical mode in which much 'recovery' work in heritage and museums is done – which seeks to tell the stories of lives previously hidden from history – is a necessary but hardly sufficient step. Indeed, in the context of exploration, there is a risk that turning the spotlight on the agency of intermediaries such as guides, consultants and interpreters simply replaces one kind of hero myth with another.

In this respect, we must tread a fine line between what might be called salvage biography and critical history. To emphasise the vulnerability of European explorers and their reliance upon local knowledge for their survival in unfamiliar environments is also to rescue local guides, interpreters and other go-betweens from what E.P. Thompson once called the condescension of posterity.[30] It may also mean celebrating their contributions as explorers in their own right. Publicity for the 2009 'Hidden Histories of Exploration' exhibition thus suggested that the true heroes of exploration had for too long remained in the shadows. This approach was reinforced by the use in exhibition marketing of Thomas Baines' oil painting entitled *A Malay native from Batavia at Coepang*, produced while he was artist and storekeeper for the North Australian Expedition in 1856.[31] At an early stage in the planning, the exhibition designer Joe Madeira referred to this painting as the 'hero image', a marketing term which refers to the focal point of a brand design, especially in the web environment. He drew from the image an attractive palette of colours which were then reproduced in banners, posters and other media. In this way the heroic mode of popular histories of exploration was wilfully exploited in order to celebrate an alternative pantheon of heroes.

However, while salvage biography has its uses, it also has some key limitations. These came home to me when I was asked on one occasion just how many 'hidden histories' we had found in the course of our research. The question was entirely reasonable so long as you assumed that discrete and readily identifiable life stories were buried in the archive, just waiting to be unearthed and celebrated. In the subject of exploration, the celebratory model of heritage practice finds a field in which the biographical mode is already dominant, and its search for alternative heroes risks reinforcing its privileging of individual agency. Furthermore, as Lowri Jones has shown in her research on Nain Singh and the Pandits, the figure of the heroic Indigene has a longer history than

---

30   The phrase comes from the preface to Thompson's *The Making of the English Working Class*, first published in 1963.

31   Carruthers and Stiebel 2012. Baines' portrait of the unnamed 'Malay native' formed the centrepiece of publicity for the 'Hidden Histories of Exploration' exhibition. Through research on Baines' diaries, he was named as Mohammed Jen Jamain, a local magistrate (Jones 2010; Driver 2013).

might be imagined.[32] During the colonial era certain kinds of local agency were not only recognised but celebrated, indeed mythologised. That is one reason we need to be wary of them today.

An alternative approach would highlight the networks, resources and practices on which exploration depended, and through which intermediaries gained their influence. So we need to consider the spatial infrastructure and logistics of expedition-making; the role of in-between places as well as people, the significance of sites of recruitment, supply and pay-off, such as Zanzibar where porters and supplies for the best-known African expeditions were obtained; Kupang where Thomas Baines and many other travellers refitted their vessels and obtained food and animals for their expeditions; Darjeeling where the British recruited their Sherpas; or ports of call on the Rio Negro beyond Manaus. At these various sites were crystallised sets of historical and geographical relationships involving regional and interregional employment practices, trading networks, political histories, family structures, large-scale migrations, and religious change. It is by considering these intermediary sites – the bases from which expeditions were planned – that a richer and more inclusive history of exploration can emerge.

Acknowledgements

This paper was originally given as a keynote lecture at The Australian National University conference on 'Local Intermediaries in International Exploration', July 2013. I would like to thank the convenors and other participants for their helpful comments. The paper has also benefitted from discussions following public lectures at the Deutscher Alpenverein in Munich and at the Gotha research institute of the University of Erfurt.

References

Armitage, Geoff 1992, 'The Schlagintweit collections', *Earth Sciences History* 11: 2–8.

Brescius, Moritz von, Friederike Kaiser and Stephanie Kleidt (eds) 2015, *Über den Himalaja: Die Expedition der Brüder Schlagintweit nach Indien und Zentralasien 1854 bis 1858*, Böhlau-Verlag, Cologne.

Bruce, Charles 1923, *The Assault on Mount Everest*, Arnold, London.

---

32   Jones 2010, chapter 2.

Burnett, D. Graham 2002, '"It is impossible to make a step without the Indians": nineteenth-century geographical exploration and the Amerindians of British Guiana', *Ethnohistory* 49(1): 3–40.

Carruthers, Jane and Lindy Stiebel (eds) 2012, *Thomas Baines: Exploring Tropical Australia, 1855 to 1857*, National Museum of Australia, Canberra.

Clendinnen, Inga 2003, *Dancing With Strangers: The True History of the Meeting of the British First Fleet and the Aboriginal Australians*, 1788, Text Publishing, Melbourne.

Craciun, Adriana 2013, 'Oceanic voyages, maritime books and eccentric inscriptions', *Atlantic Studies* 10: 170–196.

Davis, Michael 2013, 'Encountering Aboriginal knowledge: explorer narratives on north-east Queensland, 1770 to 1820', *Aboriginal History* 37: 29–50.

Dening, Greg 1996, *Performances*, University of Chicago Press, Chicago.

Douglas, Bronwen 2009, 'Art as ethno-historical text: science, representation and indigenous presence in eighteenth and nineteenth-century oceanic voyage literature', in *Double Vision: Art Histories and Colonial Histories in the Pacific*, Nicholas Thomas and Dianne Losche (eds), Cambridge University Press, Cambridge, 65–99.

Driver, Felix 2013, 'Hidden histories made visible? Reflections on a geographical exhibition', *Transactions, Institute of British Geographers* 38: 420–435.

Driver, Felix and Lowri Jones 2009, *Hidden Histories of Exploration: Researching Geographical Collections*, Royal Holloway, University of London, and Royal Geographical Society (with IBG), London.

Duff, Wilson 1969, 'The Fort Victoria treaties', *BC Studies* 3: 3–57.

Edmonds, Penelope 2010, *Urbanising Frontiers: Indigenous Peoples and Settlers in Nineteenth-Century Pacific Rim Cities*, University of British Columbia Press, Vancouver.

Finkelstein, Gabriel 2000, 'Conquerors of the Künlün? The Schlagintweit mission to High Asia, 1854–57', *History of Science* 38: 179–218.

Fogel-Chance, Nancy 2002, 'Fixing history: a contemporary examination of an Arctic journal from the 1850s', *Ethnohistory* 49: 789–819.

Govor, Elena 2010, *Twelve Days at Nuku Hiva: Russian Encounters and Mutiny in the South Pacific*, University of Hawai'i Press, Honolulu.

Greppi, Claudio 2005, 'On the spot: traveling artists and the iconographic inventory of the world', in *Tropical Visions in an Age of Empire*, Felix Driver and Luciana Martins (eds), University of Chicago Press, Chicago, 23–42.

Jones, Lowri M. 2010, 'Local Knowledge and Indigenous Agency in the History of Exploration: Studies from the RGS-IBG Collections', PhD thesis, Royal Holloway, University of London.

Karskens, Grace 2011, 'Red coat, blue jacket, black skin: Aboriginal men and clothing in early New South Wales', *Aboriginal History* 35: 1–36.

Keddie, Grant 2003, *Songhees Pictorial: A History of the Songhees People as Seen by Outsiders, 1790–1912,* Royal BC Museum, Victoria.

Kennedy, Dane 2013, *The Last Blank Spaces: Exploring Africa and Australia*, Harvard University Press, Boston, MA.

Lister, Kenneth 2010, *Paul Kane, the Artist: Wilderness to Studio*, Royal Ontario Museum, Toronto.

Lutz, John S. 2008, *Makúk: A New History of Aboriginal-White Relations*, University of British Columbia Press, Vancouver.

Mackie, Richard 1997, *Trading Beyond the Mountains: The British Fur Trade on the Pacific 1793–1843,* University of British Columbia Press, Vancouver.

Maranda, Lynn 1984, *Coast Salish Gambling Games*, Canadian Ethnology Service, National Museums of Canada, Ottawa.

Martins, Luciana 1999, 'Mapping tropical waters: British views and visions of Rio de Janeiro', in *Mappings*, Denis Cosgrove (ed.), Reaktion, London, 148–168.

Mueggler, Erik 2011, *The Paper Road: Archive and Experience in the Botanical Exploration of West China and Tibet*, University of California Press, Berkeley.

Newell, Jennifer 2010, *Trading Nature: Tahitians, Europeans and Ecological Exchange*, University of Hawai'i Press, Honolulu.

Nugent, Maria 2008, '"To try to form some connections with the natives": encounters between Captain Cook and Indigenous people at Botany Bay in 1770', *History Compass* 6: 468–487.

Pandey, Gyanendra 2000, 'Voices from the edge: the struggle to write subaltern histories', in *Mapping Subaltern Studies and the Postcolonial*, Vinayak Chaturvedi (ed.), Verso, London, 281–299.

Pratt, Stephanie 2013, 'Integrating the "Indian": the Indigenous American collections of George Catlin and Paul Kane', in *World Art and the Legacies of Colonial Violence*, Daniel Rycroft (ed.), Ashgate, Farnham, UK: 59–82.

Raj, Kapil 2002, 'When human travellers became instruments: the Indo-British exploration of central Asia in the nineteenth century', in *Instruments, Travel and Science: Itineraries of Precision from the Seventeenth to the Twentieth Century*, Marie-Noelle Bourguet, Christian Licoppe and H. Otto Sibum (eds), Routledge, London, 156–188.

——2006, *Relocating Modern Science: Circulation and the Construction of Scientific Knowledge in South Asia and Europe*, Permanent Black, Delhi.

Savard, Dan 2010, *Images from the Likeness House*, Royal BC Museum, Victoria.

Schaffer, Simon, Lissa Roberts, Kapil Raj and James Delbourgo (eds) 2009, *The Brokered World: Go-Betweens and Global Intelligence, 1770–1820*, Science History Publications, Sagamore Beach, MA.

Schlagintweit, Hermann, Adolphe and Robert 1861, *Results of a Scientific Mission to India and High Asia, Undertaken Between the Years 1854 and 1858 By Order of the Court of Directors of the Honorable East India Company, Volume 1: Astronomical Determinations of Latitudes and Longitudes and Magnetic Observations ... preceded by General Introductory Remarks*, Brockhaus, Leipzig, and Trubner, London.

Shellam, Tiffany 2009, *Shaking Hands on the Fringe: Negotiating the Aboriginal World at King George's Sound*, University of Western Australia Press, Crawley.

Smith, Bernard 1985, *European Vision and the South Pacific*, second edition, Yale University Press, New Haven.

Smith, Vanessa 2013, 'Joseph Banks's intermediaries: rethinking global cultural exchange', in *Global Intellectual History*, Samuel Moyn and Andrew Sartori (eds), Columbia University Press, New York, 81–109.

Thomas, Martin (ed.) 2015, *Expedition into Empire: Exploratory Journeys and the Making of the Modern World*, Routledge, New York.

Van Tilburg, Jo Anne 2003, *Among Stone Giants: The Life of Katherine Routledge and Her Remarkable Expedition to Easter Island*, Scribner, New York.

Veth, Peter, Peter Sutton and Margo Neale (eds) 2008, *Strangers on the Shore: Early Coastal Contacts in Australia*, National Museum of Australia Press, Canberra.

3

Explorer memory and Aboriginal celebrity

Catherine Bishop and Richard White

In the nineteenth century, those men that the British world dubbed explorers – always men – were celebrities. The designated leaders of expeditions were distinguished from other members of their parties: they wrote the journals, won the accolades, obtained the honours and had their portraits done, while those who accompanied them generally faded into obscurity. Expeditions were recorded in popular culture by the names of their leaders. We still remember Mitchell, Leichhardt and Sturt, but seldom those who accompanied them, whether European or Indigenous. Aboriginal communities remember those expeditions and the Indigenous people who accompanied them differently,[1] but this chapter is concerned with historical memory and popular celebrity in a white Australian context. The myth of the lone explorer has been debunked in late twentieth-century scholarship, with a range of historians describing the infrastructure and personnel, including Indigenous participants, that underpinned most expeditions.[2] Other studies have begun to focus on the women who accompanied various expeditions, and recently the details of the convict who guided Blaxland, Wentworth and Lawson over the Blue Mountains in 1813 have been retrieved.[3] As other chapters in this volume show, the sources for such

---

1   See Fred Cahir's chapter in Clarke and Cahir 2013.
2   See Reynolds 1990; Driver 2013; Kennedy 2013, esp. chapter 8.
3   Cadzow 2002; Yeats 2013.

studies are often sparse. Our particular concern in this chapter, by contrast, is those Indigenous guides who – despite the prevalence of the myth of the lone explorer – *were* acknowledged and even celebrated for their contribution to Australian exploration, and who are also reasonably well documented within the archives of exploration.

Throughout the nineteenth and into the twentieth century, Indigenous people accompanied European explorers in Australia. Usually but not always men, they were guides, interpreters, negotiators, collectors, hunters, providores, cooks, servants and stockmen, their multiplicity of roles similar to that of other members of the expedition, whether European or Indigenous. For convenience we use the terms 'companion' and 'guide' throughout this chapter, although, as at least one companion suggested, 'explorer', which we use for leaders of expeditions, might well be a more appropriate appellation for many of these Indigenous men. Don Baker usefully categorised Thomas Mitchell's Aboriginal companions into four groups. There were the hired help, who were independent contractors familiar with European society, essentially simply providing labour. There were those he termed 'passers on', who often had no English. These were locals met with along the way; they simply wanted to ensure the expedition passed on with as little disruption to their territory and lives as possible. A third group, camp followers, often women or young boys, attached themselves to the expedition without payment and with varying degrees of perceived usefulness.[4] Most highly valued were the professionals, who were seen as particularly skilled and were taken on for the entirety of the expedition. Recent scholarship has argued that, given the use made of their knowledge, the contribution of these Indigenous companions deserves more recognition: their particular role in ensuring the success and often the very survival of an expedition has been generally underestimated.[5]

Underestimated they may have been, but they were not entirely ignored. Given the logic of imperialism and the racial politics of the exploration era, the surprise is that, while white expedition leaders were the focus of adulation, a surprising number of Indigenous participants became quite well known and were, at different times, minor celebrities.[6] Those that Baker called 'professionals' were most likely to be individually recognised and memorialised in some form. It is remarkable how many there were and how sections of European society were willing to acknowledge them, both at the time and since. Where this recognition

---

4   Baker 1998.
5   Blyton 2012; Reynolds 1990; Host and Milroy 2001; Cahir 2010: 22.
6   See Kennedy 2013; and Driver 2013, who particularly notes that different types of indigenous assistance were accorded different levels of acknowledgement.

has been noticed in the scholarship, it has often been characterised as simply patronising, grudging and/or unavoidable. This chapter seeks to probe further the nature of that recognition.

The celebration of explorers in the nineteenth and into the twentieth century was contingent upon a particular intersection of class, gender and race. Explorers were respectable, white men and exploration was often a means of social advancement for them. Leading an expedition gave men a status that marked them apart. Thus expedition parties were constructed to varying degrees upon master–servant lines – and this extended to their fellow Europeans. Edward Eyre, for example, referred to his European companion John Baxter as a 'faithful follower', using similar language to that which he used to describe his Aboriginal companion Wylie. This was also almost by definition a masculine world, and female participants were barely acknowledged at the time and even less remembered by posterity. Turendurey, guide and negotiator for Thomas Mitchell, was one of the few, and she was not much celebrated.[7] Nevertheless, while in the popular imagination the explorer was a white male, that same popular imagination singled out particular Indigenous individuals for attention throughout the nineteenth century. Men such as Jackey Jackey, Wylie, Yuranigh, Mokare and Tommy Windich acquired some fame in their lifetime and have been celebrated in various ways since. Often, as we will see, these were men whose relationship with the expedition leader was long-standing.

In the lifecycle of celebrity, there are four periods to consider. First there is the recognition received on the completion of an expedition, in the celebrations that followed and on publication of the journal. A second moment of recognition occurs upon the guide's death, when obituaries and memorials might appear. In both of these forms of acknowledgement, the expedition's leader was usually instrumental. The third and fourth phases in the cycle reflect a broader politics of social memory. The third is the period of Stanner's 'great Australian silence', when Aboriginal Australians were generally – though not altogether – written out of history.[8] Stanner dates this from around the 1930s, although other historians find its origins in the closing decades of the nineteenth century.[9] It is in this period that guides were most likely to be forgotten, and yet during a number of local expedition centenaries they were acknowledged in various ways. Finally, there is the period since the 1960s, when white Australia began to discover a black history.

---

7   Even the few white female explorers went unheralded: the diary of Emily Caroline Creaghe, who accompanied her husband and Ernest Favenc in the late nineteenth century, remained practically unnoticed in the Mitchell Library until the end of the twentieth century.

8   Stanner 1969.

9   Henry Reynolds dates the silence from the late nineteenth century, as white explorers became the heroes of Australian history, the 'discoverers' of Australia. Reynolds 2000: 18–20.

At the end of an expedition

At the end of a successful expedition, there was generally a round of dinners and public occasions, when speeches were made, leaders were feted and exploring parties made much of. Explorers wrote up and published their journals, not only to record their achievements and to ensure and manage their public reputation, but also to make money. In the immediate aftermath of an expedition, the questions of who was recognised and for what were crucial because it could set the pattern for posterity. The focus was inevitably on the formal leader, but in their distribution of honours and credit, expedition leaders could not only acknowledge Indigenous participants but single them out for attention.

Naming places

One of the presumptions of European explorers was that they felt at liberty to name the natural features of the country through which they travelled. Some attempted to find out the local Indigenous names, regarding this as a more 'scientific' approach, but most took the opportunity to use the names of patrons, friends – or themselves.[10] As Nigel Parbury says, credit for discovery was always attributed to the white men.[11] Nevertheless the names given to places included those of both Indigenous and European expedition members, suggesting that the expedition leaders recognised something of a collaborative effort. In 1807 George Caley named Moowattin River after his Indigenous companion, Daniel Moowattin, who 'discovered' the Appin Falls. It appeared as the Moowattin River in the atlas accompanying Matthew Flinders' *Voyage to Terra Australis* in 1814, but was later renamed the Cataract River.[12] In 1846 Thomas Mitchell named Yuranigh's Ponds in honour of one his guides, although perhaps in this case it was somewhat tongue in cheek, as Yuranigh had objected to sitting close to that stretch of water because of the danger of attack by 'wild natives'.[13] In 1874 John Forrest named Windich and Pierre Springs, along the present day Canning Stock Route, in recognition of two of his Aboriginal companions. Windich Springs was an especially important find, 'a fine permanent spring', which Forrest characterised as 'the best springs I have ever seen'. According to one report, Tommy Pierre was the first to find 'his' spring, although this is not confirmed in Forrest's journal.[14] The Jardine brothers overlanding in Queensland named a welcome watercourse Eulah Creek after 'the most trusty' of their 'black boys', 'old Eulah', who found it for them in 1865.[15] Even Christie Palmerston, who is

---

10   Carter 1987.
11   Parbury 1986.
12   Smith 2005.
13   Mitchell 1848: 327 (25 September 1846).
14   *South Australian Register*, 7 November 1874: 2S; Forrest 1875, chapter 5: 28 May 1874.
15   Sharp 1992: 69; Jardine 1867, chapter 1.

remembered in some circles as 'prone to giving local Aborigines "a taste of the rifle"', named Pompo Falls in the Great Dividing Range after his 'blackboy'.[16] Given the central importance of water in Australian exploration, these namings were meaningful.

Journals

Explorers' journals are the primary surviving evidence for the roles of Indigenous guides. The mere fact that they are littered with the names of the Aboriginal men, who were finding water, hunting food, scouting new territory and negotiating with new people, shows that their role was not ignored by the journal writers. The writers could make negative comments – and when they were displeased tended to depict their Aboriginal companions as errant children, in keeping with contemporary tropes – but they also explicitly appreciated the skills they brought to the expedition. Dane Kennedy has suggested that this recognition was reluctant because admitting the contribution of Indigenous guides to the navigation and survival of the expedition potentially undermined the achievement of the European explorers themselves, particularly in a milieu in which the explorer was popularly conceived as a lone hero.[17] However, the fact that these positive and even respectful remarks survived in the published version of the journals suggests that several expedition leaders willingly and publicly articulated not only their appreciation for but their reliance on the skills of the Aboriginal members of their party.

A number of guides received specific tributes in the published journals. Mitchell acknowledged John Piper as 'the most accomplished man in the camp' because of his bush skills and ability to communicate with and elicit information from other Aboriginal people encountered by the expedition.[18] He described Yuranigh as his 'guide, companion, councillor and friend'.[19] In 1841 Eyre was less confident about the loyalty and effectiveness of Wylie after the two other Indigenous guides on the expedition killed the only other white man, overseer John Baxter. Eyre wrote 'I was now deprived of my only aid ... left alone with a single native whose fidelity I could place no dependence on'. But in the end Eyre acknowledged Wylie's 'fidelity and good conduct'.[20] It was in Eyre's published journal that the image of himself and Wylie as 'the two sole wanderers'[21] became the public face of the expedition. Long after Eyre left Australia he apparently maintained contact with Wylie.[22]

---

16   *The Queenslander*, 22 January 1881: 109; Pannell 2008: 61.
17   Kennedy 2013: 163.
18   Baker 1998: 44–45.
19   Mitchell 1848: 414, quoted in Baker 1998: 46.
20   *The Sydney Herald*, 30 August 1841: 2S; Eyre 1845: 7 July 1841.
21   Eyre 1845: 7 July 1841.
22   Dutton 1977.

Speeches, parades and dinners

At the celebratory dinners that followed successful expeditions undertaken in the second half of the nineteenth century, speakers often acknowledged the contribution of Aboriginal guides. Sometimes Aboriginal guides were present at these quintessentially European occasions. In 1874, at a 'complimentary banquet' following Major Peter Warburton's explorations in the north of Western Australia, the two guests of honour were Warburton and his Aboriginal guide 'Charley'. Warburton spoke highly of his companions, including two Afghan cameleers, but reserved 'especial praise' for Charley, to whom, Warburton said, 'the lives of the whole party were due'.[23] Charley's presence might be seen as merely providing an entertaining backdrop, but it also suggests a genuine acknowledgement of a sense of gratitude. In the same year, dinners for the Forrest brothers following their expeditions included Tommy Windich and Tommy Pierre, although the press reported that Windich seemed uncomfortable.[24] At one public banquet, the colonial secretary praised Forrest's 'friend Windich' as 'the man who had brought Mr. Forrest to Adelaide, and not Mr. Forrest him'.[25] Pierre, on the other hand, seemed quite at ease and spoke himself at the celebrations in Fremantle. His words were recorded by the papers, albeit in somewhat patronising tones. Though the inclusion of Windich and Pierre at the dinner appeared equitable, distinctions were made in other public celebrations. In the street parade in Perth 'the aborigines, [were] riding on horses, gaily caparisoned, immediately behind the carriage containing Mr Forrest and the European members of his party'.[26] The visual impact of this image is significant, underpinning their separateness and subordination, although perhaps also rendering them more visible and emphasising their role as bushmen. In contrast, in the Adelaide parade, the entire party was on horseback, and it is possible that the expedition leaders preferred to be seen that way, as men of action. The dinners and parades show a wider public were prepared to give at least some recognition to the role played by Indigenous guides.

Rewards

The material rewards bestowed on these guides were meagre and it is here perhaps that the lack of appropriate recognition is most stark. Given their roles, in which they were often responsible for the survival of their companions, they certainly benefitted less than other members of expeditions. In the hierarchies of the day there was no possibility that a reward to an Aboriginal worker might be commensurate with the value of the service provided.

---

23 *South Australian Advertiser*, 23 April 1874: 5.
24 *The Inquirer & Commercial News*, 16 December 1874: 3.
25 Cited in Kennedy 2013:191.
26 *Western Australian Times*, 15 December 1874: 3.

At the end of Leichhardt's 1845 expedition, the colonial secretary distributed £1,000 among its members: Leichhardt received £600; his adult European companions £125; a 16-year-old boy £70; a convict (who also received a government pension) £30; and Harry Brown and Charley Fisher, the Aboriginal guides, £25 each, the last deposited in a savings bank and drawn out only with the bank's approval.[27] The distribution was determined not by Leichhardt himself but by the governor, who followed military conventions,[28] perhaps underscoring the way in which expeditions were conceived as hierarchical pseudo-military enterprises by authorities, or perhaps merely reflecting a lack of imagination about alternative models of reward distribution. John Piper agreed to accompany Mitchell on his third expedition in exchange for being clothed, fed and given a horse.[29] When Mitchell's fourth expedition returned to Sydney, Yuranigh received a 'small gratuity'.[30] At the end of the Eyre expedition, Wylie received a weekly government ration of flour and meat as well as £2 and a medal from the Agricultural Society of Perth. He was also appointed a constable of Albany.[31] Tommy Windich also became a police tracker and constable, and at the time of his death was working on the overland telegraph, positions he probably acquired because of his expedition experience, although they scarcely rank as rewards.

The presentation of breastplates to local Aboriginal 'kings' is well documented and was well understood at the time, as is indicated by the reaction of John Piper.[32] When Mitchell rewarded Piper with a breastplate, it was inscribed, at Piper's insistence, not with 'King' – he said there were 'too many kings already' – but with 'Conqueror of the Inland'.[33] Jackey Jackey, celebrated survivor of Edward Kennedy's ill-fated 1848 expedition, also received a breastplate and a government gratuity. Uniquely, Jackey Jackey's breastplate was solid silver. The inscription read:

> Presented by His Excellency Sir Charles Augustus Fitz Roy K.H., Governor of New South Wales, to Jackey Jackey, An Aboriginal Native of that Colony, In testimony of the fidelity with which he followed the late Assistant Surveyor E.B.C. Kennedy, throughout his exploration of York Peninsula in the year 1848; the noble daring with which he supported that lamented Gentleman, when mortally wounded by the Natives of Escape River, the courage with which, after having affectionately tended the last moments of his Master, he made his way through hostile Tribes, and an unknown Country, to Cape York; and finally the unexampled sagacity with which he conducted the succour that there awaited the Expedition to the rescue of the other survivors of it, who had been left at Shelbourne Bay.[34]

27 Leichhardt 1847, Appendix.
28 Thomas 2015: 124.
29 Baker 1993: 17.
30 Anon 1967.
31 *West Australian*, 25 June 1941: 8.
32 See Troy 1993; McCarthy 1952.
33 Mitchell 1839: 338–339 quoted in Baker 1998: 45. See also Baker 1993.
34 [Silver breastplate] Presented by His Excellency Sir Charles Augustus Fitz Roy K.H., Governor of New South Wales, to Jackey Jackey …, item description, State Library New South Wales, 143.119.202.10/item/itemDetailPaged.aspx?itemID=446737.

The breastplate was displayed in the Australian Museum in the 1860s, presented not by Jackey Jackey or his family but by the governor.[35] Jackey Jackey was particularly celebrated because his presence at Kennedy's death provided a highly sentimentalised and idealised image of the relationship between explorer hero and Aboriginal companion (see Nugent in this volume).

The inadequacy of rewards was recognised by some at the time. Edward Read Parker, who had himself explored and then settled in the area around Dangin, 160 kilometres east of Perth, wrote a letter to the *West Australian Times* shortly after the return of Forrest's 1874 expedition. He commented perceptively that the 'laudations and presents, and the greetings shown towards Forrest and his party, will shortly become things of the past … when the quiet ploddings of the every-day life are again resumed by each individual'. He argued that it was the duty of the government to give 'a small and lasting pension, that is, for life, to Tommy Windich "in recognition of his valuable and long tried service in so many expeditions"'. He challenged readers to 'name an expedition into the interior without naming Tommy Windich as one of the party'.[36]

Portraits

While Aboriginal people appear as exotic background scenery in early paintings of Australia, individuals, including guides, also had their portraits painted. Many explorers' journals were illustrated with portraits of their participants and this included the Aboriginal guides. Artists depicted them in various ways but generally acknowledged the individuality of the guides themselves.

Leichhardt's published journal (1847) included distinctive personal portrayals of Charley Fisher and Harry Brown.[37] They are dressed in plain shirts and have individual expressions – contemplative, intelligent and, in Fisher's case, sad. These are not caricatures, nor are they cheap exploitations of indigeneity. They are respectful portraits and could be seen as depicting these two men as (unhappily) trapped in European disguise, with no recognition of their cultural difference. Whatever the interpretation, the artist's depiction of Leichhardt's Aboriginal guides appears sympathetic, in keeping with Leichhardt's positive, albeit tempestuous, relationship with the two men.[38]

---

35   *Sydney Morning Herald*, 1 October 1868: 5.
36   *West Australian Times*, 29 December 1874: 3.
37   'Charley [and] Harry Brown' in Leichhardt 1847.
38   Clarke 2008: 97; Kennedy 2013: 159–162. On Leichhardt's second expedition in 1847, Harry Brown was acknowledged for a time as de facto commander, Kennedy 2013: 161.

CHARLEY.   HARRY BROWN.

Figure 3.1 Charley Fisher and Harry Brown, guides on Leichhardt's expedition, 1844–45.

Source: Ludwig Leichhardt, *Journal of an Overland Expedition in Australia, from Moreton Bay to Port Essington, during the years 1844–1845*, T&W Boone, London, 1847. Courtesy National Library of Australia.

Aboriginal guides were also often subjects of portraits outside the published journals. While exoticism was part of their appeal to prospective buyers, these were very definitely pictures of individuals who were important to European society. After Mitchell's 1836 expedition, John Piper was much feted in Sydney. W.H. Fernyhough included Piper, 'the native who accompanied Major Mitchell in his expedition to the interior of N.S.W.', in his series of 12 lithographic silhouette portraits of Aborigines. Fernyhough and his publisher John Austin recognised Piper's marketability. He was depicted in his trademark costume, having become a recognisable figure 'strutting about Sydney [in] a red coat and cocked hat with long white feathers'.[39] As Elisabeth Findlay notes, Piper's deliberate swagger in such conspicuous clothing suggests he was consciously cultivating his celebrity. Piper reappeared in Fernyhough's portrait of Thomas Mitchell, who is shown holding the artist's silhouette of Piper. While this might merely be indicating the close relationship between the two men, or just be clever cross promotion, Findlay has drawn attention to the significant timing of the portraits, with the second appearing for sale when Mitchell was attempting to blame Piper for Aboriginal deaths on the expedition.[40]

---

39 *Sydney Gazette and New South Wales Advertiser*, 20 December 1836: 2; 'Piper' at National Portrait Gallery, www.portrait.gov.au/site/collection_info.php?searchtype=advan&searchstring=&irn=52&acno=1999.23.2&onshow=.

40 Findlay 2013: 20–21.

PIPER.

[V]E WHO ACCOMPANIED MAJOR MITCHELL
IN HIS EXPEDITION TO THE INTERIOR.

Figure 3.2 W.H. Fernyhough, 'Piper. The Native who accompanied Major Mitchell in His Expedition to the Interior', c. 1836.

Source: Album of portraits, mainly of New South Wales officials, c. 1836, PXA 617, Mitchell Library, State Library of New South Wales.

Figure 3.3 W.H. Fernyhough, 'Sir Thomas Mitchell', c. 1836.
Source: Album of portraits, mainly of New South Wales officials, c. 1836, PXA 617, Mitchell Library, State Library of New South Wales.

Jackey Jackey's fame was reinforced by the 1849 lithographic portrait by Charles Rodius, who had already produced two sets of lithographs of Aboriginal identities. Identified as 'Jackey Jackey – Expedition of Kennedy 1849', he was portrayed as a steadfast, contemplative man, shirtless but wearing trousers. Kennedy's death meant that there was no sense of celebration but instead of melancholy and loss. When the NSW Legislative Council commissioned a monument to Kennedy in St James' Church, Sydney, it included a bas-relief of Jackey Jackey holding Kennedy in his dying moments and a tribute to the guide:

JACKEY JACKEY

WHO WAS MR. KENNEDY'S SOLE COMPANION IN HIS CONFLICT WITH THE SAVAGES,

AND THOUGH HIMSELF WOUNDED

TENDED HIS LEADER WITH A COURAGE AND DEVOTION WORTHY OF REMEMBRANCE,

SUPPORTING HIM IN HIS LAST MOMENTS,

AND MAKING HIS GRAVE ON THE SPOT WHERE HE FELL.

This sense of loss was repeated in the major 1865 painting of 'The Death of Kennedy' by Eugene Montague Scott. It was regarded as 'the best of all' his paintings and attracted 'considerable notice' when exhibited in 1873.[41] The painting was bought by a Sydney café owner for display in his establishment, clear evidence of the popularity of heroic explorers at that time. The *Sydney Morning Herald* approved of the painting and of Jackey Jackey, 'whose homely name has, in New South Wales, since that time, been permanently associated with the idea of manly courage, gentle affection and dog-like fidelity'.[42] The high praise of 'manly courage', normally a quality reserved for white colonial males, was somewhat undercut by the attribution of 'dog-like fidelity'. Rodius's portrait had been similarly well-received, although the comment in *Bell's Life in Sydney* underlined how these guides were seen as exceptional; 'the intelligence of his countenance, (so unlike the mass of Aborigines,) is very happily caught'.[43]

---

41   *Sydney Morning Herald*, 17 April 1873: 5.
42   *Sydney Morning Herald*, 21 September 1865: 10.
43   *Bell's Life in Sydney*, 24 March 1849: 2.

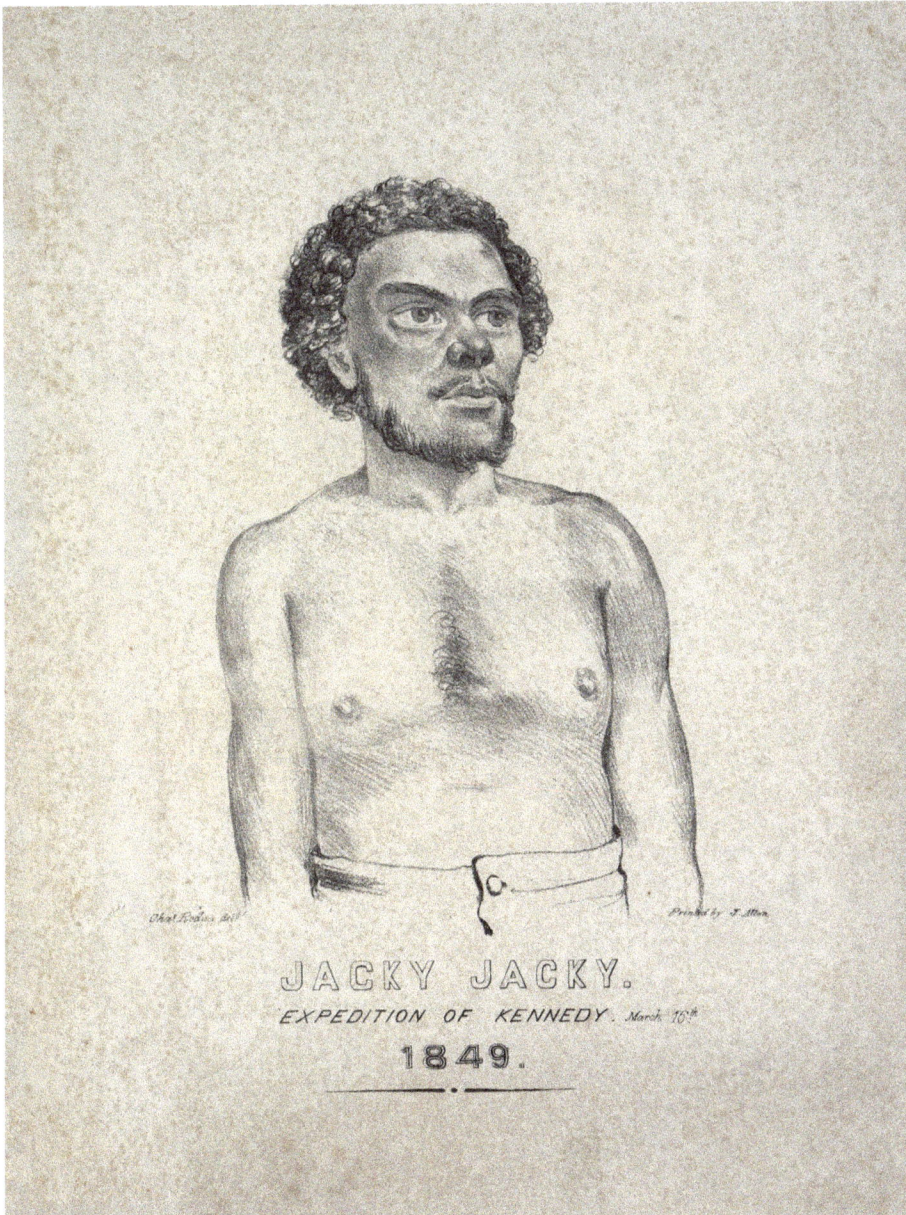

Figure 3.4 Charles Rodius, 'Jacky Jacky, Expedition of Kennedy, March 16th 1849'.

Source: Collection of portraits, predominantly of Aborigines of New South Wales and Tasmania, c. 1817–1849, SAFE/PXA 615, Mitchell Library, State Library of New South Wales.

Less racially charged are the photographic studio portraits of the Forrest brothers' expeditions. In these the Aboriginal and European men are grouped together. In one, from 1874, Alexander and John Forrest are seated in front, clearly leaders of the expedition. Behind them, all in a row, are Tommy Pierre, Tommy Windich and two European participants. In another photograph of an earlier expedition in 1871, Jemmy Mungaro, an Aboriginal guide, squats beside Alexander Forrest and James Sweeney, who are seated on chairs. Behind them stand two other European participants and Tommy Windich. In a publicity photograph from the 1869 expedition in search of Leichhardt's remains, Tommy Windich is at the centre of the picture. He is posed on bended knee, flanked by Malcolm Hamersley and John Forrest, who are standing; but Windich is very much the centre – the focus – of the portrait.[44]

Figure 3.5 'Forrest expedition exploring party, 1874'.

Left to right, back row: Tommy Pierre, Tommy Windich, James Kennedy, James Sweeney; front row: Alexander Forrest, John Forrest.

Source: State Library of Western Australia, 004541D.

---

44 'Malcolm Hamersley, Tommy Windich and John Forrest, part of an exploring expedition in search of the remains of the late Dr Leichhardt and party', 1869, National Library of Australia, picture 174393417. These portraits are in sharp contrast to, for example, African explorer Henry Stanley's use of his boy guide Kalulu. Stanley took Kalulu to London and he is included in several photographic portraits of the white explorer, as much an accessory as the gun, spear and shield also included. This is emphasised by the possessive title of Stanley's later pamphlet 'My Kalulu'. See Kennedy 2013: 171–173. Stanley created a celebrity for Kalulu because it augmented his own status.

Figure 3.6 'Six members of the exploration party to the eastward and southward of Hampton Plains, led by Alexander Forrest', 1871.

Left to right, standing: Richard Burges or Hector McLarty, George Monger, Tommy Windich; sitting: Jemmy Mungaro, Alexander Forrest, James Sweeney.

Source: State Library of Western Australia, 001297D.

Images of Aboriginal guides continued to be produced and to sell well into the twentieth century. In the plethora of images depicting stages of the Eyre expedition, Wylie was usually included. And in January 1919 the *Northern Herald* contained portraits not only of Palmerston but also of Pompo. The *Cairns Post* noted that these would 'appeal to old-timers'.[45]

There is a notable exception to artists' recognition of individuality in their Indigenous guide subjects. That this exception is a woman is perhaps indicative of the way in which this was very much a masculine world. In Mitchell's journal, Turandurey and her daughter, who is on her shoulders, are shown as part of the environment 'with the scenery on the Lachlan'. Facing away from the artist, as if observing the countryside, the woman and girl are naked. This is less about the individual than the idyllic.

---

45   *Northern Herald* (Cairns), 23 January 1919: Magazine section; *Cairns Post*, 19 January 1919: 8

Figure 3.7 Thomas Mitchell, 'Portraits of Turandurey (the female guide) and her child Ballandella, with the scenery on the Lachlan (10th May 1836)'.

Source: Major T.L. Mitchell, *Three Expeditions into the Interior of Eastern Australia*, T. and W. Boone, London, 1839. Courtesy National Library of Australia.

Deaths, burials and obituaries

While some Aboriginal guides became police trackers, their celebrity did not necessarily convert into a better life. Indeed their minor celebrity status was possibly a hindrance to their returning to their own communities, and yet it was never enough to lead to acceptance in white society. Perhaps Tommy Dower, who was the third 'Tommy' to accompany the Forrest brothers, had the most notable later life, becoming something of a media personality in the 1880s. The *Inquirer* reported that Dower 'wishes to know how it is he has not been remunerated either in money or land' for his services on the exploring trip to Port Darwin.[46] It is difficult to tell whether this story was instigated by Dower or the *Inquirer* itself, but Geoffrey Bolton suggests Dower knew how to make his concerns noticed by exploiting his position as an explorer's guide, his value as entertainment and his status within Aboriginal society. He was known as the 'King of West Australia' when he died in 1895, 20 years after his two Aboriginal companions.

Most of the others were left in limbo and died earlier deaths than might have been expected. Moowattin's fate was an extreme example. In 1810 Caley took him to England, where he was paraded around 'in the pink of fashion', but then he returned alone to Sydney, where he was hanged for the rape of a white girl in 1816.[47] Mokare, Yuranigh, Jackey Jackey, Tommy Windich, Tommy Pierre, Pompo and Dick Cubadgee all died within six years of their exploring exploits. Wylie was still alive seven years after his moment of fame but then disappeared from the (white) public view.

Dying so soon after acquiring celebrity status, these men often inspired obituaries in the local press. In the case of Jackey Jackey, who died after falling into a campfire, apparently drunk, there was a sense of disappointment that such a 'faithful guide' had succumbed to the evils of drink. The fate of Jackey Jackey was seen as being particularly poignant, as he was a hero, yet ultimately unsurprising. Others died more respectable deaths. Expedition leaders often took the opportunity to comment on the loyalty of their erstwhile companions. Upon Tommy Windich's death in 1876, John Forrest wrote to the *Inquirer* that he had 'lost an old and well-tried companion and friend'.[48] Four years later he used the same phrase when Tommy Pierre died, telling the *Herald* 'I feel that

---

46   *Inquirer*, 22 November 1882 in Bolton 1988: 80.

47   Smith 2005.

48   *Inquirer and Commercial News*, 15 March 1876: 3.

I have lost an old companion and friend'.[49] A year after Pompo died, Palmerston recorded in the *Brisbane Courier* that the loss of his 'faithful little follower' was 'irreparable' and

> plunged me in great misery. Even now it is with an overwhelming sense of grief and with swimming eyes I copy these lines. It is not in me to express how much this little aborigine had endeared himself to me by his bright intelligence and fidelity.[50]

The sentimentality was heightened by exaggerating Pompo's youth. Given Palmerston's bloody reputation with regard to Aboriginal people, his public expression of grief for Pompo underscores the way in which guides could be considered quite separately from the rest of the Indigenous population.

Expedition leaders also publicly recognised their Aboriginal guides by arranging formal commemorations, often contributing to their burial and gravestone. Palmerston was reported as having had a tombstone erected on Pompo's grave.[51] Yuranigh died in his own country and was buried by his community near Molong in New South Wales. His grave was fenced at government expense and Mitchell paid for an adjacent monument, which was inscribed:

To

Native Courage

Honesty and Fidelity.

Yuranigh

who accompanied the

expedition of discovery

into tropical Australia in

1846

lies buried here

according to the rites

of his countrymen

and this spot was

dedicated and enclosed

by the

Governor General's authority

in 1852.

---

49   *Herald* (Fremantle), 22 November 1879: 3.
50   *Brisbane Courier*, 27 September 1883: 2.
51   *The Queenslander*, 22 January 1881: 109.

Mitchell, in an unusual moment of modesty, did not include his own name on the tombstone. Twenty years later, the Forrest brothers saw value in emphasising their patronage of their guides. They paid for Windich's tombstone, on which was inscribed the words:

Erected by

John and Alexander Forrest

in Memory of

Tommy Windich,

Born near Mt Stirling 1849

Died at Esperance Bay 1876.

He was an aboriginal native of Western Australia,

of great intelligence and fidelity, who accompanied them on EXPLORING EXPEDITIONS

into the interior of Australia, two of which were from

PERTH to ADELAIDE.

Be ye also ready!

When Tommy Dower died in 1895 he was buried in East Perth cemetery, the only Aboriginal person to be interred there. His tombstone and burial were organised by the Aborigines Protection Board, although Bolton suggests the Forrest brothers were instrumental. Billy Noongale was another of John Forrest's guides, described on his tombstone in 1905 as 'one of his faithful companions'. As Bolton aptly summed up, the Forrests 'were at least punctilious in ensuring that their Aboriginal offsiders were given decent funerals'.[52] The Forrest family continued that sense of responsibility: in 1950, Alexander's son John Forrest paid £15 for preservation work on Tommy Windich's grave in Esperance.[53]

But the most remarkable example of an explorer's involvement in the burial of his guide was also one of the earliest. Mokare, an experienced guide, went exploring in Western Australia with Alexander Collie in 1830. When Mokare died in June 1831, his family chose a burial site on Alexander Collie's property. Four years later, Collie died. At his specific request he was buried next to Mokare. In 1840 Collie's bones (or bones assumed to be Collie's)[54] were disinterred and reburied in the new Albany cemetery. Mokare was apparently forgotten, although in Aberdeen, Scotland, Alexander Collie's brother, George, named his house 'Morkeu' after his brother's friend. This recognition and the intensity of friendship and feeling suggested by Alexander Collie's burial instructions were unique; unlike the flowery phrases and declarations of other explorers, these

---

52   Bolton 1988: 82.
53   *Kalgoorlie Miner*, 18 March 1950: 4.
54   Green 2005. See also Bladon et al. 2011.

were actions that cannot be misinterpreted. Perhaps at this stage of European colonisation in Western Australia explorer–guide relations had not yet settled into formal separation of patron and patronised. By the same token, the official reburial of Collie but not Mokare nine years later is similarly telling – suggesting that Collie's personal wishes were less important than the need to have such a celebrity as Collie as the first occupant of the new town cemetery. Ironically, in spite of local citizens' concerns to celebrate Collie, by 1935 his grave had vanished and his importance lost in local memory.[55]

This celebration of a particular set of Aboriginal guides, in the heyday of exploration – through naming places, acknowledgements in print, on public occasions and after death – seems odd in a society that was also brutally dispossessing Indigenous people, dismissing them as primitive savages or children; a society that was, at the same time, actively promoting the ideal of the lone explorer as hero. One explanation for this conundrum lies with that lone explorer himself.

It is striking that in most of these cases the expedition's leader seems to have taken the initiative in publicly acknowledging the contribution of their Indigenous 'professional' guides. On the face of it this seems to go against their self-interest in identifying with the explorer myth. But by emphasising their relationship with these individuals, these explorers were positioning *themselves* as intermediaries between the cultures, as adept at engaging with Indigenous cultures. It positioned them as people who can speak for and inspire loyalty from 'the other'. Sometimes, it is true, they emphasised the childlike 'faithfulness' of their companions, but they also publicly appreciated their skills. It is also probably significant that some of the most definite in their praise of specific Aboriginal companions – Mitchell, Palmerston and Warburton – were also criticised for being too ready to use force against Indigenous people. Yet we should not discount the importance of genuine affection and regard explorer and guide could have for each other.

This still does not explain the wider public celebrity given to these men. Explorers were heroes whose words carried weight among a respectful public. The guides were also colourful characters, providing an exotic backdrop to the imperial enterprise. Their skills in bushcraft were widely acknowledged. The public was well aware of the dangers of the Australian environment and of the accompanying potential threat from Indigenous people hostile to the spread of European settlement. Guides were 'friendly natives' in a landscape of potential enemies. They appeared to be reassuring, living proof that it was possible to co-opt Aboriginal people in European interests. Just as Edward Eyre felt supremely grateful to Wylie for not deserting him in the wake of Baxter's murder, so did

---

55   *Albany Advertiser*, 27 May 1935: 3; 1 July 1935: 3.

citizens of small frontier towns sing the praises of such men, perhaps with a sense of relief. The guides were a model for how Australians felt Aboriginal people should be.

A great Australian silence? Forgetting Indigenous guides

It is clear that recognising the assistance of Indigenous guides was a regular feature of the celebration of exploration in its heyday in the nineteenth century. But subsequently they were increasingly written out of the history of exploration. Part of the explanation for this forgetting lies in the way exploration became part of a national historical narrative.[56] In a *local* setting, and for a range of motives, explorers might acknowledge some debt to those who guided them and others might accord some individuals recognition. But in a national story, in which exploration was the origin myth that brought the nation into being, and in which convention required a history of great white men, Indigenous guides were an inconvenience.

The first comprehensive account of Australian exploration was published in 1888 as part of the colonial centenary celebrations, with the support of the New South Wales government and 'under the auspices of the Government of the Australian Colonies'. The somewhat excessively titled *The History of Australian Exploration from 1788 to 1888. Compiled from State Documents, Private Papers and the most authentic sources of information* was 'a rather formidable volume', according to the *Daily Telegraph*, but it nevertheless became a popular success. The author was an established journalist, Ernest Favenc, himself an explorer of some note (if not as much as he received from his own pen) who went on to write novels, poetry and short stories. Favenc almost single-handedly created the canon of notable explorers. His inclusions and omissions, peppered with forthright opinions on their achievements, their effectiveness and the quality of their bushcraft (compared implicitly with his own), were definitive. As a late romantic, he focused on the individual explorer as hero, in the belief that 'the great charm of Australian exploration' was 'the spectacle of one man pitted against the whole force of nature'.[57] In his account there was little room for recognising the contribution of guides (or indeed of any other members of the expedition). Among many others, Moowattin, Mokare, Piper, Yuranigh, Pompo and Cubadgee received no mention, and those that did were depicted as the possessions of their masters. Wylie was only seen as important because he did not participate in Baxter's murder, after which 'Eyre proceeded on his journey', and Windich figured only as the 'black

---

56   Reynolds 2000: 18–21.
57   Favenc 1888: v–vi.

boy' whom Forrest acknowledged in the naming of Windich Springs. Ernest Giles's 'black boy' Tommy and the 'pompous' Warburton's 'black boy, Charley' were recognised as finding water at crucial times, and Eulah received a mention as the Jardines' 'most-trusted black boy'. Various other anonymous 'black boys' were mentioned as accompanying other expeditions, including Favenc's own explorations, but their actual contribution was ignored. Occasionally they provided an opportunity for Favenc's malicious humour. Leichhardt and 'the black boy, Charlie, managed to get lost for two or three days, a faculty which apparently most of the party happily possessed'.[58] Turandurey also became an opportunity for humour in the account of Mitchell's punitive raid on the Aborigines who had been harassing his progress, in which seven were killed. Turandurey, unnamed except as 'the black boy's gin', had been left as

> the sole protector of the drays, and equipment. On his return, the Major found her standing erect at the head of the leading horse, with a drawn sword over her shoulder.

> Her appearance was, above all, both laughable and interesting. She was a tall, gaunt woman, with one disfigured eye, and her attitude, as she stood there with the naked weapon in her hand, faithful guard of all their belongings, was a picture that Mitchell did not soon forget.[59]

The one exception to brief or 'humorous' mentions was Jackey Jackey. He was still merely 'the black boy Jacky-Jacky' or 'a naked blackfellow', but Jackey Jackey's own well-publicised account of the last days of Kennedy was given at length:

> The one brightening touch in the whole gloomy picture is the simple devotion shown by poor Jacky: 'He then fell back and died, and I caught him as he fell back and held him, AND THEN I TURNED ROUND MYSELF AND CRIED,' was the funeral oration over the brave and unfortunate Kennedy.[60]

Favenc's exclusion of a meaningful Indigenous contribution in his story of exploration reflected a far more deliberate social Darwinism than many of his peers. A later novel, *The Secret of the Australian Desert* (1895), a fictional account of Leichhardt's disappearance among a 'depraved, bloodthirsty cannibalistic tribe of savages', was a warning to Australians that mixing too closely with Aboriginal people would lead to the white race's degeneration.[61] In addition, he explicitly argued that Indigenous knowledge was of little assistance to Australian exploration on the grounds that 'the blackfellow of Australia' was

---

58   Favenc 1888: 135, 262, 266, 193, 257, 242, 153.
59   Favenc 1888: 112–113.
60   Favenc 1888: 171, 169, 172–173.
61   Anon 2010.

circumscribed by the boundaries of his own country, so 'information he was able to impart was, as a rule, meagre and misleading, and without any good result in the way of assistance to the explorer'.[62]

Favenc's interpretation dominated explorer historiography and heralded 'the great Australian silence' for the next 80 years, when Aboriginal people had little place in a national history. Nevertheless, as a number of historians have noted recently, this was not necessarily true at a local or regional level.[63] The silence could be broken by an expedition anniversary, or an occasional historical feature in a local newspaper, usually prompted by a zealous local historian or an enthusiastic commemoration committee. Aboriginal guides were being recognised, still within a framework of 'faithful henchman',[64] but recognised nonetheless, and often to a greater degree than the other European members of the party. Recognition was easier when there was already a site, such as a grave, that could be a focus. In 1908 the state government renovated Yuranigh's grave and replaced the headstone.[65] In 1935 there was a 'pilgrimage' to the site by the local historical society, and in 1952 the Orange Historical Society organised a similar excursion.[66] A creek near Molong and a county in Queensland were also named after Yuranigh.

When Alexander Collie was rediscovered and memorialised in Albany in 1935 on the anniversary of his death, a local Albany historian, Robert Stephens, began to take an interest in Mokare, requesting information about the whereabouts of his grave in the local paper. He also took an interest in Eyre's companion, Wylie, another local. Ten years later, Stephens publicly pushed for recognition of those he called 'Black Helpers'.[67] In 1946 Wylie Crescent appeared at the same time as Mokare Park was gazetted, and the following year, further afield, Wylie Head and Wylie Bay were named by the surveyor general.[68]

For over a century explorers themselves were perhaps the most acceptable face of Australian history for the establishment. The authorities, who often deplored the popular interest in convicts and bushrangers, encouraged the celebration of explorers, along with pioneer settlers, because they were respectable. Similarly, Aboriginal guides could be considered acceptable in ways that other Indigenous people – fringe dwellers, cattle-killers and 'myalls' – were not. The guides

---

62   Favenc 1888: 286.
63   Healy 1997; Curthoys 2001; Nettlebeck and Foster 2010; Griffin-Foley 2011.
64   This term was applied to Jackey Jackey by L.M.R., a correspondent to the *Sunday Mail*, 17 July 1932: 3. It was also used for 'Jacky, who was for years [Tom] Petre's faithful henchman', who is buried at Maroomba in Queensland, in an article in *The World's News*, 10 April 1948: 22.
65   *Evening News* (Sydney), 24 August 1908: 8.
66   *Molong Express and Western District Advertiser*, 23 March 1935: 8; 28 April 1950: 1.
67   *Albany Advertiser*, 15 July 1935: 6; 3 December 1845: 8. They were also represented as 'black helpers' in the *West Australian*, 4 April 1936: 18.
68   *West Australian*, 5 March 1947: 5.

continued to represent a success story of peaceful coexistence, as 'faithful' and 'loyal' servants to the various famous white explorers. They were the epitome of cooperation and assimilation. In 1934 Alexander Petrie Campbell, a Congregational minister, wrote to the *Sydney Morning Herald* applauding the public's enthusiasm for explorers, suggesting that 'with the rounding of the century we seem to have awakened a proper interest in the development of our land'. But the purpose of the article was to draw attention to the 'quality and worth' of Aboriginal people, by pointing to the role of the Aboriginal participants on the expeditions. Underpinning his argument was the fact that 'Our early explorers were not slow to recognise the partnership of the aboriginal in the work'. His choice of the word partnership is uncharacteristic for the era, although the title of the piece was more typical: 'Yuranigh, Nature's Gentleman'.[69]

Rediscovering Indigenous explorers

In the last third of the twentieth century, academic historians began to write Indigenous Australians into what had been a predominantly white history. In popular culture, in the development of school curricula, in tourism and in various forms of public commemoration, Aboriginal history also became more visible. In the case of explorers' Aboriginal companions, the emphasis was initially on their role as faithful servants, a continuation of their depiction in popular culture in the 1930s. For historians in a post-colonial age, explorers were becoming problematic – rather than being respectable celebratory historical figures, they were part of an imperial invasion. Their guides could be seen as collaborators, with questions asked about their motivation in assisting the European imperial project. Others emphasised the guides' role as independent agents. Ironically, this emphasis on their agency, skill and knowledge of their country, along with explorers' acknowledgement of their reliance upon them, was a way of returning explorers themselves to a recast version of Australian history.

The changes can be seen in a 1986 school text: in accounts of specific expeditions we learn of Wylie's 'loyal service' to Eyre and of Kennedy's 'faithful Aboriginal companion, Jacky Jacky', but a later chapter discusses explorers' relations with Aboriginal people and points to their dependence on the skills of their guides.[70] It is even clearer in the differences in the style and tone of entries for 'indigenous guides' in the *Australian Dictionary of Biography* (*ADB*). The entries for Wylie, Yuranigh and Jackey Jackey were written in 1967, Tommy Windich appeared in 1976, and Cubadgee, Mokare and Broughton in 2005, part of the millennium 'catch-up' of entries for individuals previously not considered as material for a

---

69   *Sydney Morning Herald*, 15 September 1934: 11.
70   Foster 1986: 87, 90, 105.

national dictionary of biography. The entry for Jackey Jackey (1967) refers to an attack by 'blacks' and the loyalty and attachment of Jackey Jackey to his 'master'.[71] Wylie (1967) was described as 'sulky and disobedient' when food supplies became low, because his 'good temper largely depended on prodigious meals rich in protein'.[72] Earlier *ADB* entries focusing on expedition leaders either ignored the guides[73] or depicted them in similar ways: in the 1966 entry for Collie, Mokare was his 'faithful exploring companion'.[74] These depictions of guides as childlike or devoted are not found in the later entries. Philip Jones insisted that Cubadgee (2005) was 'not simply "Lindsay's boy"', while the entry for Mokare (2005) similarly avoided perpetuating 'loyal native' stereotypes.[75] In addition, more attention was paid to their place within the Aboriginal world, increasing the sense of their more fully rounded individuality.

In the 1980s and 1990s there was a surge of interest in historical commemoration generally, and the shift in approach, giving some recognition to Indigenous guides as independent agents, carried over into a range of civic activity. Local historians once again led the way, sometimes with an eye to the tourist potential of a guide's distinctive historical associations with a particular region. Streets were named, sculptures were commissioned and interpretative panels began to litter civic parks. A monument to Warburton erected in 1989 not only acknowledged Charley but also the expedition's two Afghan men, who were named:

> PETER EDGERTON WARBURTON
> Left the known here for the unknown
> On April 18th 1873
> With his son Richard, J.W. Lewis, Dennis
> White, Charley, Sahleh and Halleem.
> After suffering many privations, hunger
> and thirst crossing the Great Sandy
> Desert the party reached Roebourne W.A.
> with no loss of life on Jan. 26th. 1874
>
> Erected by his relatives
> To commemorate the 100th Anniversary of
> His death November 5th 1889

The Europeans were still listed first, but interestingly the order of precedence for the Afghan and Aboriginal members was reversed from what it might have been in the nineteenth century.

---

71   Beale 1967.
72   Birman 1967.
73   Pompo was not mentioned in Geoffrey Bolton's 1974 *ADB* entry on Palmerston.
74   Cohen 1966.
75   Jones 2005; Green 2005.

The 1991 sesquicentenary of the Eyre expedition prompted a number of memorials. It was not coincidental that hundreds of 'grey nomads' and other tourists crossing the Nullarbor were now following Eyre and Wylie's route. Explorers do not generally generate popular tourist attractions – their impact on the land is too ephemeral – but when there is little else, a monument can attract tourist interest and town councils along the route were aware of the fact. The town of Eucla, near the start of the journey, acquired a monument to commemorate the entire party. In recognising the contribution of the Indigenous guides alongside the Europeans, there was no mention of Baxter's subsequent murder by Joey and Yarry. The inscription simply reads:

EDWARD JOHN EYRE,
BAXTER, WYLIE, JOEY, YARRY.
On 11 March 1841
camped in this vicinity
during the 1500km journey
from Fowlers Bay to Albany.
Unveiled by
the HON. IAN TAYLOR M.L.A.
Deputy Premier of Western Australia
11 March 1991.
Presented by the Post Office Historical Society of WA
for the Sesquicentenary Celebration 1841 – 1991.
Royal Western Australian Historical Society.[76]

The Shire of Esperance also erected a monument in 1991 to Eyre and Wylie, who 'passed this way' at Pink Lake.[77] The Kimba District Council commissioned a giant sculpture of Eyre and an Aboriginal guide, unveiled in 2011 and partly funded by a Tourism Commission grant. Curiously, although the statues, both double life-sized, represent Eyre and an Aboriginal man and are closely allied to conventional popular images of Eyre and Wylie, the assemblage is known as 'The Edward John Eyre Statue' – Wylie had not joined the expedition at that point. The accompanying text describes it as 'an artistic tribute to Edward John Eyre and the indigenous men on whose bush skills he so often relied', and merely notes that Baxter perished, with no mention of how.[78] The collective coyness about the murder contrasts with the efforts made by the Western Australian Historical Society in 1930 to erect a memorial to Baxter on the site of his remains.[79]

---

76   'Eyre, Baxter & Wylie Expedition', Monument Australia, monumentaustralia.org.au/themes/landscape/discovery/display/60462-eyre,-baxter-&-wylie-expedition.
77   'Eyre & Wylie Sesquicentenary', Monument Australia, monumentaustralia.org.au/themes/landscape/discovery/display/60454-eyre-&-wylie-sesequicentenary/photo/1.
78   'Edward John Eyre Sculptures', District Council of Kimba Attractions, www.kimba.sa.gov.au/page.aspx?u=297, accessed 3 July 2013.
79   *The Queenslander*, 28 August 1930: 65.

Figure 3.8 'The Edward John Eyre Statue', Kimba, South Australia (Marcus Possingham and Roland Weight, sculptors), unveiled 2011.
Source: Courtesy Roland Weight.

Other guides were being recalled at the same time. Perhaps one of the more bizarre commemorations was the naming of a variety of barley after Tommy Windich in 1988.[80] A Windich Street materialised in Esperance Bay and

---

80 *Countryman* (Perth), 6 October 1988: 14.

a statue of Windich in a Coolgardie park. Tommy Windich's gravesite has been problematic. Tourists are encouraged to visit 'the final resting place' of Tommy Windich in the Port Authority Park, Esperance.[81] Oddly, this is not Windich's final resting place but is called a 'memorial grave' and was constructed in 1988.[82] The original grave, complete with white picket fence and granite headstone, overlooked the ocean in the sandhills on what became Port Authority property. The original gravesite, now without its original headstone or fence, sits between the Port's entry and exit roads. Recently a 'Historical Site' sign has been added.[83] The siting of the 'memorial grave' in a public park suggests both that Windich was considered important but also that, as with other public memorial sites, accessibility was sometimes more important than accuracy in determining a place of public memory.[84]

Figure 3.9 Windich 'memorial' grave, Esperance, Western Australia, erected in 1988.

Source: Courtesy Maryann Lankester, Esperance Museum.

---

81 'Australia's Golden Outback Holiday Planner 2014/2015': 58, www.wheatbelttourism.com/wp-content/uploads/2012/04/ago-planner-2014_web.pdf, accessed 20 May 2014.

82 The original headstone was replaced in 1973 by a granite rock. See *Esperance Advertiser*, 5 January 1973. This rock was moved to the new site in the park in 1988 and a second plaque added. This plaque used the term 'memorial grave'.

83 The headstone was apparently damaged in the 1960s but was restored and is now in the Esperance Museum.

84 We are grateful to Maryann Lankester of the Esperance Museum for her research into the history of Tommy Windich's grave and memorial.

Figure 3.10 Original Windich grave with headstone, photographed 1938.
Source: Courtesy Maryann Lankester, Esperance Museum.

Figure 3.11 Original site of Windich's grave, as it is now, Esperance, Western Australia. The headstone is now in the Esperance Museum.
Source: Courtesy Maryann Lankester, Esperance Museum.

The new suburb of Ngunnawal in Canberra, created in 1995, focused on honouring a range of Aboriginal Australians, and included Bungaree Crescent, Mokare Street, Yuranigh Court and Windich Street. In north Queensland, a Jackey Jackey Coffee Shop appeared in Cooktown, and the very active Eacham Historical Society erected a statue commemorating Palmerston and Pompo in Millaa Millaa. In Western Australia, a 'Mokare heritage walk' was developed near Denmark, and local Albany residents commissioned a large statue of Mokare in 1997 as part of a Reconciliation project. This statue itself led to another type of recognition: it prompted historian Tiffany Shellam's exploration of contact history in the Albany district. Her research demonstrated the critical role of Mokare in establishing communication and mutual respect between the two cultures.[85]

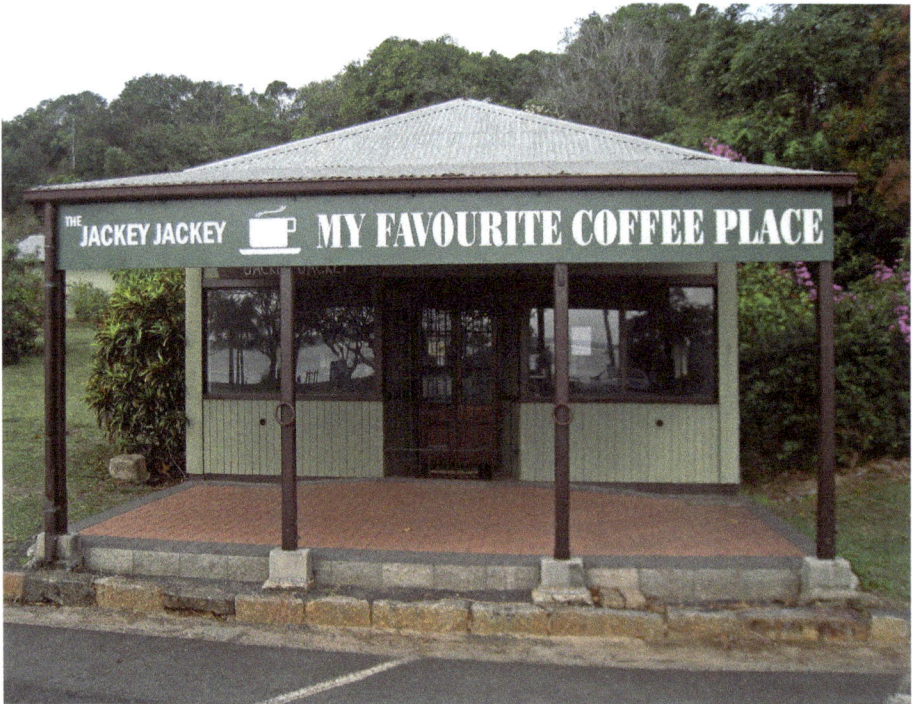

Figure 3.12: Jackey Jackey coffee shop, Cooktown, Queensland, 2010.
Source: Courtesy Richard White.

---

85   Shellam 2009.

Conclusion

In the end we cannot say Indigenous participants in Australian exploration received no recognition. A number clearly were singled out for a particular kind of celebrity, and arguably they were – at the time, and now conclusively – given more recognition than other members of exploring parties apart from the leader. So the questions then become: what form did their recognition take, who promoted their celebrity and why did the popular recognition of their exploits ebb and flow over the years and in different contexts? We have argued that expedition leaders often genuinely acknowledged their debt to Aboriginal guides and recognised their particular skills, though they may have had self-interested motives in doing so. Many in the wider society accepted this acknowledgement. From the end of the nineteenth century, however, their celebrity waned, punctuated by the occasional local commemorations, until the breaking of the great Australian silence in the 1960s, after which commemoration and recognition became more apparent and tied into tourism and civic promotion.

A separate question is whether the recognition they received was sufficient or appropriate, given their contribution, and whether numbers of Indigenous participants who were not singled out should have been. That goes into larger and ultimately unanswerable questions of who gets recognised in history and who should be. Is history the story of 'Great Men' or of the collective souls of history – including Indigenous men and women – who never get a mention?

Finally, we know little of how these guides saw their own roles, but three interesting pieces of evidence suggest they saw themselves as in no way inferior to the designated leader of the expedition. From an Indigenous perspective, who was led and who was leader could be quite different. In the one extended account of an expedition given by an Aboriginal guide, Jackey Jackey talked consistently of what he 'told' Kennedy to do – 'to put the saddles on', 'to leave the horses', 'to look behind always', 'to sit down' – without any sense of this being unusual.[86] On Leichhardt's second expedition, according to one member of the party, the explorer 'put himself under the guidance' of Harry Brown, who then successfully led the party home. When Leichhardt momentarily took over the lead and went the wrong way, 'Brown called out loudly – "He don't know the Road"' and returned to the lead.[87] And finally there is Tommy Windich's

---

86   Carron 1849: 84–85.
87   Hely, Hovenden 1846–47, Journal of an Expedition Overland …, Mitchell Library, C264: entries for 2 July 1847, 12 July 1847; Kennedy 2013: 162.

much-publicised self-identification upon reaching the Overland Telegraph line during John Forrest's expedition in 1874, when he 'called out with enthusiasm, "Three cheers for Tommy Windich, the West Australian Explorer"'. [88]

Acknowledgements

We would like to thank the editors for their suggestions and acknowledge the support of the Australian Research Council.

References

Anon 1968, 'Yuranigh (?–1850)', *Australian Dictionary of Biography*, National Centre of Biography, The Australian National University, adb.anu.edu.au/biography/yuranigh-2829/text4059, accessed 12 January 2014.

Anon 2010, 'Jungun, white prince of the red desert', *The Batavia Legacy: Shipwrecks, Castaways, Lost Explorers and White Tribes in Australia's History and Mythology*, batavialegacy.wordpress.com, accessed 12 January 2014.

Baker, Don W.A. 1993, 'John Piper, "Conqueror of the interior"', *Aboriginal History* 17: 17–37.

——1998, 'Exploring with Aborigines: Thomas Mitchell and his Aboriginal guides', *Aboriginal History* 22: 36–50.

Beale, Edgar 1967, 'Jackey Jackey (?–1854)', *Australian Dictionary of Biography*, National Centre of Biography, The Australian National University, adb.anu.edu.au/biography/jackey-jackey-2264/text2897, accessed 12 January 2014.

Birman, Wendy 1967, 'Wylie (?–?)', *Australian Dictionary of Biography*, National Centre of Biography, The Australian National University, adb.anu.edu.au/biography/wylie-2823/text4047, accessed online 18 July 2015.

Bladon, Paul, Ian Moffat, David Guilfoyle, Alice Bealand and Jennifer Milani 2011, 'Mapping anthropogenic fill with GPR for unmarked grave detection; a case study from an alleged location of Mokare's grave, Albany, Western Australia', *Exploration Geophysics* 42: 249–257.

Blyton, Greg 2012, 'Aboriginal guides of the Hunter region 1800–1850: a case study in Indigenous labour history', *History Australia* 9(3): 89–106.

---

88   *South Australian Register,* 7 November 1874: 2S; *Inquirer,* 15 March 1876: 3.

Bolton, Geoffrey C. 1974, 'Palmerston, Christie (1850–1897)', *Australian Dictionary of Biography*, National Centre of Biography, The Australian National University, adb.anu.edu.au/biography/palmerston-christie-4361/text7089, accessed 12 January 2014.

——1988, 'Tommy Dower and the Perth newspapers', *Aboriginal History* 12: 79–84.

Cadzow, Allison 2002, 'Waltzing Matildas: A Study of Select Australian Women Explorers', PhD thesis, University of Technology, Sydney.

Cahir, Fred 2010, '"Are you off to The Diggings?": Aboriginal guiding to and on the goldfields', *Latrobe Journal* 85: 22–36.

Carron, William 1849, 'The Statement of the Aboriginal Native Jackey Jackey, who Accompanied Mr. Kennedy', in *Narrative of an Expedition undertaken under the Direction of the Late Mr. Assistant Surveyor E. B. Kennedy*, Kemp & Fairfax, Sydney.

Carter, Paul 1987, *The Road to Botany Bay: An Essay in Spatial History*, Faber & Faber, London.

Clarke, Ian D. and Fred Cahir (eds) 2013, *The Aboriginal Story of Burke and Wills: Forgotten Narratives*, CSIRO Publishing, Collingwood, Vic.

Clarke, Philip A. 2008, *Aboriginal Plant Collectors: Botanists and Australian Aboriginal People*, Rosenberg Publishing, Kenthurst, NSW.

Cohen, B.C. 1966, 'Collie, Alexander (1793–1835)', *Australian Dictionary of Biography*, National Centre of Biography, The Australian National University, adb.anu.edu.au/biography/collie-alexander-1911/text2267, accessed 14 January 2014.

Curthoys, Ann 2001, 'National narratives, war commemoration and racial exclusion in a settler society: the Australian case', in *The Politics of War Memory and Commemoration*, T.G. Ashplant, Graham Dawson and Michael Roper (eds), Routledge, London.

Driver, Felix 2013, 'Hidden histories made visible? Reflections on a geographical exhibition', *Transactions of the Institute of British Geographers* 38(3): 420–435.

Dutton, Geoffrey 1977, *Edward John Eyre, the Hero as Murderer*, Penguin, Ringwood, Victoria.

Eyre, Edward John 1845, *Journals Of Expeditions Of Discovery Into Central Australia*, T. & W. Boone, London.

Favenc, Ernest 1888, *The History of Australian Exploration from 1788 to 1888. Complied from State Documents, Private Papers and the most authentic sources of information*, Turner & Henderson, Sydney.

Findlay, Elisabeth 2013, 'Peddling prejudice: a series of twelve profile portraits of Aborigines of New South Wales', *Postcolonial Studies* 16(1): 2–27.

Forrest, John 1875, *Explorations in Australia*, London, gutenberg.net.au/ebooks/e00051.html, accessed 12 February 2014.

Flinders, Matthew 1814, *A Voyage to Terra Australis*, G. and W. Nicol, London.

Foster, Elizabeth 1986, *Explorers of Australia*, Oxford University Press, Melbourne.

Green, Neville 2005, 'Mokare (1800–1831)', *Australian Dictionary of Biography*, National Centre of Biography, The Australian National University, adb.anu.edu.au/biography/mokare-13106/text23711, accessed 13 February 2014.

Griffin-Foley, Bridget 2011, 'Digging up the past: Frank Clune, Australian historian and multi-media personality', *History Australia* 8(1): 127–150.

Healy, Chris 1997, *From the Ruins of Colonialism: History as Social Memory*, Cambridge University Press, Melbourne.

Hely, Hovenden 1846–47, Journal of an Expedition Overland from Sydney to Darling Downs under Dr Leichhardt, 1 October 1846–July 28, 1847, Mitchell Library, State Library of New South Wales, ML C264.

Host, John and Jill Milroy 2001, 'Towards an Aboriginal labour history', in *Wordal*, Studies in Western Australian History no. 22, Jill Milroy, John Host and Tom Stannage (eds), University of Western Australia, Nedlands.

Jardine, Frank 1867, *Narrative of the Overland Expedition of the Messrs. Jardine from Rockhampton to Cape York, Northern Queensland / compiled from the journals of the brothers, and edited by Frederick J. Byerley*, J.W. Buxton, Brisbane.

Kennedy, Dane 2013, *The Last Blank Spaces: Exploring Africa and Australia*, Harvard University Press, Cambridge, MA.

Leichhardt, Ludwig 1847, *Journal of an Overland Expedition in Australia from Moreton Bay to Port Essington ... during the Years 1844–1845*, T. & W. Boone, London.

McCarthy, Frederick 1952, 'Breast-plate: the Blackfellows' reward', *The Australian Museum Magazine* 10(10): 326–331.

Mitchell, Thomas Livingstone 1839, *Three Expeditions into the Interior of Eastern Australia: With Descriptions of the Recently Explored Region of Australia Felix, and of the Present Colony of New South Wales,* T. & W. Boone, London, gutenberg.net.au/ebooks/e00036.html#mitchell2-07, accessed 14 February 2014.

——1848, *Journal of an Expedition into the Interior of Tropical Australia: In Search of a Route from Sydney to the Gulf of Carpentaria,* Longman, Brown, Green, and Longmans, London.

Nettlebeck, Amanda and Robert Foster 2010, 'Commemorating foundation: a study in regional historical memory', *History Australia* 7(3): 53.1–53.18.

Pannell, Sandra 2008, 'Aboriginal cultures in the Wet Tropics', in *Living in a Dynamic Tropical Forest Landscape,* Nigel E. Stork and Stephen M. Turton (eds), Blackwell, Oxford.

Parbury, Nigel 1986, *Survival – A History of Aboriginal Life in New South Wales,* Ministry of Aboriginal Affairs, Sydney.

Reynolds, Henry 1990, *With the White People,* Penguin, Ringwood, Victoria.

——2000, *Black Pioneers: How Aboriginal and Islander People Helped Build Australia,* Penguin, Ringwood, Vic.

Sharp, Nonie 1992, *Footprints along the Cape York Sandbeaches,* Aboriginal Studies Press, Canberra.

Shellam, Tiffany 2009, *Shaking Hands on the Fringe,* University of Western Australia Press, Perth.

Smith, Keith Vincent 2005, 'Moowattin, Daniel (1791–1816)', *Australian Dictionary of Biography,* National Centre of Biography, The Australian National University, adb.anu.edu.au/biography/moowattin-daniel-13107/text23713, accessed 12 February 2014.

Stanner, W.E.H. 1969, *After the Dreaming: Black and White Australians – an Anthropologist's View,* ABC, Sydney.

Thomas, Martin 2015, 'The expedition as a cultural form: on the structure of exploratory journeys as revealed by the Australian explorations of Ludwig Leichhardt', in *Expedition into Empire: Exploratory Journeys and the Making of the Modern World,* Martin Thomas (ed.), Routledge, London.

Troy, Jakelin 1993, *King Plates, A History of Aboriginal Gorgets,* Aboriginal Studies Press, Canberra.

Yeats, Christine 2013, '1813 Blue Mountains crossing convict identified: Samuel Fairs – an extraordinary life', *History: Royal Australian Historical Society Magazine*, June, 10–11.

4

Jacky Jacky and the politics of Aboriginal testimony

Maria Nugent

One obstacle to writing detailed histories and rounded biographies of Aboriginal guides who participated in nineteenth-century exploration is the dearth of source material, especially accounts provided by Aboriginal guides themselves. Within the epistemology of exploration, Indigenous guides and other intermediaries were rarely accorded the status of author, an honour preserved for the expedition leader or expedition scientists and naturalists.[1] Published exploration narratives sometimes disavowed Aboriginal guides and their contributions, a situation influenced by the premise that scientific knowledge was gained by an explorer's unmediated and unfettered encounters with places and people.[2] Even though intermediaries were indispensable to many expeditions, the knowledge and labour they provided became 'hidden' or 'invisible' (or only 'partially visible') within exploration texts, as Felix Driver and Lowri Jones have shown.[3] And although it was quite common for Aboriginal guides to be given some form of public recognition once an expedition was completed, such as monetary reward or public testimonials

---

1   Kennedy 2013: 2.
2   Kennedy 2013: 193–194; Driver and Jones 2009: 11.
3   Driver and Jones 2009: 5.

(see Bishop and White, this volume), this did not usually extend to making a lasting record of their own lives and exploration experiences.[4] It required exceptional circumstances for that to happen.

An exploration narrative produced by an Aboriginal guide under exceptional circumstances is the focus of this chapter. Jacky, also known as Jacky Jacky (often spelt Jackey Jackey), accompanied the expedition led by E.B. Kennedy to Cape York in 1848.[5] His account of its last phase is one of the few, perhaps the only, exploration narrative recorded by an Australian Aboriginal guide in the nineteenth century.[6] The exceptional circumstance – or crisis – that provided the catalyst for his account to be produced and preserved was Kennedy's death. According to Jacky's testimony and other evidence, it is believed that Kennedy died from spear wounds inflicted by some Aboriginal men encountered in the Cape York region of Queensland.[7] As the only member of the 13-man strong expedition to witness the demise of its leader, Jacky's account of what happened gained currency, not only to titillate colonial audiences hungry for stories about tragic hero-explorers, but for legal purposes as well. Kennedy's death required explanation.[8] As eyewitness, Jacky's account had evidential value, but the question of its veracity and faithfulness, and by extension Jacky's reputation as trustworthy guide, would come to be determined according to the terms of imperial and colonial knowledge, commentary and assessment, and in which the courts and the press were highly influential institutions.

As survivor, Jacky found himself in a nebulous position. Returning to colonial society as a young Aboriginal guide, a long way away from his own 'place' and people, and without his employer, made his verbatim testimony especially charged. This is also what makes it particularly fruitful for engaging with questions about the terms on which he (and intermediaries like him) could negotiate the intricate social situations they faced, not only within expeditions but also in the colonial contexts to which they returned.

Recent scholarship on intermediaries – or brokers or go-betweens – has stressed qualities such as ambivalence, ambiguity and doubleness. David Turnbull has argued, for instance, that the mark of the go-between is fluidity in character and attachments, but he notes that subtly shifting alliances and deft political

---

4   Reynolds 1990: 5.
5   Beale 1977 [1970]: 145–146; Paice 1976.
6   Kennedy (2013: 299, footnote 11) notes that for his chapter on intermediaries the 'only verbatim testimony by an Aboriginal intermediary I have found is that of Jackey Jackey'.
7   The most detailed history of E.B. Kennedy's expedition to Cape York is Beale 1977 [1970].
8   For discussion of storytelling provoked by catastrophes in the context of imperial exploration, see Driver 2004: 89–90.

machinations can be difficult to represent. 'The narration of cultural encounters and the interpellation of actors in those stories are profoundly problematic', he writes:

> Acts of translation and betrayal, oppression and resistance occur on both sides of the encounter and in its *narration*. The figure of the go-between is always two-sided, always both enabler and betrayer; but the duality and the centrality of their role is suppressed in the narration of colonial history. In this duality and denial the nature of the go-between is like that of the contemporary historian, who as a teller of narratives, a crosser of boundaries, is also, something of a jester or a trickster.[9]

Drawing on contemporary scholarship of Aboriginal 'texts', colonial knowledge, and the production and politics of archives, my suggestion is that closer attention to the making of Jacky's exploration narrative and its circulation and treatment within interlocking colonial sites of evidence-gathering, knowledge production and 'truth-making', is a useful way to engage critically with the 'slipperiness' that is so often ascribed to intermediaries.[10] By tracking the production and circulation of Jacky's accounts of his exploits, some of the processes – political, cultural, discursive – of his 'becoming', as well as negotiation, however limited, of the subjectivities and speaking positions that were available to him, come to the fore.

Crisis and testimony

It is often at moments of crisis that Indigenous people become visible in the records of exploration. They come into view, for instance, when they abscond or obstruct, or when they cause (or are blamed for) trouble.[11] A similar observation might be made regarding what it takes for an Aboriginal guide to become the 'author' of an exploration narrative. It requires, in the Australian context at least, special circumstances. As already noted, the crisis that provided Jacky with a rare opportunity to speak on record about his exploration experiences was the expedition leader Kennedy's premature and violent death.

From the outset, Kennedy's expedition had been difficult – and perhaps doomed. For the last desperate stretch of it, Kennedy and Jacky travelled alone because they had been forced to leave behind the other 11 men, all sick, exhausted or injured, at two separate camps – eight at one and three at another. Kennedy and Jacky pressed on together, desperately attempting to reach the supply ship,

---

9   Turnbull 2009: 388 (emphasis added).
10   See Johnston 2011; Burton 2005; Paisley and Reid 2014; Stoler 2009; Ballantyne 2013.
11   See Kennedy 2013: 179.

the *Ariel*, which was waiting for the expedition at Port Albany near the tip of Cape York. Near the mouth of Escape River, not far from their destination, Kennedy was fatally speared by some local (Yadhaykenu) men. After burying him, Jacky proceeded to Port Albany, where he found the *Ariel* still at anchor, and so was rescued.[12]

This is the juncture that marks the beginning of Jacky's public storytelling. Immediately upon coming aboard the *Ariel*, he assumed a privileged position as the sole source of knowledge about what had happened during the expedition and, in particular, to Kennedy and the other men. Deaths under violent or mysterious circumstances require explanation. The death of a young, promising and celebrated explorer – killed 'in the line of duty' – was of heightened interest.[13] Like other catastrophic failures in the course of colonial exploration, the death of Kennedy and the demise of his expedition 'had first to be represented, and then accounted for'.[14] It was inevitable it would become the subject of public and judicial inquiry. It is not surprising, then, that as soon as he came on board the *Ariel*, and despite his seriously weakened state, Jacky's account was coaxed from him and taken down in the form of a deposition. Depositions are verbatim transcriptions of information given orally, often in response to a standard set of questions (at least in part), which can be used to inform a legal investigation.[15] Less an account prepared for posterity, Jacky's statement was created with a specific future purpose in mind: to establish the circumstances surrounding Kennedy's killing and to identify, if possible, those responsible. Matters of causality, negligence and blame would be paramount. The story he told would need to work as evidence.

Initiating this evidence-gathering and storytelling process was a man named Adoniah Vallack, a medical doctor and coroner, who had sailed to Port Albany with the *Ariel* in expectation of joining Kennedy's expedition.[16] As a coroner, he was familiar with procedures regarding inquiries into deaths, including preparation of depositions, and given the circumstances, he was particularly anxious to get a statement from the key witness. Later explaining his procedure, Vallack said that he had taken down the bulk of the statement the same day Jacky came aboard and on the next, and that the urgency was borne of fear 'that anything might happen to him [Jacky] from overexcitement'.[17]

---

12   Beale 1977 [1970]: 205–223.
13   Kennedy (2013: 242) notes that: 'Explorers who had died or disappeared during their journeys stirred especially strong passions in settler communities. They became public martyrs in the colonial struggle to conquer a harsh and intractable continent.'
14   Driver 2004: 90.
15   Depositions and other transcripts of oral evidence are rich sources in histories of non-literate or subaltern people. See, for instance, Anderson 2012; Frost and Maxwell-Stewart 2001; Atkinson 1997, esp. chapter 8. See also Zemon Davis 1987.
16   Sullivan 2003: 106–120. See also Beale 1977 [1970]: 146.
17   Carron 1849: 89.

As chiefly verbatim accounts, depositions are one type of text within the broader colonial archive through which it is possible to hear, with less interference than usual, Aboriginal voices. In a critical survey of various modes in which Aboriginal speech was rendered in writing during the first 60 years of British colonisation, Penny van Toorn emphasises the part played by 'white' scribes and editors in rendering, and sometimes imagining, Aboriginal speech as writing. Of Jacky's statement, she says it 'was less encumbered with literary flourishes' than comparable examples.[18] She contrasts it, for example, to the ways in which in his published expedition journals the explorer and later governor George Grey presented the verbal account given to him by Warrup, an Aboriginal guide on his expedition, about, as it also happens, the death of a white man. In Grey's hands, van Toorn argues, 'Warrup's "testimony" drifts between fiction and fact, prose and poetry, scientific reportage and literary narrative', and concludes that ultimately 'readers engage with little other than Grey's literary stylisations of Aboriginal speech'.[19] The judgement is perhaps overly harsh, but nevertheless she detects much less stylisation in the written version of Jacky's testimony, although she does not offer any reasons for this. One difference might be that, unlike George Grey with his literary and professional ambitions, Adoniah Vallack did not see himself as explorer-author and was not seeking publication (nor promotion). His task was more prosaic. As medical man and coroner, he was intent on getting the details down and the facts straight.

Transcribing spoken words, shared in dialogue, is always a complicated process. All texts of this kind are best described as 'co-productions', the result of many small negotiations over the narrative, the order in which details will appear, the ways in which dialogue and other speech will be rendered in writing, and so forth.[20] In this particular instance, the fraught process of textual production might have been smoothed by the fact that the interlocutors – the speaker and the scribe – shared a past. There is some suggestion that they were already acquaintances before they encountered each other on board the *Ariel*.[21] Both men came from the Hunter region near Sydney, and Vallack's own records indicate that he drew on this bond when eliciting Jacky's statement. In his personal journal, he recorded that he had been 'conversing with Jackey, taking down in pencil what he had to say, changing the subject now and then by speaking of his comrades at Jerry's Plains. I did so as he told me what kept him awake all last night was thinking about Mr Kennedy'.[22] No doubt needing to reinforce

18   van Toorn 2007: 172.
19   van Toorn 2007: 172.
20   van Toorn 2006; Paisley and Reid 2014.
21   Sullivan 2003: 110. See also Paice 1976: 18.
22   Enquiry relative to death of Kennedy, Vallack's evidence, 6 March 1849, E. Wise's papers, Mitchell Library, ML A857, p. 77; *Sydney Morning Herald*, 7 March 1849; Papers collected by Sir William Dixson relating to Edmund Kennedy, Mitchell Library, ML CY4279.

the authenticity and veracity of Jacky's statement, Vallack later claimed that 'it was taken down in my own handwriting'. A journalist claimed 'it is nearly as possible exactly the narration of the black'.[23]

Even so, Penny van Toorn suspects some editorial intervention. '[Jacky's] narrative of Kennedy's final days', she writes, 'is lucid and engaging, if perhaps rendered melodramatic by a white editorial hand.'[24] While much of Jacky's statement is recounted in a rather matter-of-fact manner, it certainly has some dramatic sections, especially when it comes to the scenes leading up to and describing Kennedy's spearing. Reported deathbed dialogue between Kennedy and Jacky ('"Mr Kennedy, are you going to leave me?" and he said, "Yes, my boy, I am going to leave you"'); bracketed descriptions to Jacky's mimicry of actions (i.e. 'Jackey rolling his eyes'); and expressions of emotions ('I then turned around myself and cried; I was crying a good while, until I got well'), all add to the pathos. This was, in fact, a quality that was noted, approvingly, at the time. For instance, when it was first published in the *Sydney Morning Herald*, Jacky's statement was prefaced with the journalistic comment that 'anything more affecting than the simple description of poor Kennedy dying in the wilderness, and Jackey crying over him until he got better, we never read'.[25] But rather than ascribe this quality solely or primarily to a 'white editorial hand', my preference is to contemplate the contribution Jackey might have made, because circumstances demanded it, to the narration of his story in this affecting way.

Arriving alone at Port Albany without Kennedy, nor any of the other 11 expedition members, Jacky was, it must be said, in a delicate position. He was the sole witness to what had happened. In that situation, he was surely not free from suspicion; Aboriginal guides rarely were. Their loyalties, actions and motivations were always open to question. They provoked ambivalence. Historian Dane Kennedy suggests that this was because a 'common thread' among intermediaries was that 'they were deracinated figures, wrenched from their families, friends, communities and localities by traumatic events such as war, slave raids, colonial conquest, and other forms of social violence'.[26] Since they were adrift in the world, with few or only weak personal attachments to other people or places, this could make them, he says, 'fairly fluid in their

---

23 *Sydney Morning Herald*, 7 March 1849.
24 van Toorn 2007: 172.
25 *Sydney Morning Herald*, 6 March 1849.
26 Kennedy 2013: 164. For his discussion of the conditions in Australia that contributed to 'deracination' of Aboriginal youths, see pp. 174–175. There is little biographical information about Jacky regarding his life before and after Kennedy's expedition, so it is not possible to know the extent to which he conformed to this description of 'deracination'. The fact that Vallack spoke to him about his 'comrades' at Jerry's Plains suggests that he was not completely severed from his community. See also Tiffany Shellam's chapter in this volume. The point here, though, is less about Jacky as an individual, and more about the ways in which Aboriginal people could easily become suspects in violent deaths of white men.

loyalties'.[27] Their faithfulness to fellow travellers could be contingent and fleeting, lasting only for as long as it suited them. And when that time came, they exercised their autonomy, another trait that Dane Kennedy identifies as evident within the employment category of guides. Their independence, he suggests, was enabled by their superior and much-needed knowledge and skills.[28] More broadly, though, it was not unprecedented for an Aboriginal man – or youth – to be wrongly accused of a white man's death at this time in colonial New South Wales or to be sent to trial for murder on hearsay and flimsy evidence. A number of such cases had occurred within living memory.[29] Suspicion of Jacky – or merely the whiff of it – surely, then, required of him a mode of storytelling that not only provided a credible narrative, but also one that would work to exonerate him.

Given the opportunity to speak, Jacky would have to use his words carefully to create a viable space for himself in the immediate aftermath of Kennedy's death. The scope and options available to him were quite circumscribed. Aboriginal guides were either regarded as loyal and faithful, or they were damned as unreliable and treacherous. Dane Kennedy points out that 'most of the indigenous intermediaries whose contributions generated public praise were portrayed as "highly sentimentalized emblems of fidelity, loyalty and obedience"'.[30] And those who absconded, caused trouble, were deemed difficult to 'manage', or committed (or were suspected of committing) violent acts were cast in equally heightened terms as unreliable, irredeemable and treacherous. Although it has become common in the scholarship to portray Aboriginal guides as occupying a 'middle ground',[31] a metaphor that emphasises in-between-ness, when it came to judgements about their character, whether individually or collectively, less leeway was given. In appraisals and portrayals of Aboriginal guides, there was, it seems, little scope for appreciating human complexity. Keeping in mind the very real constraints faced by Aboriginal youths in colonial New South Wales, then it makes good sense for men like Jacky to convey an image of themselves that conforms with the idea (or ideal) of the loyal and faithful companion and guide. Essentially, these were the only terms available to Jacky under the circumstances. This is not to say that what he described to Vallack about what had happened, what he had done, and what he had thought, was a complete fabrication. Nor is it to diminish the ways in which Vallack might have massaged Jacky's story to accentuate these particular

---

27 Kennedy 2013: 192.
28 Kennedy 2013: 162.
29 See Johnston 2011: 186–209; Harman 2012.
30 Kennedy 2013: 190, and citing Pettitt 2007: 142.
31 White 2005 [1991].

personal qualities. It is rather to point out that to shore up innocence and to secure a future, Jacky's own actions and reactions could not be cast as anything much less than self-sacrificing service.

At the same time, Jacky's statement portrays the expedition leader E.B. Kennedy as partly responsible for his own demise because, as he tells it, the explorer's mistake was to misjudge the motivations of the local Aboriginal men who allegedly speared him. Explorers were prone to mistakes of this order. According to Jacky, Kennedy had believed the local Aboriginal men they encountered were 'friends' when it turned out they were foes.[32] And Kennedy's fatal error, as Jacky saw it, was to fail to heed his Aboriginal guide's advice. 'I told Mr Kennedy that very likely those blackfellows would follow us, and he said, "No, Jacky, those blacks are very friendly;" I said to him, "I know those blackfellows well, they speak too much."'[33] Soon after this exchange, Kennedy and Jacky were 'ambushed', and it was at that point that Kennedy was fatally wounded.

Shipboard talk

As already explained, the main portion of Jacky's account was taken down during the first two days he was taken on board the *Ariel* at Port Albany.[34] This narrative spanned the period from when Jacky, E.B. Kennedy and three others (Luff, Dunn and Costigan) had continued on after leaving the other eight men of the expedition behind at a camp near Shelbourne Bay. When Jacky came aboard, the *Ariel* departed from Port Albany almost immediately, and on the way back down the coast, he was able to pinpoint the location of the Shelbourne Bay camp, where miraculously two survivors were found, although in a dire state.[35] These two men – the expedition's naturalist William Carron and a labourer named William Goddard – were rescued, taken aboard the *Ariel*, and gradually recovered. Their accounts of their own experiences would be added to Jacky's already recorded statement, creating a piecemeal archive of the expedition to substitute Kennedy's own journals and records.

---

32   One of Kennedy's maps, later retrieved, has marked on it 'friendly natives' and 'unfriendly natives'. See Edmund Kennedy Papers on an expedition from Rockingham Bay to Cape York in 1848, Mitchell Library, ML, MAV/FM3/72. The landscape that explorers encountered was not just mapped by them in terms of geographical features, but also in terms of the features of human presence. An analogue to this is the ways in which Aboriginal people living in colonised landscapes 'mapped' the terrain through which they moved in terms of friendly and hostile whites. For a discussion of this, see Byrne and Nugent 2004.

33   Enquiry, Jackey's statement, 6 March 1849, ML A857: 82.

34   Enquiry, Vallack's evidence, 6 March 1849, ML A857: 77.

35   Enquiry, Dobson's evidence, 6 March 1849, ML A857: 120–121.

The *Ariel* took about two months to make its way back to Sydney, and this provided necessary time for further accounts of Kennedy's expedition to be assembled. Carron compiled a day-by-day narrative from the start of the expedition up until his rescue, drawing on some of his own journals that were salvaged when he was found. Goddard recorded a shorter, less detailed account, for which he did not have the advantage of recourse to written records.

The voyage to Sydney also provided an opportunity for Jacky to recollect and share further details of his experiences.[36] This extra section, which Vallack included separately from the narrative he had transcribed over those first two days, reads something like a compendium of random thoughts. For example, one section reads:

> he [Jacky] planted [sic] Mr K's saddle-bags and papers until he got so weak that he could not carry them further leaving some things 5 miles from where Mr Kennedy was buried, and planted them. Mr K once got into a bog after leaving Pudding-pan Hill up to his shoulders and was like a pig in mud. Jacky says he lifted him out – He tried to bring the barbs of the spears which he cut out with him, but lost them – The blacks he says were very saucy in far from the coast, but very civil at Rockingham Bay – When the spears came from all quarters at Escape River Jacky would break them in pieces when he came across them …[37]

This small extract gives a sense of the brevity of description, the shifts from topic to topic, and the almost complete absence of any temporal coordinates. Despite this, or because of it, it offers some revealing glimpses into Jacky's experiences, his exploration methods and the nature of the relationship he had with Kennedy. For instance, one part provides a catalogue of things Jacky buried (i.e. planted) after Kennedy's death: 'Jacky planted a sextant and a Macintosh Cloak of Mr K's – also gloves … Jacky says he planted besides the Papers, a Looking Glass Comb dress brush and bone of a steel pen a pair of Compasses Kettle lots of paper.'[38] Vallack interpolated: 'It appears Jacky would have with him latterly a pencil and paper to describe rudely any mountain he might see when on a tree, &c.'[39] As though to prove the utility of the method, Vallack immediately adds: 'In passing Escape River in the vessel [i.e. the *Ariel*] Jacky knew the place well.'[40] Here, then, are provided, almost incidentally, details about Jacky's own exploration methods, and what emerges is a portrayal of him as a partner in Kennedy's explorations. In respect to the conditions of his employment, this appended section of his deposition includes the detail that:

---

36   Enquiry, Vallack's evidence, 6 March 1849, ML A857: 77, notes: 'I took the statement produced from Jacky the Aboriginal Native on that [i.e. first] day and the following, principally, except the latter part which was taken on the voyage to Sydney.'

37   Enquiry, Jacky's statement, 6 March 1849, ML A857: 87–88.

38   Enquiry, Jacky's statement, 6 March 1849, ML A857: 89.

39   Enquiry, Jacky's statement, 6 March 1849, ML A857: 89.

40   Enquiry, Jacky's statement, 6 March 1849, ML A857: 89.

'Mr K. told Jacky, from Shelbourne Bay that he would give him 5/- per week to look out for opossums for him, and Jacky did so all the way to Escape River.'[41] Later on it records that 'Mr Kennedy promised to take Jacky to England with him on his return', and Vallack adds 'and appears to have made a Companion of him during the latter part of the journey'.[42] With Kennedy's death, neither of these promises would be fulfilled, emphasising the vulnerability of Aboriginal guides and the uncertainty of their employment conditions.

In this non-linear section of his deposition, one encounters Jacky quite directly, as he mentions matters that clearly concerned him. He gives bare details that shed some light on his own experiences of exploration, and which he was not recalling or marshalling solely to give an account and explanation of Kennedy's death. Here, within the more leisurely, less pressured context of ordinary shipboard talk, Jacky asserts some further authorial control over his story. For this section, Vallack did little, almost nothing it appears, to turn the text of the deposition into a coherent narrative, although he is quite present in the text as interlocutor. Vallack appears simply to have written down the various titbits in the order in which he heard them. And rather than incorporate them into Jacky's original statement, even though some of them deal directly with Kennedy's death, Vallack instead simply appended this additional section to the original statement. In this form, these extra details do not threaten the integrity of the main part of Jacky's deposition. But for that very reason, this section became the most disposable part of Jacky's account. It is published the least often, especially when his testimony was mobilised for popular, colonial storytelling about Kennedy and his fate.

As soon as the *Ariel* arrived back in Sydney, Jacky's testimony became incorporated into colonial modes of truth-making and storytelling, some of it sensational, about the dead Kennedy, and in that process only certain sections of it were to be valued. The newspapers and the courts would play a pivotal role in storytelling about Kennedy and the survivors of his expedition. These two sites were, as literary scholar Anna Johnston points out, especially powerful institutions in colonial Sydney for producing and arbitrating truth, for discursively constructing and authorising certain kinds of subjectivities and subject positions, and for creating and destroying reputations.[43] Initially, Jacky's return to Sydney was heralded by the publication on page two of the *Sydney Morning Herald* of his entire statement – the two parts of it (as discussed above). On that occasion, it was published on its own, as the sole, authoritative account attesting to Kennedy's fate.[44] Reinforcing its veracity, it was introduced with this

---

41   Enquiry, Jacky's statement, 6 March 1849, ML A857: 87.
42   Enquiry, Jacky's statement, 6 March 1849, ML A857: 90.
43   Johnston 2011: 8–13, 181–182.
44   *Sydney Morning Herald*, 6 March 1849: 2.

retraction: 'We are glad to find that the first reports of the fate of poor Kennedy's expedition were so far incorrect, that the black natives are only answerable for one death, that of Mr Kennedy himself, and that the other unfortunate men died from other causes.'[45] Jacky's eyewitness account was, then, presented as a corrective to rumour and hearsay, those other currencies in which newspapers so often traded. And it came with unequivocal endorsement, both of its literary quality ('anything more affecting ... we have never read') and of the worthiness of its author ('we hope some means of giving Jackey a small annual pension will be devised').

However, this would, it appears, be one of the very few, perhaps the only, times when Jacky's statement was published on its own and in full. The next day it was published in the same newspaper as part of the suite of evidence that had been presented at the judicial inquiry into the circumstances of Kennedy's death. An editor noted on this occasion: 'We ... have arranged [the evidence] in order different to that in which it was taken, to give intelligibility and consistence to the facts it narrates.'[46] In what would quickly become convention, the account provided by William Carron, the expedition's naturalist, and based largely on his salvaged journal notes, led. This placement made sense chronologically, given that Carron's account began with the expedition's commencement at Rockingham Bay, but it also gave him authorial precedence, establishing a hierarchy in which Carron would become the lead, indeed only, author of the expedition's narrative. And while Carron's evidence given to the judicial inquiry was published in full in the newspaper, only the first part of Jacky's statement appeared.[47] As would become increasingly common, it was missing its second section. For colonial readers, the first section ended more appropriately with the reported comment that Jacky was 'murry murry glad when the boat [i.e. the *Ariel*] came for me', a remark expressing due gratitude. The second section, by contrast, concluded with the detail that [a]fter Mr K had been bogged his feet were swollen much', a less than edifying image of a hero-explorer.

More consequentially, though, this politics of publication represented the diminution of Jacky as authority, a process that had begun during the judicial inquiry held into Kennedy's death.[48] Under colonial court procedures, Jacky, as an Aboriginal man, had been forced to remain almost completely silent. Legal procedures in New South Wales created Aboriginal people, as a category, as unreliable witnesses. Law courts denied them the right to be sworn in as

45 *Sydney Morning Herald*, 6 March 1849: 2.
46 *Sydney Morning Herald*, 7 March 1849: 2.
47 *Sydney Morning Herald*, 7 March 1849: 2.
48 The inquiry was held at the Water Police Court on 6 March 1849, and presided over by J.L. Innes and H.H. Browne. It heard sworn testimony from Goddard and Carron, Vallack and the *Ariel*'s captain William Dobson. Jacky's deposition was tendered as part of Vallack's evidence. Transcripts of proceedings are in E. Wise's papers, Mitchell Library, ML A857.

witnesses.[49] Indeed, upon reviewing the evidence presented to the inquiry, the NSW Attorney-General stated in a memo (22 March 1849) that '[t]his melancholy case furnishes an additional proof of the necessity that exists for altering the law of evidence so as to allow the Aboriginal natives to be competent witnesses in the court of Justice of the colony'.[50] Aboriginal people were disqualified from acting as witnesses ostensibly for not being Christian. As Johnston notes, 'even if Aboriginal witnesses could use English competently, their evidence was inadmissible because, unless baptized Christians, they could not swear to the truth of their testimony'.[51] This was the narrow reasoning behind the convention, but this prohibition went to larger questions about hierarchies of knowledge, judgements about Aboriginal capacity, and the status of oral evidence in an increasingly literate and text-based culture and society.[52] In a general sense, these were the same kinds of issues that shaped the epistemology of exploration, which also largely denied Aboriginal people a speaking part. As Paul Carter notes, 'Australia's indigenous population … rarely enjoy any narrative status' in Australian exploration literature,[53] to which 'authorial' status can be added as well.

Although the court had denied Jacky a speaking part, it had in effect, and in tandem with the colonial press, accorded him a speaking position. The judicial inquiry had valorised Jacky's statement as a *true* statement of what happened, even if it could not admit him as a reliable witness. It had treated his deposition as evidence, and on par with the evidence given by the other two survivors. And the court endorsed Vallack's claim when he presented Jacky's statement that he had 'reason to believe [it] to be true'.[54]

From the time the *Ariel* returned to Sydney, and as public interest in Kennedy and his failed expedition grew apace, it was almost impossible to tell its story without some reference to Jacky's statement. But it was also the case that rarely would Jacky's account of Kennedy's final days appear on its own. As the judicial inquiry had demanded, and as colonial expectations enforced, Jacky's account – as the testimony of an Aboriginal man – would be presented and framed by others. The truth of it was not self-evident; its veracity would have to be established every time it appeared. A common method for doing this was to attest to Jacky's own character as faithful, contributing to his growing reputation as the exemplary loyal guide. This is evident when William Carron's narrative was published. In the wake of the inquiry, it quickly became the substitute official

---

49   See Johnston 2011; Smandych 2004.
50   Papers … relating to Edmund Kennedy, ML CY4279.
51   Johnston 2011: 80.
52   See Atkinson 2002.
53   Carter 1992: 11.
54   Enquiry, Vallack's sworn evidence, 6 March 1849, ML A857: 77.

account of the expedition, following a tradition in which scientists could be authors but Aboriginal guides not. Within Carron's published account, Jacky's statement, minus its second section, was the first in a series of appendices.[55] Although Jacky's statement in essence completed Carron's interrupted exploration narrative, interrupted because he was not able to continue with the expedition, it was not part of it. Carron alone was the book's author. And in that role, he could commend to his readership Jacky's statement in ways that sought to emphasise its credibility by reference to Jacky's own virtues. To preface it, Carron wrote: 'it would ill become me to add anything to the artless narrative of the faithful and truehearted Jackey, who having tended his [i.e. Kennedy's] last moments, and closed his eyes, was the first, perhaps the most disinterested, bewailer of his unhappy fate.'[56] This is just one of many such endorsements which, along with other modes of memorialisation, contributed to the mythologisation of Jacky as the exemplary Aboriginal guide, a legacy that he has not been able to shake, and which has obscured those other more complex aspects of his identity and experience.[57]

Tracking back

Even though he could not speak as a sworn witness, the silence imposed on Jacky during the judicial inquiry was not total. He was accorded one small and limited opportunity to speak at the conclusion of the day's proceedings, when he was asked to identify remnants of things brought back by the *Ariel*. They included a patch of fabric, a piece of iron, a small strap of leather and a strip of sinew; they had been wrested from some local Aboriginal men near Port Albany, violently it turns out.[58] The story of this incident is too complicated to tell for the purposes of this chapter. The point I want to make is that these scraps of things would become another means by which Jacky could make his case. These ordinary objects, the detritus of encounters with Europeans, became, in the wake of Kennedy's death, apparently damning evidence, and thus also part of the archive. When shown a piece of blue cloth, Jacky said it was part of Kennedy's trousers; a scrap of leather from a bridle; and a strip of sinew from a horse.[59] Here, Jackey was being cast in the role of tracker, one of the 'authorised' positions available to Aboriginal men within mid-nineteenth-century colonial courts and policing procedures.[60] Although he could not speak

---

55   It is also published in later exploration texts, such as MacGillivray 1852.
56   Carron 1849: 79. See also *NSW Government Gazette*, 9 March 1849.
57   Other modes of memorialisation include a portrait of Jacky, a silver breastplate, and a monument stone in St James Church in Sydney.
58   Enquiry, Vallack's sworn evidence, 6 March 1849, ML A857: 93–94.
59   Enquiry, 6 March 1849, ML A857: 121.
60   See Richards 2008: 120; Langton 2006: 55–56; Finnane 2013: 407–408; Fels 1988: 42.

directly to his own experience, as an Aboriginal guide-cum-tracker, and one who had survived a harrowing journey when a dozen or so others had not, he was acknowledged as an accomplished interpreter of signs.

The remaking of him as tracker did not end in the courtroom. Once the judicial inquiry was over, the colonial government commissioned a recovery voyage to attempt to retrieve Kennedy's body and his books and papers, many of which Jacky had buried or hidden, in a bid to salvage something remotely useful from this failed expedition. Jacky was commandeered to lead the search party and, in a sense, to *track* his own movements. Drawing on Ludwig Leichhardt's writings, Paul Carter argues that the key distinction between guide and tracker was that:

> The tracker operated in familiar territory; in any case, he was not responsible for finding his way back by the same route. On the other hand, the guide was taken along in order to make sense of the unfamiliar. Hunting animals, interpreting signs of Aboriginal occupation, he acts as tracker; but in addition, he is the expedition's spatial memory, connecting up the changing views into a coherent track. While the tracker might be skilled at interpreting broken branches, it is the guide who needs to be able to recognize 'Trees peculiarly formed'.[61]

Jacky's exploration skills, especially as the expedition's memory, and his verbatim evidence about what had happened, recently presented in court, were to be put to the test. He passed. By recognising the evidence of his previous travels, and by successfully retracing his route, Jacky was able to lead the party to where he had buried and hidden Kennedy's things, his books and papers especially, and to the place where he had interred him, although his body was not found. In this way, the recovery voyage served – and perhaps was even designed by the colonial government – to corroborate Jacky's original evidence as he 're-enacted' his story for a small audience. One newspaper report, announcing the return of the recovery party to Sydney, noted that:

> The Captain and some of the crew who went with Jacky-Jacky to the spot, were unremitting in their exertions *to ascertain the truth of his statement* as regarded the unfortunate gentleman, and to recover his papers, and they speak in the highest terms of the intelligence and assiduity of the Aboriginal, the last companion of Mr Kennedy.[62]

The captain and crew on this second expedition became another source of testaments to Jacky's character, contributing further to his reputation as the exemplary faithful servant and true character.[63]

---

61   Carter 1992: 47.

62   *Bell's Life in Sydney*, 7 July 1849: 2 (emphasis added). See also Sheridan 2009: 120, in which she notes that 'It seems to have been an unstated purpose of the expedition to confirm the truth of Jackey's account'.

63   See, for instance, Carron 1849: 97. See also Sheridan 2009: 118–122, for her discussion of Simpson's narrative.

Jacky did not give an account of the return voyage and recovery expedition, even though he was apparently asked for one. One local newspaper reported that when he eventually returned home to the Hunter region, after two strenuous journeys in Cape York in quick succession, Jacky was 'too weak and ill to give an account of his last trip'.[64] He was willing, however, to testify to, even boast about, the acuity of his memory when it came to locating 'the spots where he had buried or "planted" Mr Kennedy's papers'.[65] His remembrance was, according to the report, 'so clear, that on the landing of the recovery party, he at once struck inland for them in a direct line, and on reaching their neighbourhood had just to study the bearings for a few moments, when he at once found them'.[66] Happy to lay claim to his own proven ability as guide, explorer and tracker, he would now leave the storytelling – about Kennedy and about himself – to others.

Negotiations and struggles over his narrative, as well as his authority or otherwise to speak, reveal efforts to suppress or contain any ambiguities and anxieties that Jacky might have provoked in his immediate circle, and in colonial society more broadly. It also suggests a fair amount of self-fashioning on his own part as he sought to manage the invidious position in which he found himself in the wake of Kennedy's death. Close attention to these processes and performances provides, I suggest, the material from which to create an alternative portrait of Jacky, one less starkly drawn than his enduring reputation as 'faithful follower' – and its obverse 'race traitor'.[67] An approach that focuses on the creation of his unique exploration archive shines a sliver of light on the ways in which Jacky engaged with the limited 'subject' and speaking positions available to him, not only within the context of Kennedy's expedition but also in its aftermath. This necessarily situates questions about the archives and epistemologies of exploration within the broader politics of knowledge production and subject formation in mid-nineteenth-century Australian colonial society. While Jacky's composite statement is, in a very real sense, an exploration narrative, the story of its production and publication also tells us much about the constraints that Aboriginal guides faced, not least of all to have their experiences recorded and their voices heard, once an expedition was over. In this way, it serves as a good reminder, somewhat paradoxically, for why there are so very few verbatim accounts from Aboriginal guides to draw on in attempts to tell new cross-cultural histories of Australian exploration; and why the few that do exist demand interpretive approaches that go beyond treating them merely as archival sources to be mined for content.

---

64 *Maitland Mercury*, 25 July 1849: 2.
65 *Maitland Mercury*, 25 July 1849: 2.
66 *Maitland Mercury*, 25 July 1849: 2.
67 See, for instance, Maloney 2008: 74; Langton 2008: xxiv.

References

Anderson, Clare 2012, *Subaltern Lives: Biographies of Colonialism in the Indian Ocean World, 1790–1920*, Cambridge University Press, Cambridge.

Atkinson, Alan 1997, *The Europeans in Australia: Democracy*, Vol. 2, Oxford University Press, Melbourne.

——2002, *The Commonwealth of Speech: An Argument about Australia's Past, Present and Future*, Australian Scholarly Publishing, Melbourne.

Ballantyne, Tony 2013, 'Strategic intimacies: knowledge and colonization in southern New Zealand', *Journal of New Zealand Studies* NS14: 4–18.

Beale, Edgar 1977 [1970], *Kennedy of Cape York*, Seal Books, Sydney.

Burton, Antoinette (ed.) 2005, *Archive Stories: Facts, Fictions, and the Writing of History*, Duke University Press, Durham, NC.

Byrne, Denis and Maria Nugent 2004, *Mapping Attachment: A Spatial Approach to Aboriginal Post-contact Heritage*, NSW Department of the Environment, Sydney.

Carron, William 1849, *Narrative of an Expedition undertaken under the direction of the late surveyor E. B. Kennedy for the exploration of the country lying between Rockingham Bay and Cape York*, Kemp and Fairfax, Sydney.

Carter, Paul 1992, *Living in a New Country: History, Travelling and Language*, Faber and Faber, London.

Driver, Felix 2004, 'Distance and disturbance: travel, exploration and knowledge in the nineteenth century', *Transactions of the Royal Historical Society* 14: 73–92.

Driver, Felix and Lowri Jones 2009, *Hidden Histories of Exploration: Researching the RGS-IBG Collections*, Royal Holloway, University of London, and Royal Geographical Society (with IBG), London.

Enquiry taken at Sydney before J.L. Innes and H.H. Browne Relative to the Death of E.B. Kennedy and others who left Sydney on an Exploring Expedition, Wise, E., Pamphlets collected by Justice Wise, Mitchell Library, State Library of New South Wales, ML A857.

Fels, Marie Hansen 1988, *Good Men and True: The Aboriginal Police of the Port Phillip District, 1837–1853*, Melbourne University Press, Carlton, Vic.

Finnane, Mark 2013, 'Law and regulation', *Cambridge History of Australia*, vol. 1, Alison Bashford and Stuart MacIntyre (eds), Cambridge University Press, Port Melbourne, VIC, 391–413.

Frost, Lucy and Hamish Maxwell-Stewart (eds) 2001, *Chain Letters: Narrating Convict Lives*, Melbourne University Press, Carlton South, VIC.

Harman, Kristyn 2012, *Aboriginal Convicts: Australian, Khoisan and Maori Exiles*, NewSouth Publishing, Sydney.

Johnston, Anna 2011, *The Paper War: Morality, Print Culture, and Power in Colonial New South Wales*, UWA Publishing, Crawley, WA.

Kennedy, Dane 2013, *The Last Blank Spaces: Exploring Africa and Australia*, Harvard University Press, Cambridge, MA.

Kennedy, Edmund Papers on an expedition from Rockingham Bay to Cape York in 1848, Mitchell Library, State Library of New South Wales, ML MAV/FM3/72.

Langton, Marcia 2006, 'Out from the shadows', *Meanjin* 65(1): 55–64.

——2008, 'Prologue', in *First Australians: An Illustrated History*, Rachel Perkins and Marcia Langton (eds), The Miegunyah Press, Carlton, VIC.

MacGillivray, John 1852, *Narrative of the Voyage of the* H. M. S. Rattlesnake, T & W Boone, London.

Maloney, Shane 2008, 'Jackey Jackey and the Yadhaykenu', *The Monthly* 33: 74.

Paice, Margaret 1976, *Jackey Jackey*, Collins, Sydney.

Paisley, Fiona and Kirsty Reid 2014, 'Introduction', in *Critical Perspectives on Colonialism: Writing the Empire from Below*, Fiona Paisley and Kirsty Reid (eds), Routledge, New York.

Papers collected by Sir William Dixson relating to Edmund Kennedy's expedition to Cape York, 13 September 1848–7 March 1849, Mitchell Library, State Library of New South Wales, ML CY 4279.

Pettitt, Clare 2007, *Dr. Livingstone, I Presume? Missionaries, Journalists, Explorers, and Empire*, Harvard University Press, Cambridge, MA.

Reynolds, Henry 1990, *With the White People: The Crucial Role of Aborigines in the Exploration and Development of Australia*, Penguin, Melbourne.

Richards, Jonathan 2008, *The Secret War: A True History of Queensland's Native Police*, University of Queensland Press, St Lucia.

Sheridan, Susan 2009, 'Some versions of coastal: Thea Astley, Captain Simpson and the North Queensland coast', in *Something Rich and Strange: Sea Changes, Beaches and the Littoral in The Antipodes*, Susan Hosking et al. (eds), Wakefield Press, Adelaide, 114–126.

Simpson, Thomas Beckford, Logbook of the brig Freak from Sydney to Shanghai and back, vol. 1, 1849–50, Mitchell Library, State Library of New South Wales, ML A2619.

Smandych, Russell 2004, 'Contemplating the testimony of "others": James Stephen, the Colonial Office, and the fate of Australian Aboriginal Evidence Acts, circa 1839–1849', *Australian Journal of Legal History* 11.

Stoler, Ann Laura 2009, *Along the Archival Grain: Epistemic Anxieties and Colonial Commonsense*, Princeton University Press, Princeton, NJ.

Sullivan, Jack 2003, *A Fortunate Liaison: Dr Adoniah Vallack and Jackey Jackey*, Paterson Historical Society, Paterson.

Turnbull, David 2009, 'Boundary-crossings, cultural encounters and knowledge spaces in early Australia', in *The Brokered World: Go-Betweens and Global Intelligence, 1770-1820*, Simon Schaffer, Lissa Roberts, Kapil Raj and James Delbourgo (eds), Science History Publications, Sagamore Beach, MA, 387–428.

van Toorn, Penny 2006, *Writing Never Arrives Naked: Early Aboriginal Cultures of Writing in Australia*, Aboriginal Studies Press, Canberra.

——2007, 'Wild speech, tame speech, real speech? Written renditions of Aboriginal Australian speech, 1788–1850', *Southerly* 67(1–2): 166–178.

White, Richard 2005 [1991], *The Middle Ground: Indians, Empires, and Republics in the Great Lakes Region, 1650–1815*, Cambridge University Press, Cambridge.

Zemon Davis, Natalie 1987, *Fiction in the Archives: Pardon Tales and their Tellers in Sixteenth-Century France*, Stanford University Press, Stanford, CA.

5

Mediating encounters through bodies and talk

Tiffany Shellam

Until recently, Australian exploration historiography has tended to cast and interpret the encounters between European explorers and Aboriginal people in terms of a dyadic, hierarchical relationship. This has strengthened the assumption that within the context of exploration, encounters are only ever between Indigenous people and Europeans, and only ever occur in a binary relationship. Yet exploration archives indicate that European explorers were well aware of the extra dynamic that the presence of a 'native aid', or 'intermediary', brought to encounters. They stress, for instance, their unfamiliarity with new environments, the limits of their languages, and the misunderstandings that sometimes arose between them and the Aboriginal people and communities they encountered. That they were surprised at all by this illustrates the ways in which explorers in the early nineteenth century were not always aware just how much complexity and regional diversity there was across Aboriginal Australia until they commenced travelling. The midshipman on Phillip Parker King's 1818 Australian hydrographic survey, John Septimus Roe, for instance, noted with surprise that Aboriginal 'languages can change within 50 or 60 miles' along the coast.[1] Allan Cunningham,

---

1   Roe, John Septimus, to William Roe, 6 June 1821, Mitchell Library, MLMSS 7964.

the botanist on the same survey, registered difference between the expedition's intermediary, Boongaree, and Aboriginal people met along the way by referring to the latter as 'Stranger-Aborigines'.[2]

Scholars working on the exploration and colonisation of Africa and the Americas have, in recent years, highlighted the role of the go-between in the brokering between indigenous people and European newcomers, facilitating knowledge collection and valuable local information. Felix Driver's project with the Royal Geographical Society engaged with the 'hidden histories' of go-betweens in British exploration history by unearthing the experiences of indigenous people, local guides and interpreters who were part of exploration expeditions.[3] Driver has recast intermediaries as central figures in exploration enterprises and has written their histories into the narrative of exploration and empire. Other scholars have focused on the lasting effect of go-betweens, from first encounters to possession and colonial settlement. For example, in Alida Metcalf's book *Go-Betweens and the Colonization of Brazil, 1500–1600*, she argues that 'go-betweens clearly took centre stage, for they were the means of communication in the middle grounds of encounters'.[4] Metcalf focuses on the 'opening up' that go-betweens enabled for the colonisers and themselves. In this triangular relationship that the presence of a go-between produced in encounters, Metcalf argues, 'they occupied an intermediate space between worlds where a boundary could become a borderland'.[5] She also stresses that go-betweens were not neutral figures, they had 'complex and shifting loyalties that are difficult for modern historians to reconstruct'.[6] Australian scholar David Turnbull has also reflected on this idea of slippery loyalty, stating that '[g]o-betweens can both dissolve and create boundaries in the process of linking people, practices, and places in networks'.[7] David Philip Miller, in his review of the book *The Brokered World: Go-Betweens and Global Intelligence 1770–1820*, referred to this renewed focus on intermediaries as 'history from between', a literature which he argues 'has presented a corrective to top down Eurocentric histories' in the same way that 'history from below' reacted against and sought to remedy the earlier political history's top down approach.[8] Similarly, Dane Kennedy's recent comparative history *Last Blank Spaces: Exploring Africa and Australia* considers the role of overland guides and mediators in the British exploration of Australia and Africa in the nineteenth century. Discussing examples of intermediaries' autonomy in Australian exploration, Kennedy gives these men the identity

2   Cunningham. Allan Journal and Correspondence, 20 September 1816 – 7 May 1819, State Library of Victoria [hereafter Cunningham 1816–19].
3   Driver and Jones 2010.
4   Metcalf 2005: 8.
5   Metcalf 2005: 8.
6   Metcalf 2005: 10.
7   Turnbull 2009: 396.
8   Miller 2011: 610.

of 'deracinated' figures, or 'marginal men', who had been ripped from their communities and 'forced by the circumstances of their estrangement to forge a new niche for themselves at the intersection of cultures'.[9] This chapter utilises this recent international scholarship on go-betweens in an attempt to highlight the role and effects of Australian Aboriginal intermediaries in British maritime expeditions along the north-west coast of the continent in the early to mid-nineteenth century.

Following Matthew Flinders' map of the continent, made during his circumnavigation in 1801, the British Admiralty, in concert with the Colonial Office, required hydrographic expeditions to fill in the missing parts of Flinders' coastal survey. The north-west and northern coasts of Australia needed the most clarification, and the surveys of 1818–22, captained by Phillip Parker King on the brig *Mermaid* and then *Bathurst*, and of 1837–41, captained by John Wickham on the *Beagle*, made successive visits to the north-west coast. Both expeditions took Aboriginal intermediaries on board and this meant that the north-west coast became a site of repeat visits and exchange between intermediaries, expedition members and Aborigines on shore.

This chapter will draw out some of these 'histories from between'. In particular, my aim is to elucidate the experiences of Boongaree, a Garigal man from Broken Bay, and Miago and Tommy, Nyungar men from the south-west of Western Australia, and to tease out the effects their presence had in engagements with Aboriginal strangers, as well as speculate about their own feelings about voyaging and mediating. We might ask: How did these people converse with strangers? What skills or techniques did they draw on? Were they directed about *how* to mediate by the crew, or free to broker in ways they desired? All three intermediaries had different experiences, and while their presence, to an extent, encouraged an 'opening up' of boundaries, it is the effect of the space of the expedition on their identities and histories that is most revealing. The episodes discussed below highlight the three intermediaries' techniques of brokering, with particular attention given to the use of their bodies and their talk, which I then discuss in further detail at the end.

---

9   Kennedy 2013: 166.

Boongaree

Boongaree, often referred to as Bungaree, was a Garigal man, probably from the Broken Bay–West Head group to the north of Port Jackson, and born around 1775.[10] He has become one of the most famous and iconic of all go-betweens in early colonial Australia, with a reputation as a man who moved with ease between the Aboriginal world and that of the newcomers. 'His activities in Port Jackson as a self-appointed Aboriginal ambassador' and welcomer of ships has been the topic of much discussion and myth-making.[11] However, besides the work of Bronwen Douglas and David Turnbull, who have written about Boongaree's mediation during Flinders' circumnavigation in 1803, historians have generally placed little emphasis on what is arguably Boongaree's most important role: intermediary on the maritime expeditions of Matthew Flinders and Phillip Parker King.[12] Instead, as David Hansen has argued, Boongaree's legacy was framed in the decade before his death (1820–30) through anecdotes and many portraits conveying the image of him as an 'eccentric low life'.[13] Hansen writes: 'He is not remembered as the explorers' aide, the first Aborigine to circumnavigate Australia … No he is remembered as a comic metonym of early colonial Sydney: mimic, beggar, drunk.'[14] Here I will examine what Boongaree did as a 'native aid' on board the *Mermaid*.

From December 1817 to July 1818, Boongaree joined the Australian hydrographic expedition captained by Phillip Parker King. While Boongaree did not keep a written record of his own experience of voyaging (and was probably illiterate), some of the crew recorded details about his experience and described him in their journals and letters. The expedition's botanist, Allan Cunningham, referred in his journal to Boongaree affectionately as 'our friend', 'our witty friend' or 'our Native chief'.[15] Prefacing Boongaree's name with 'ours' placed him in possession of the expedition; it also served to set up a dichotomy between Boongaree and other Indigenous people they encountered, and also a triangular relationship which included the crew, Aboriginal strangers on shore and Boongaree in-between. By contrast, the midshipman, John Septimus Roe, made only brief and disapproving, although revealing, comments of Boongaree in his letters home to his father, while King wrote of him with a mixture of frustration and gratitude. The encounters discussed here will help to explain why.

---

10   In the explorers' texts that I am using, his name is spelt Boongaree, however, he was also commonly recorded as Bungaree, Bongree, Bongary, and largely known as Bungaree today.

11   See Smith 1992.

12   Douglas 2007: 18; Turnbull 2009.

13   Hansen 2007: 30.

14   Hansen 2007: 30.

15   Cunningham 1816–19: 25 January 1818, at King George's Sound; 25 February 1818, Enderby Island.

Figure 5.1 Phillip Parker King, 'Boon-ga-ree Aboriginal of New So. Wales 1819 who accompanied me on my first voyage to the NW Coast'.

Source: Phillip Parker King, album of drawings and engravings, 1802–1902, PXC 767, Mitchell Library, State Library of New South Wales.

On 26 February 1818, the *Mermaid* was sailing close to the islands of Dampier's Archipelago, near present-day Karratha, when three Jaburara men were seen in the water 'floating on logs'.[16] Steering their course directly for these men, a jolly boat was lowered and Frederick Bedwell, the second midshipman, pulled one of the men by his hair into it.[17] King wrote that this man was 'unwilling' to be brought on board the ship until 'Boongaree showed himself to him when he obtained a little more confidence and he allowed himself to be conducted over [the side] and [into this vessel]'. A conversation between Boongaree and this man must have been attempted, because Cunningham recorded that 'he occasionally made signs towards the land, and talk'd but his language was neither understood by Boongaree our Port Jackson native or ourselves'.[18]

This kidnapped man was clearly unsettled. The crew tried to put him at ease by giving him food and gifts, but King remarked that this man 'looked round discontented [appeared anxious] and with a sort of inquiry when Boongaree was away from him and on his return he appeared pleased'.[19] Cunningham likewise wrote that this man 'took much notice of Boongaree, who had reluctantly at our persuasion, strip'd and exhibited a scarified body'. The Jaburara captive had scars too, on his breast and stomach. Cunningham referred to Boongaree's nudity in the presence of this captive as a 'counterpart of the strangers', linking their naked 'native' bodies.

Boongaree was also a key figure when the crew went ashore to meet with the 30 Jaburara people who had collected on the beach later that day. The man who had been kidnapped earlier soon noticed Boongaree and 'pointed him out to his Comrades, who addressed themselves to him, wishing him more particularly to land with them'.[20] King also added: 'they were all much struck with Boongaree's appearance and appeared to be very anxious to talk with him but for Boongaree who upon all occasions forgets his native tongue addressed them in Broken English – it is of little consequence for he does not understand one word uttered by them and therefore he would have been misunderstood in English as in his Port Jackson language.' But the effect of Boongaree's presence was clear. King explained: 'When Boongaree opened his mouth to speak they were all quite silent awaiting for his answers to the question which every one was putting to him.'[21] Several other encounters occurred over the following days; at each meeting Boongaree removed his clothes. As the crew departed Dampier's Archipelago, King wrote that 'Boongaree was made very much of' by

---

16   King, Phillip Parker December 1817–July 1818, 'Remark Book', Mitchell Library, MLMSS.5277 [hereafter King 1817–18]: 26 February 1818.
17   King 1817–18: 26 February 1818.
18   Cunningham 1816–19: 26 February 1818.
19   King 1817–18: 26 February 1818.
20   Cunningham 1816–19: 26 February 1818.
21   King 1817–18: 26 February 1818.

the Jaburara who 'appeared quite delighted to find his shoulders scarified like their own he always spoke to them in Broken English – He however, is of great use to us … on the appearance of a Black man being with us [has] given them a confidence what it could be difficult otherwise to instill'.[22]

From this brief episode it is possible to see the ways in which Boongaree's presence was crucial in these encounters, as he was looked to and depended upon by explorers and locals alike. He was sought out by the Jaburara, who are described as being less anxious in his presence. And King and Cunningham were aware of and grateful for Boongaree's usefulness in encouraging a mutual confidence between strangers. As I will discuss in more detail, it was the points of similarity rather than strangeness that were emphasised in these encounters between Aboriginal people.

Miago

Miago was a Nyungar man from the Upper Swan country to the north of the Perth township, and by 1833 was well known to colonial settlers at Swan River. He was represented in the local newspapers as a mediator between the Aboriginal groups living around Perth and described by colonial observers as a 'messenger of peace' and an 'ambassador'. He acted as broker between the Swan River groups, Governor Stirling and the Pinjarra group soon after the Pinjarra massacre in 1834.[23] As well as his mediating skills, he was considered a useful tracker and guide, assisting survey parties and tracking lost settlers in the bush.[24]

In planning for the Beagle's Australian survey, the Admiralty encouraged its captain, John Wickham, to 'hire, at a low rate, some person acquainted with the dialects of the natives, which you are subsequently to visit, and with whom it will be essential to be on friendly terms'.[25] John Septimus Roe, who had been midshipman on King's earlier expedition, had travelled with Miago overland to King George's Sound from Swan River in 1835, and he advised the next maritime surveyor of the north-west coast to take Miago on board the Beagle in 1837. Lieutenant John Lort Stokes, Wickham's assistant surveyor, wrote that:

---

22   King 1817–18: 26 February 1818.
23   *Perth Gazette,* 3 January 1835; CSR 37/178, 230 State Records Office of Western Australia [hereafter SRO WA]; *Perth Gazette,* 29 March 1835.
24   CSR 29/157–9, SRO WA.
25   F. Beaufort, 8 June 1837, printed in Stokes 1846, vol. 1.

> Among the many useful hints, for which we were indebted to Mr Roe, was that of taking a native with us to the northward; and accordingly, after some trouble, we shipped an intelligent young man, named Miago; he proved in some respects, exceedingly useful, and made an excellent gun-room waiter.[26]

In Stokes's published narrative of this voyage, he described how he questioned Miago about particular aspects of Aboriginal culture on which he wanted clarification. In the contained space of the expedition, Miago became the archetype or axis upon which all other Aborigines encountered were compared or contrasted.

Unlike the east coast intermediary Boongaree, who probably had little or no prior knowledge of Aborigines of the north-west before travelling there, Miago had stories and deep knowledge of the northern Aboriginal groups of the west coast. Like many south-western Aboriginal people in this period, Miago feared his northern neighbours, the Waylo or weel men, who were considered to be physically large and violent by the southerners. This, I suggest, contributed to Miago's belief that even far-distant north-westerners were men to be feared, and was perhaps the cause of the 'trouble' that Stokes referred to in coaxing Miago to join the expedition. As Stokes noted, Miago 'evidently holds these north men in great dread ... They are, according to his account, "Bad men – eat men – Perth men tell me so: Perth men say, Miago, you go on shore very little, plenty Quibra men [men of the ship] go, you go."' Stokes's rendition suggests that Miago used the explorers as *his* mediators when they encountered these northern men, a position he was advised to take by his countrymen.[27] Stokes further recorded: 'These instructions' to stay close to the ship and the crew 'appear to have been very carefully pressed upon him by his associates, and certainly they had succeeded in inspiring him with the utmost dread of this division of his fellow countrymen'.[28]

The *Beagle* was anchored at Cape Villaret, near present day Broome, on 18 January 1838. When Miago heard that Aborigines had been sighted on shore, he was 'delighted that these blackfellows, as he calls them, have no throwing sticks'.[29] Of his landing the following day, Stokes further recorded Miago's fear:

> Miago had accompanied this party on shore, though he evidently showed no great devotion to the deed. They said he watched everything, aye, every bush, with the most scrutinising gaze: his head appeared to turn upon a pivot, so constantly was it in motion.[30]

---

26   Stokes 1846, I: 58.
27   Stokes 1846, I: 74–75.
28   Stokes 1846, I: 75.
29   Stokes 1846, I: 74.
30   Stokes 1846, I: 78.

A few days later at Beagle Bay, Stokes recorded an encounter with a group of Nyul Nyul people, and their reaction to Miago:

> Their speech was shrill and quick, perfectly unintelligible to our friend Miago, who seemed greatly in fear of them: they seemed astonished to find one apparently of their 'own clime, complexion, and degree' in company with the white strangers, who must have seemed to them a distant race of beings; nor was their wonder at all abated when Miago threw open his shirt, and showed them his breast curiously scarred after their fashion … as a convincing evidence that he, though now the associate of a white man, belonged to the same country as themselves.[31]

It is worth remembering the possibility that go-betweens, rarely neutral, influenced the power dynamics at play in the relations between the Aboriginal and European worlds. 'There is a further dimension of power' in the triad relationship, as Alida Metcalf has written: 'go-betweens may exploit their positions for their own benefit', because he or she is indifferent to the outcome.[32] According to Stokes, Miago frequently expressed a desire to kidnap an Aboriginal woman from the north-west to take back to Swan River. Stokes believed that she would be tangible evidence to his kin of his far travels.[33] This theme of evidence of experiences – a desire by Aboriginal intermediaries to bring evidence of their new knowledge and experience of travel back to their countrymen – is apparent in other exploration accounts in Western Australia. For instance, when Manyat, a Nyungar man from King George's Sound, travelled beyond his known geographic domain with colonial surgeon and naturalist Alexander Collie in 1833, he brought back bark from trees he had hitherto not seen to show his countrymen how far he had travelled.[34] Miago's desire to kidnap a woman also reveals that Miago had in mind the expedition's aftermath: he was thinking about his return home, and perhaps already anticipating the reception he might receive from his countrymen. Miago certainly used the crew to his own advantage, whether placing them in a mediating position for him in his fears of the northern strangers or using his in-between position for gain in quite specific ways. However, whether he really desired to take a woman, or, as Stokes suggested, it was just bravado, Miago's fear outweighed his desire: 'all his boasting', Stokes wrote, 'about killing some of them and taking one of their women as proof of his prowess, back to Perth, failed to concern.'[35] At Hanover Bay, much to Miago's protest, the crew went ashore to meet a group of Worora men. These men very closely examined the heroic Miago, who submitted to be handled by these much dreaded northern men

> with a very rueful countenance, and afterwards construed the way in which one of them had gently stroked his beard, into an attempt to take him by the

---

31   Stokes 1846, I: 91–92.
32   Metcalf 2005: 3.
33   Stokes 1846, I: 75.
34   Shellam 2010.
35   Stokes 1846, I: 75.

throat and strangle him! An injury and indignity which, when safe on board, he resented by repeated threats, uttered in a sort of wild chant, of spearing their thighs, backs, loins, and indeed, each individual portion of the frame.[36]

While Miago's fear is prominent in Stokes's account, the episode suggests other interpretive possibilities. It is clear, for instance, that these encounters were also intimate: a Worora man had 'gently stroked' Miago's beard, even if he later chose to render it an intrusive gesture.

Miago may have benefitted from his fluid position as go-between, but he was also frequently described as being homesick and unsettled at sea. Being away from kin may have been difficult for some intermediaries. On their return, journey Miago was, according to Stokes, increasingly impatient for Swan River and would stand by the gangway singing mournful songs. Stokes recorded:

> Miago, who was as anxious as any one on board for the sight of his native land. He would stand gazing steadily and in silence over the sea, and then sometimes, perceiving that I watched him, say to me 'Miago sing, by and by northern men wind jump up:' then would he station himself for hours at the lee-gangway, and chant to some imaginary deity an incantation or prayer to change the opposing wind. I could never rightly learn to whom this rude melody was addressed; for if any one approached him near enough to overhear the words, he became at once silent; but there was a mournful and pathetic air running through the strain, that rendered it by no means unpleasing; though doubtless it owed much of its effect to the concomitant circumstances.[37]

While Stokes suggests Miago's songs were mournful and evidence of his homesickness, it is also clear that some of his songs were intended for the northern men he had met with. The explorer and later governor George Grey, who was picked up by the *Beagle* on the north coast, recorded in his journal that '[i]f a native [is] afraid, he sings himself full of courage; in fact under all circumstances he finds aid and comfort from a song'.[38] Grey also described the song that Miago's mother sang constantly during his absence at sea: 'ship bal win-jal bat-tar-dal gool-an-een', which he translated as 'whither is that lone ship wandering'.[39] On Miago's safe return, another song was composed by a Nyungar man after hearing the stories about his adventures at sea.[40] The lyrics go: 'Unsteadily shifts the wind-o, unsteadily shifts the wind-o, The sails-o handle, the sails-o handle-ho.' Martin Gibbs has written about the Nyungar songman and whaler Nebinyan, and how 'the novel experience of whaling'

---

36   Stokes 1846, I: 99.
37   Stokes 1846, I: 221–222.
38   Grey 1841: 404.
39   Grey 1841: 409–410.
40   Grey 1841: 10.

provided him with 'material to translate into song and dance, and consequently further facilitated his rise in standing within … Nyungar society'.[41] Shipboard experience gave Miago material for a story-song too.

Boongaree also utilised songs during his expeditioning. Rather than a medium to recount his adventures, his singing was a mediating technique. When meeting with Undambi people at Skirmish Point while travelling with Matthew Flinders in 1791, the Undambi sang and Boongaree reciprocated with a song of his own.[42] Flinders wrote that the Undambi 'singing was musical and pleasing', but 'the song of Bong-ree', which he gave at the conclusion of theirs, sounded barbarous and grating to the ear and 'annoyed his auditors'. Both Flinders and Stokes disliked the sound of their intermediaries' singing, but, perhaps, they were missing the meaning of this music. Rather than music to be enjoyed, it was it seems an improvised, and unpractised or unrehearsed, technique required of them in the context of their brokering.[43]

Tommy

In 1839 Tommy replaced Miago on the *Beagle*'s voyage for a successive expedition to the north-west. His Nyungar name was Yee-lal-nar-nap – but the crew called him Tommy. He was a young man who had joined the expedition with his 'mother's consent'. Mr Pasco, a master's mate, wrote that 'Poor Tommy soon felt homesick or mammy-sick, for I noticed [him] one evening under the lee of the spanker crying. "What are you crying about, Tommy?" I inquired. "Cos my mudder cry now, I know, so I cry."'[44] Like Miago, Tommy also feared the northern men, and his encounters too were shaped by his history and knowledge of them. After Fitzmaurice, who had taken a whaler to survey the coast, had been confronted by Aboriginal people on shore and had chosen to retreat rather than use his guns, Stokes made note of Tommy's bravery:

> It was of much the same complexion as that of Miago; and he threatened magnanimously to inflict the most condign punishment on the fellows who opposed Mr Fitzmaurice's landing. He had a strong impression that these northern people were of gigantic stature; and in the midst of the silent and gaping interest

---

41 Gibbs 2003: 12.

42 Collins 1804: 512.

43 The explorers themselves were not shy of improvising with song and dance when they were in a dangerous encounter with Aborigines. Keys and Fitzmaurice from the *Beagle* voyage 'danced for their lives' and sang a 'Scottish reel' when faced with 'hostile' Aborigines at Adam Bay near Port Essington. Stokes recorded: 'No one could recall to mind, without laughing, the ludicrous figure necessarily cut by our shipmates, when to amuse the natives they figured on the light fantastic toe; they literally danced for their lives.' Stokes 1846, II, frontispiece.

44 Pasco 1897: 112.

with which he listened to Mr Fitzmaurice's account of his adventure, the words 'big fella' often escaped from his lips; and he appeared quite satisfied when assured that his opinion was correct.[45]

Such stories about the north-west coast being inhabited by 'giants' or 'big men' were not specific to southern Aboriginal groups. Shino Konishi has written about French descriptions of Aboriginal people at Shark Bay in 1803. François Péron, the naturalist on board Nicholas Baudin's scientific expedition, recorded the 'extraordinarily big, strong men' who were 'like giants' that had been seen by their sailors when they went turtle fishing.[46]

Pasco also recorded Tommy's impression of Coepang in Timor and an encounter that took place there. At Coepang,

> members of the monkey tribe were numerous. There are also a number of Chinese engaged in business on the island. Both monkeys and Chinamen were novelties to Tommy, but from seeing the Chinese wear tails [tail shirts?], he thought there must be some connection between man and monkey. Taking him into a Chinese store, the China boy, who had never seen an Australian aboriginal before, said to Tommy, 'You go away, you eat him man.' 'No', said Tommy, very indignantly, 'my not yeat him man, but you yeat him monkey, look you tail'.[47]

Mediating sameness and strangeness

In thinking about the experience of these Aboriginal men and their border crossings in the context of maritime exploration it is obvious that their bodies and their talk were crucial vehicles for, as well as points of, connection during meetings with Aboriginal people who were strangers to them. According to Phillip Parker King, Boongaree's skill as 'native aid' was inseparable from his body. His physique, his clothes – or absence of them – were crucial aspects of his presence and effect in encounters. His nudity was frequently commented upon in the crews' journals, when they regularly drew connections between the removal of his clothes and the success of encounters. Indeed, soon after leaving Port Jackson in December 1817, the expedition met with some Aborigines on the east coast at Twofold Bay. King was frustrated on this occasion that Boongaree had refused to remove his elaborate English attire when meeting Aborigines there. The failed communication at this site, King thought, was due to Boongaree's clothes, which had been given to him especially for the

---

45   Stokes 1846, II: 173–174.
46   Konishi 2008: 12.
47   Pasco 1897: 112.

expedition and might explain why he was loath to remove them so early on in the journey. He was, according to King, 'looking quite fierce with a new blue jacket and trousers, a red frock and cap'.[48]

King recognised the language of the body in human encounters. He had done enough pantomiming himself to know that the body, more than words, was an effective way to communicate with strangers. He recognised too that Boongaree's body – his skin colour, physical features and decoration – would speak a language that his white, clothed body could not. For all the differences between Boongaree and the other Aboriginal people they met, their bodies could be a point of sameness or at least similarity.

Yet King still yearned for the security of language, commenting each time in disappointment when Boongaree used broken English to speak with 'Strangers', and voicing his frustration when it was not possible to record a vocabulary. Likewise, at Beagle Bay, Miago, according to Stokes, 'very sagaciously addressed' the Nyul Nyul people

> in English; shaking hands and saying, 'How do you do?' and then began to imitate their various actions, and mimic their language, and so perfectly did he succeed that one of our party could not be persuaded that he really understood them; though for this suspicion I am convinced there was in truth no foundation.[49]

Boongaree and Miago's use of broken English rather than their native language is revealing. As David Turnbull suggests, it was 'the improvised resort of a go-between trying to create an auditory common ground, but relying on the language he had acquired during an earlier boundary crossing'.[50] But it was precisely these acquisitions that expedition leaders sometimes wished their intermediaries to downplay. While explorers were often well aware of the strangeness between their guides and the Aboriginal locals, they also, as the episodes above attest, attempted on many occasions to render these people more familiar to each other: encouraging Boongaree to forget his broken English, remove his clothes – to be an 'authentic Aborigine' and not the 'civilised native' he had become.

Grace Karskens recently pointed out the strategic use of clothes by Aborigines in colonial Sydney, overturning earlier historiographies that interpreted Aborigines wearing clothes as a sign of degradation and cultural disintegration.[51] In these encounters we see something else: Boongaree, content in his European clothes, was encouraged – sometimes coerced – to remove them, while some of

---

48   King 1817–18: 26 December 1817.
49   Stokes 1846, I: 91.
50   Turnbull 2009: 415.
51   Karskens 2011.

the Aborigines he encountered, such as the captive at Dampier's Archipelago, were dressed, their presentation altered then applauded, when they came on board the ship. European clothing was practical and meaningful for Boongaree and being forced to remove them may have chagrined him. Yet there were times when he was content to remove his clothing of his own volition. In settlements 'it was frequently remarked upon by settlers that Aborigines removed their European clothes when they went back to their own camps'.[52] Boongaree visited Frenchman Rene Lesson in 1822 on his way to corroborees. Lesson contests that Boongaree 'appeared a transformed man. The coat and plumed hat were gone, his powerful body was dusted with red ochre and painted with red and white clay, his canoe filled with spears and clubs.'[53] Karskens persuasively shows that for Aboriginal people in colonial Sydney, European clothing was meaningful, and rather than a symbol of degradation, Aboriginal people wore clothes in distinctive ways. There was, she argues, an Aboriginal style of dressing – jacket with the collar turned up, and without a shirt, keeping the cicatrices on the chest visible. This Aboriginal mode, Karsken argues, was established in the mid–late 1790s.[54]

It was not simply black naked bodies that were important in these exchanges, but the inscriptions that they revealed. Both Boongaree and Miago were initiated men, having gone through the process of ritual scarification. These 'deliberately-made cuts and keloid cicatrices engrave social and cultural meaning and brand bodies as inextricably part of the social collective'. As Anna Haebich has written, they speak of inclusion of membership; projecting affiliated lineage on identity within a social hierarchy.[55] Boongaree had been inscribed by both his Aboriginal and colonial worlds. He was the first Aborigine to be given a king plate. Historians have read these metal gorgets, hung around the necks of designated wearers, as a form of colonial branding or labelling. Such inscriptions identified people like Boongaree as useful, worthy individuals; they also could be read by other settler-colonials as a badge of protection against frontier violence. As Ray Evans has written: 'Bearing the "imprint of the master's control" and testifying to the wearers' deracination, they eradicated one identity and imposed another.'[56] For contemporary Aboriginal people, as Kate Darian-Smith has argued, breastplates remain emotionally ambiguous 'Aboriginal-European' objects, reflecting both 'imperial oppression and violence' as well as 'Aboriginal adaptation and resilience'.[57] However, I would suggest that Boongaree not only wore his king plate like his English dress – with pride – he also used it and

---

52   Karskens 2011: 26.
53   Karskens 2011: 26.
54   Karskens 2011: 17.
55   Haebich 2008: 3.
56   Quoted in Van Toorn 2008: 233.
57   Darian-Smith 2015: 55.

the status it brought to benefit him in the fairly crazy and rapidly shifting context of colonial life in Sydney. Rather than losing an identity, he added to his existing one.

Was this push and pull between Aboriginal and European worlds something that Boongaree was accustomed to and part of a survival strategy? Some explorers utilised the suspended space of the expedition – on board a ship, away from the go-betweens' country – to conduct experiments in civilisation. All crew members commented on the rapidity with which Boongaree and Miago went back to their uncivilised ways at the end of the expedition, suggesting their failure to convert. Boongaree did not rejoin King's expedition as he had cultural obligations to fulfil, yet the crew represented this as a step backwards and an abandonment of the expedition. As Roe, the midshipman, stated: 'he had secreted himself in the Woods'.[58] Miago's much anticipated return to Swan River is constructed by the expeditioners as a crisis of identity. The master's mate, Benjamin Francis Helpman, found it amusing, representing it in the following way:

> A great piece of fun! Miago the New Hollander, went ashore. He had one of the Captain's old dress coats; a gold-laced cap with feathers in it; my old sword and belt, with a pair of new trowsers. He looked more like a stuffed monkey. On landing he was distant with his old friends and brothers. He would not allow them to kiss him, because he said they were not 'wilgayed'. And the cream of the joke is, he would not speak his own language, but would persist in speaking English, although they did not understand a word of what he said.[59]

Soon, Stokes records, he rejoined his kin and went back to his 'uncivilised' ways, and when asked to rejoin the expedition he decided to remain at home with his wife. Stokes describes it in the following way:

> We were considerably amused with the consequential air Miago assumed towards his countrymen on our arrival, which afforded us a not uninstructive instance of the prevalence of the ordinary infirmities of our common human nature, whether of pride or vanity, universally to be met with both in the civilized man and the uncultivated savage. He declared that he would not land until they first came off to wait on him ... During the time that Miago was on board we took great pains to wean him from his natural propensity for the savage life by instilling such information as his untutored mind was capable of receiving, and from his often expressed resolutions we were led to hope a cure had been effected; great was our disappointment then on finding that in less than a fortnight after our arrival,

---

58   Roe, John to William, 6 June 1821, MLMSS 7964.
59   Christie 1943–44: 13.

he had resumed his original wildness, and was again to be numbered amongst the native inhabitants of the bush. To us he had been the source of great mirth, by the absurd anecdotes he sometimes related about his countrymen.[60]

Later, George Grey commented on this tension for Miago, comparing the 'apparently perfectly civilised' native he had first met on board the *Beagle* who 'waited at the gun room mess, was temperate (never tasting spirits), attentive, cheerful, and remarkably clean' with the 'savage, almost naked [man] painted all over … (who) had been [involved] in several murders'.[61]

Conclusion

David Phillip Miller has warned against too much focus on intermediaries. This, he argues, could lead 'us to neglect the larger forces within which they operated'. He states that it is 'easy in our fascination' with these colourful, puzzling characters to overstate their agency.[62] Miller is right to urge us to find a balance between the mythic explorer-hero narrative from which intermediaries were excluded, and an 'add guides and stir approach'. By conceptualising the expedition as an experiment undertaken by both intermediaries and explorers, we can include in our analyses the colonial and imperial contexts in which Boongaree and Miago were operating, as well as allow space for an exploration of the experiments and improvisational techniques utilised by them with their bodies and their talk when meeting with strangers. It is possible to see these techniques as part of an emerging repertoire for Aboriginal intermediaries as they found themselves to be momentarily key protagonists in slippery, triangular relationships.

References

Christie, E.M. 1943–44. *Being Extracts and Comments on the Manuscript Journals of Benjamin Francis Helpman of H.M. Sloop 'Beagle' 1837-38-39-40*, Extract from Proceedings 1943–1944, Royal Geographical Society of Australasia South Australian Branch Incorporated, Adelaide, 1–59.

Collins, David 1804, *An Account of the English Colony in New South Wales, from its first settlement in January 1788, to August 1801*, second edition, T. Cadwell and W. Davies, London.

---

60   Stokes 1846, I: 226–229.
61   Hordern 1989: 88.
62   Miller 2011: 613.

Cunningham, Allan Journal and Correspondence, 1816–19, 20 September 1816 – 7 May 1819, Colonial Secretary's Office Records, Australian Joint Copying Project, GM47, Reel no.6034, State Library of Victoria.

Darian-Smith, Kate 2015, 'Breastplates: re-enacting possession in North America and Australia', in *Conciliation on Colonial Frontiers: Conflict, Performance and Commemoration in Australia and the Pacific Rim*, Kate Darian-Smith and Penelope Edmonds (eds), Routledge, New York, 54–74.

Driver, Felix and Lowri Jones 2010, 'Hidden Histories? Local knowledge and indigenous agency in the history of geographical exploration', *Proceedings of the 14th International Conference of Historical Geographers*, Kyoto University Press, Kyoto.

Douglas, Bronwen 2007, 'The lure of texts and the discipline of praxis: cross-cultural history in a post-empirical world', *Humanities Research* XIV(1): 11–30.

Gibbs, Martin 2003, 'Nebinyan's songs: an Aboriginal whaler of south-west Australia', *Aboriginal History* 27: 1–15.

Grey, George 1841, *Journals of Two Expeditions of Discovery in North-West and Western Australia, during the years 1837, 1838 and 39, in two volumes*, vol. II, The Echo Library, Middlesex.

Haebich, Anna 2008, 'Marked bodies: a corporeal history of colonial Australia', *Borderlands e-journal* 7(2).

Hansen, David 2007, 'Death dance' [A salute to Bungaree of the Carigal clan of the Kuringgai tribe from Broken Bay, NSW.], *Australian Book Review* 290(April): 27–32.

Hordern, Marsden 1989, *Mariners be warned: John Lort Stokes and HMS Beagle in Australia, 1837–1843*, Melbourne University Press, Carlton, Vic.

Karskens, Grace 2011, 'Red coat, blue jacket, black skin: Aboriginal men and clothing in early New South Wales', *Aboriginal History* 35: 1–36.

Kennedy, Dane 2013, *The Last Blank Spaces: Exploring Africa and Australia*, Harvard University Press, Cambridge, MA.

King, Phillip Parker December 1817–July 1818, 'Remark Book', Mitchell Library, MLMSS.5277, item 1, 1–103.

Konishi, Shino 2008, '"Inhabited by a race of formidable giants": French explorers, Aborigines and the endurance of the fantastic in the great south land, 1803', *Australian Humanities Review* 44(March): 7–22.

Metcalf, Alida C. 2005, *Go-Betweens and the Colonization of Brazil: 1500–1650*, University of Texas Press, Austin.

Miller, David Philip 2011, 'History from between', *Technology and Culture* 52(3): 610–613.

Pasco, Crawford 1897, *A Roving Commission: Naval Reminiscences,* George Robertson and Company, Melbourne, Adelaide and Sydney.

Roe, John Septimus, Letter to his brother William Roe, off Cape Capricorn on east coast of Australia, 6 June 1821. Series 05: John Septimus Roe letters, the Australian survey completed: the voyage of the Bathurst 2 June 1821 – 1 June 1823, Mitchell Library, State Library of New South Wales, MLMSS 7964 / vol. 5 (Safe 1 / 468), Item 160.

Shellam, Tiffany 2010, '"Manyat's sole delight: travelling knowledge in Western Australia's south west, 1830s', in *Transnational Lives: Biographies of Global Modernity, 1700-Present*, Desley Deacon, Penny Russell and Angela Woollacott (eds), Palgrave Macmillan, Basingstoke, England, 121–132.

Smith, Keith Vincent 1992, *King Bungaree: A Sydney Aborigine Meets the Great South Pacific Explorers: 1799–1830*, Kangaroo Press, Kenthurst, NSW.

Stokes, John Lort 1846, *Discoveries in Australia; with an account of coasts and rivers explored and surveyed during the voyage of H.M.S. Beagle in the years 1837–38–38–39–40–41–42–43*, T. & W. Boone, London, 2 vols.

Turnbull, David 2009, 'Boundary-crossings, cultural encounters and knowledge spaces in early Australia', in *The Brokered World: Go-Betweens and Global Intelligence 1770-1820,* Simon Schaffer, Lissa Roberts, Kapil Raj and James Delbourgo (eds), Science History Publications, Sagamore Beach, MA, 387–428.

Van Toorn, Penny 2008, 'Slave brands or cicatrices? Writing on Aboriginal skin in *Tom Petrie's Reminiscences of early Queensland*', *Biography* 31(2): 223–244.

6

Agency, affect, and local knowledge in the exploration of Oceania

Bronwen Douglas

Since the early 1990s, a rich series of critical studies by historians of science, cultural geographers and cartographic historians has acknowledged the significance of indigenous agency, knowledge and spatialities in records of encounters with Euro-American travellers and colonisers.[1] In the process, imperial science, geography and cartography have been reconfigured as dialogic, if usually unequal processes of knowledge co-production by global and local, metropolitan and colonial, colonising and colonised agents.[2]

My own heuristic strategy parallels these approaches but is applied to contexts that are in no sense colonial, set in the first phase of fleeting coastal or seaborne encounters between indigenous people and European scientific voyagers in Oceania (Island Southeast Asia, Australia, New Guinea, New Zealand and the Pacific Islands). In exploiting travellers' written and visual representations, including maps, as ethnohistorical texts, I position local people as shadowy but often potent agents in

1   For example, Bravo 1996b; Burnett 2002: 27–34; Safier 2008: 254–255. I gratefully acknowledge research support from the Australian Research Council (project numbers DP0665356 and DP1094562) and the National Library of Australia which awarded me a Harold White Fellowship in 2010 and gave generous permission for the reproduction of images and maps.
2   For example, Bravo 1996a, 1999; Driver and Jones 2009; Raj 2010 [2007]: 60–94, 223–234; Safier 2010; Schaffer et al. 2009; Short 2009; Wagoner 2003.

the formulation of such knowledge. Going beyond the now common inference that there must have been local agency in encounters, I identify its textual residues as overt signs or inadvertent countersigns in the content, language and iconography of outsiders' representations. Filtered through the prejudices, perceptions and emotions of foreign observers, signs and countersigns of indigenous behaviour, appearance and lifestyle are intrusive elements in written and graphic texts. They are variously manifest in word usages, names and motifs; in tense, mood and voice; in tone and style; and in presence, absence, emphasis, ambiguity and contradiction.[3]

Most indigenous signs and countersigns were triggered by obscure, unnamed persons, collectivised and stereotyped as 'natives', 'Indians', or 'savages'. But some indigenous individuals feature more prominently in voyage writings, art and maritime surveys. Most obvious are persons identified as local leaders, so-called 'kings' or 'chiefs' whom naval commanders had to flatter, mollify, bribe or intimidate, and who themselves tried to control or exploit the presence of potent, dangerous, needy strangers. However, other Islanders greatly influenced voyagers' knowledge and representations by joining their vessels, whether coerced or voluntarily, and acting as guides, interpreters, assistants and informants. They were forerunners of thousands of mostly anonymous Oceanians who, from the early sixteenth century, sailed and worked on European vessels, visited foreign places as far away as the Americas and Europe, and arguably initiated the modern Pacific diaspora. Usually sidelined in marginalia and footnotes or patronised as exotica, their actions and textual impact demand greater scholarly attention. So, too, do the contributions of another category of subaltern – ordinary sailors and castaways of varied nationalities whose enigmatic traces also litter archives and master narratives. With reference to the concepts of agency and affect or emotion, this chapter examines the crucial assistance given to the work of scientific travellers by indigenous auxiliaries, often mediated by seamen or itinerant foreigners. Detailed examples are taken from the copious textual legacy of Jules Dumont d'Urville's voyage to Oceania on the *Astrolabe* in 1826–29.

Traces of indigenous intermediaries populate voyage texts from the onset of European entry into Oceania after the capture of Malacca (Melaka, Malaysia) in 1511. The Spanish routinely abducted Islanders to serve as pilots, interpreters, informants, hostages and potential converts. Dependence on indigenous cooperation and expertise is a subtext in their writings and cartography. Local interlocutors are a ghostly presence behind the vocabularies collected in 1519–21 in Brazil, Patagonia, the Philippines and the Moluccas (Maluku, eastern Indonesia) by Antonio Pigafetta, the Italian chronicler of Ferdinand Magellan's expedition.[4] In the Philippines, Magellan relied on the communication skills of his Malaccan slave-interpreter Enrique, while the continuation of the remnants of the expedition after the commander's death depended for navigation and local knowledge on

---

3   For full exposition and application of my theory of countersigns, see Douglas 2013, 2014a, 2014b.
4   For his vocabularies, see Pigafetta 1906 [1525?], I: 44, 74–78, 182–192; II: 116–144.

pilots kidnapped or recruited in Mindanao and the Moluccas.[5] Pigafetta's narrative interleaves a wonderful set of maps that order the physical world traversed according to universalist Renaissance principles.[6] Yet the regional geography of Island Southeast Asia and many of the places depicted were unknown to the Spanish pilots or to Pigafetta, whose cartography indirectly rehearses indigenous geographic knowledge. A legend adorns the island of Gafi (North Maluku), alluding to local stories: 'In this island pygmies live.'[7] Pigafetta's narrative relates this terse dictum to a European performance genre: 'in this island of Caphi live small men like the agreeable dwarfs who are pygmies.'[8] Legend, remark, and the maps in general are countersigns of dialogue with indigenous agents.

In 1606, Pedro Fernández de Quirós led a Spanish expedition from Peru to 'discover the unknown Southern part' of the globe. He exalted abduction as an avenue for saving souls and gained ecclesiastical sanction to do it. But he also admitted pragmatically that the 'manifest risk' to ships and people made kidnapping a 'necessity' to obtain vital supplies of water and wood – the admission is another indigenous countersign.[9] Quirós's second-in-command Luis Váez de Torres 'caught' 20 persons 'of different nations' along the south coast of New Guinea in order to make a 'better report' to the king and noted that they provided 'much news on other peoples'.[10] Such information, conflated as personal observation, is an undercurrent in Spanish writings. In Taumako (eastern Solomon Islands), the 'chief' Tumai used signs to give Quirós sailing directions for 'more than sixty islands, and a large land' whose inhabitants and products he described. On departure, Quirós ordered Torres to seize four men. Three leapt overboard but the fourth, who was originally from another island and had been 'serving' Tumai 'like a captive', stayed cheerfully on board; he was later baptised Pedro, learned some Spanish and eventually died in Mexico. Pedro confirmed and extended the geographical knowledge Quirós had gleaned in Taumako.[11] Not all the place names learned by Quirós are identifiable but they conceivably stretch from the main Solomons chain to Tuvalu and Fiji, a maximum span of more than 2,000 kilometres and a potent countersign of the range and skills of Austronesian voyagers.[12]

Since about 1990, as the idea of local agency in encounters has become steadily more thinkable, some Polynesian and Micronesian travellers figure in voyage historiography.[13] They include two men who joined James Cook's expeditions.

---

5   For example, Pigafetta 1906 [1525?], II: 54, 62, 110, 154, 158, 168.
6   For Pigafetta's maps, see Pigafetta [c. 1525].
7   Pigafetta [c. 1525]: folio 87, brbl-media.library.yale.edu/images/1069116_quarter.jpg, accessed 8 February 2014.
8   Pigafetta 1906 [1525?], II: 144.
9   Quirós 1973a: 23; 2000: 225; Quirós and Valera 1963. For examples of such kidnappings in Rakahanga (Cook Islands) and Espíritu Santo (Vanuatu), see Quirós 2000: 223–229, 276–278.
10   Torres 1878: 21.
11   Munilla 1963: 77; Quirós 1973b; 2000: 241–243, 305; Torres 1878: 18.
12   Lewis 1994 [1972]: 37–38; Parsonson 1966.
13   Chappell 1997; Newell 2005.

The high-ranking Ra'iatean priest-navigator Tupaia left Tahiti with the naturalist Joseph Banks in 1769 and died in Batavia 18 months later en route to England. Cook called him 'a Shrewd Sensible, Ingenious Man', with great 'understanding' but 'proud and obstinate'. His exceptional contributions as navigator, cartographer, interpreter, mediator and ethnographic artist have inspired a welter of historical appreciations.[14] The middle-ranking but politically ambitious Ra'iatean Ma'i reached England in 1774, was lionised in 'genteel company', and was the subject of numerous portraits. Exoticised in Joshua Reynolds's celebrated oil (Figure 6.1) and in James Caldwall's engraving of a drawing by William Hodges, who had travelled with Cook, Ma'i was also painted by Hodges in more naturalistic mode.[15] Ma'i did not impress Cook, despite his value as an interpreter.[16]

Two other prominent indigenous auxiliaries and knowledge brokers on European voyages have also attracted greater historical notice. The high-ranking Tahitian Ahutoru accompanied Bougainville in 1767, spent a year in France, and much influenced Bougainville, notwithstanding ethnocentric doubts expressed about the Islander's intellect and capacity to communicate.[17] Signs of his contributions are patent in Bougainville's Tahitian wordlist.[18] Countersigns of conversations with Ahutoru on which Bougainville based his mature account of Tahitian polity are implicit in comparing his shipboard journal with his published narrative.[19] The Caroline Islander Kadu spent eight months with Otto von Kotzebue's Russian expedition in 1817. The aristocratic French-German naturalist Adelbert von Chamisso acknowledged him as 'our friend and companion' and – after each had learned enough of the other's language – as his prime source of ethnographic information on what is now Micronesia. The German-Russian artist Louis Choris, who based his ethnographic commentary partly on 'Kadou's stories', remarked on the Islander's ability 'to make himself loved by the officers and esteemed by the sailors'. Kotzebue, an aristocratic Baltic German from a literary family, affirmed that he had 'grown very fond' of Kadu.[20] Choris's naturalistic lithograph of his friend (Figure 6.2) contrasts sharply with an engraved appropriation of Choris's portrait in the English edition of Kotzebue's narrative (Figure 6.3). The engraving civilises Kadu with European dress and embellishes him racially with Roman nose and thin lips, befitting one so admired by urbane gentlemen.

---

14   For contemporary signs of Tupaia, see Banks 1962, I: 312, 323, 401; Cook 1955–67, I: 138, 156–157, 169, 442; 1955–67, II: 275, 356; Forster 1778: 511–525. For a selection of modern histories of his significance, see Carter 1998; Salmond 2003: 38–162; 2008; Smith 2010: 189–198; Thomas 1997: 1–5; Turnbull 1998; Williams 2003.

15   Caldwall 1777; Hodges [c. 1775].

16   For contemporary signs of Ma'i, see Solander in Cook 1955–67, II: 949–950, cf. Cook 1955–67, II: 428, note 2; 1955–67, III: 62, 79, 105–106, 136–8, 241; Forster 1777, I: xiv–xvii, 388–389, 444; II: 77, 83, 92, 457. For modern evaluations, see Guest 2004; Hetherington 2001; Rensch 2000: 52–55; Smith 2010: 199–212.

17   Bougainville 1771: 224–226; Hervé 1914; Pereire 1771. See also Smith 2010: 182–189.

18   Bougainville 1771: 389–402.

19   Bougainville 1771: 207–232; cf. 1977: 310–331. For modern appreciations of Ahutoru, see Liebersohn 2006: 142–149; Rensch 2000: 15–17, 46–51; Staum 1996: 161–162.

20   Chamisso 1821: 86–142; Choris 1822: 'Iles Radak', 14–22; Kotzebue 1821, II: 84–122. See also the modern evaluation of Kadu by Liebersohn (2006: 157–162).

Figure 6.1 Joshua Reynolds, 'Omai', 1776, oil.

Source: Wikimedia Commons: commons.wikimedia.org/wiki/File:Joshua_Reynolds_-_Portrait_of_Omai.jpg, accessed 9 February 2014.

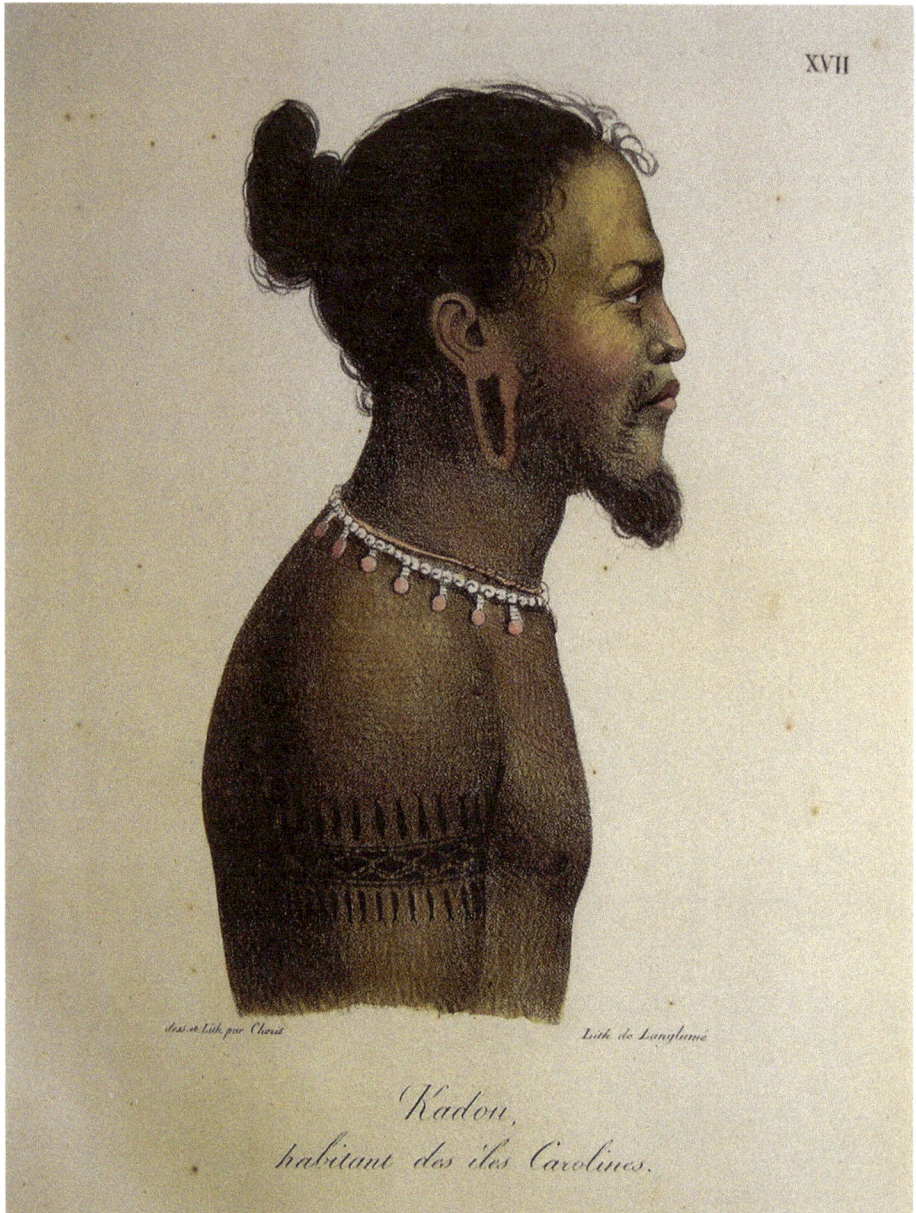

Figure 6.2 Louis Choris, 'Kadou, habitant des îles Carolines', 1822.

Lithograph, in *Voyage pittoresque autour du monde, avec des portraits de sauvages d'Amérique, d'Asie, d'Afrique, et des îles du Grand Océan …*, J.B.B. Eyriès (tr.), Firmin Didot, Paris: 'Iles Sandwich': plate 17.

Source: Service historique de la Défense, département Marine, Vincennes, France. Photograph: B. Douglas.

Figure 6.3 I. Clark after Louis Choris, 'Kadu', 1821.

Engraving, in Otto von Kotzebue, *A Voyage of Discovery, into the South Sea and Beering's Straits, for the Purpose of Exploring a North-east Passage, Undertaken in the Years 1815–1818 … in the Ship Rurick …*, Hannibal Evans Lloyd (tr.), Longman, Hurst, Rees, Orme, and Brown, London, vol. 3, frontispiece.

Source: National Library of Australia, Canberra: NK 921.

Far less prominent historically than these more or less iconic figures was a multinational array of intermediaries who left scattered but telling traces in the texts of Dumont d'Urville's voyage of 1826–29. Anticipating the event, his official instructions hoped that the perils of surveying the little-known Fiji archipelago might be avoided by obtaining 'information on the position of neighbouring islands' and the 'main shoals or reefs' from the inhabitants – notwithstanding their reputation for 'ferocity' amongst both nearby Tongans and the handful of navigators who had so far ventured into Fijian waters. Whatever its 'imperfections', this local knowledge would complement the admittedly 'very incomplete' map of the 'Viti Islands' included in Adam Johann von Krusenstern's recent *Atlas de l'Océan Pacifique* – the first such work devoted to the great ocean (Figure 6.4).[21] In the event, the French passage through the archipelago was successively directed by a Tongan and a Fijian, interpreted by Spanish-speaking castaways who knew the vernacular languages. In the process, the French acquired a rich body of linguistic, ethnographic, demographic and geographic knowledge, the latter epitomised in a 'Map of the Archipelago of the Fiji Islands' drafted by the *enseigne* (sub-lieutenant) Victor-Amédée Gressien (Figure 6.5).

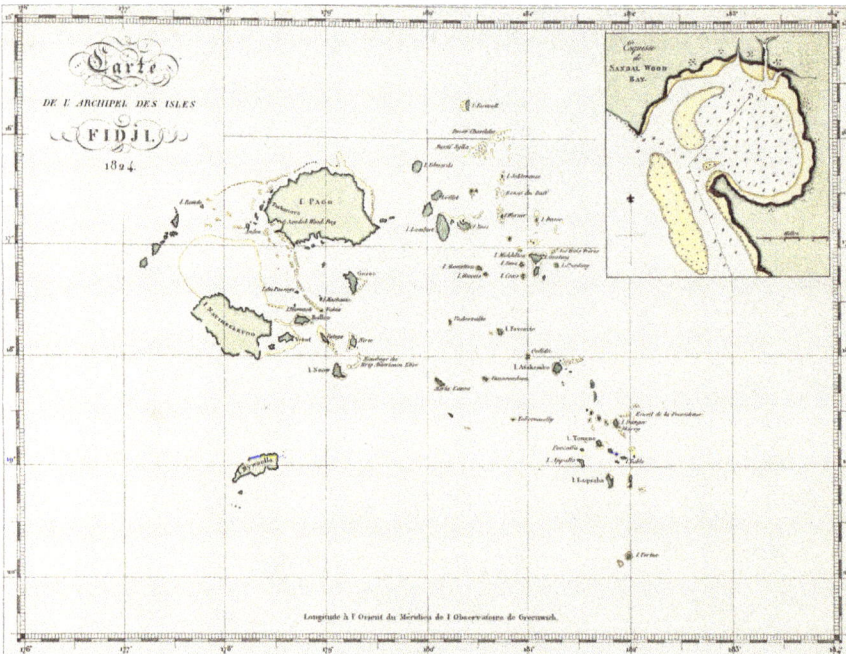

Figure 6.4 Adam Johann von Krusenstern, 'Carte de l'archipel des îles Fidji', 1824.

Engraving, in *Atlas de l'Océan pacifique*, par ordre de Sa Majesté impériale, Saint-Petersbourg, vol. 1: plate 14.

Source: National Library of Australia, Canberra: MAP Ra 100 Plate 14.

---

21   Dumont d'Urville 1830–33, I: lxv; Krusenstern 1824a; 1824b: 231–235.

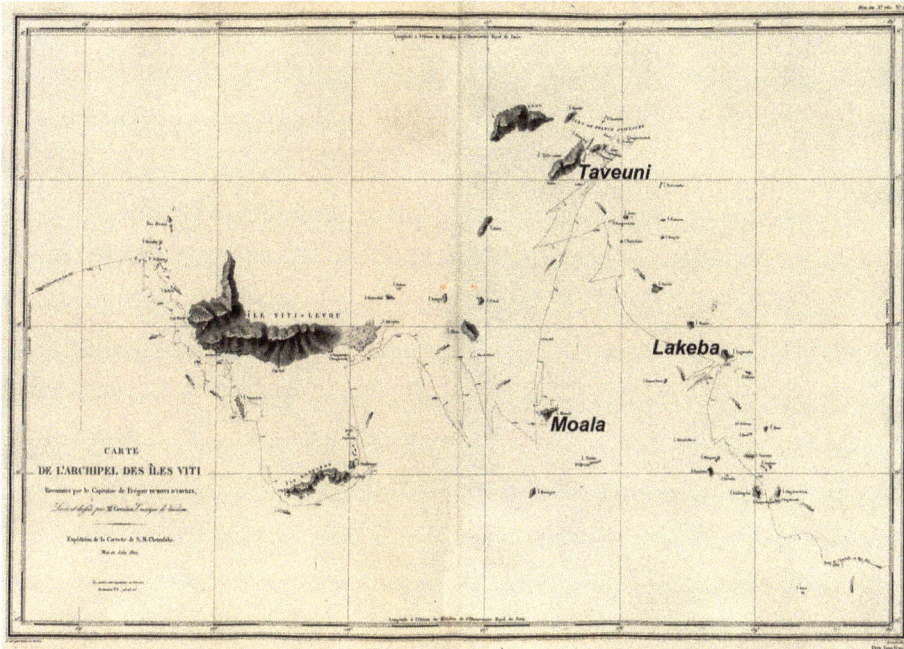

Figure 6.5 Ambroise Tardieu after Victor-Amédée Gressien, 'Carte de l'Archipel des Iles Viti, reconnues par le capitaine de frégate Dumont d'Urville … expédition de la corvette de S.M. l'Astrolabe, mai et juin 1827', 1833.

Engraving, in Jules Dumont d'Urville, *Voyage de la corvette l'Astrolabe exécuté pendant les années 1826–1827–1828–1829 … Atlas [hydrographique]*, J. Tastu, Paris: plate 23.

Source: National Library of Australia, Canberra. Annotation. Photograph: B. Douglas.

On 25 May 1827, as the *Astrolabe* sailed through the southern islands of the Lau group in eastern Fiji, five men boarded the corvette from a canoe. Four were Tongans, including the 'chief, named Mouki', and his son. Proud owner of 10 firearms, Mouki had visited Port Jackson, New Zealand and Tahiti on an English vessel. He now lived and traded at Lakeba 'under the protection of the chief Touï-Neao [Tui Nayau]' who had only six guns. The surgeon-naturalist Joseph-Paul Gaimard was amazed to discover that the fifth visitor was 'one of our former acquaintances from Guam', a young Islander named José Mediola whom Gaimard had met during his earlier circumnavigation of the globe under Louis de Freycinet. On 26 May 1819, then aged 14 years, Mediola was among 76 'Metis, descendants of Filipinos, and Chamorros, or natives of the Marianas Islands', whose strength Gaimard tested on a dynamometer. His performance was above average for his age and Gaimard described him as 'a well built young man'. Several years later, Mediola had either deserted or been abandoned by a Manila-based Spanish trading ship and 'attached himself' to Mouki's service. He begged to be allowed to join the *Astrolabe* and Dumont d'Urville admitted him on grounds of 'humanity' and his likely utility as an interpreter. The next day, three young Spanish survivors of the trading vessel's subsequent shipwreck came on board and also pleaded successfully to be added to the crew. One of them, Guttierez, reputedly spoke Fijian 'fluently' and became the key link in an interpretive chain with Gaimard who spoke Spanish.[22] Gaimard was the expedition's main ethnographer due to his great enthusiasm for working ashore, his linguistic interests, and – said Dumont d'Urville – the 'good opinion he usually enjoyed amongst savage nations'.[23]

Mouki, who claimed some 'authority' in Lakeba, initially made himself 'very useful' to the French. During two days on board, he helped pilot the vessel to Lakeba, impressing Dumont d'Urville with his knowledge of the position of reefs, islands, and their 'true names'.[24] Keeping the other three Tongans 'as hostages', Dumont d'Urville sent Mouki to Lakeba in the longboat, with Mediola as interpreter, to negotiate the acquisition of an anchor reportedly abandoned there, though none of the boat's crew knew much Spanish. Once on shore, Mouki's inability to exercise 'any influence' over a 'turbulent', 'noisy' crowd of armed Fijians led the prudent *enseigne* Victor-Charles Lottin to retreat without landing. It was, Lottin decided, 'evident that he had no rights over the anchor, and probable that he enjoyed no authority in the island'. Mouki was seemingly so overcome by 'fright' at the height of the affair that he hid, flat on his stomach, in the bottom of the boat. Yet a 'brother' of the Tui Nayau known to the French as Toki (Figure 6.9), who had also come aboard the *Astrolabe*, insisted that the Fijians meant no harm and wanted only to trade. Mediola, the Spaniards, and Mouki maintained that they were extremely curious rather than hostile and Lottin himself later agreed, blaming the debacle on 'the pilot' Mouki who afterwards left the *Astrolabe* and did not return.[25]

From 27 May, persistent storms drove the corvette away from Lakeba. Marooned on board were the three remaining Tongans, a half-Tongan 'cousin' of the Tui Nayau, and two Fijian 'chiefs' – Toki of Lakeba and a man the French knew as Tomboua-Nakoro (Tubuanakoro). When Dumont d'Urville, per Guttierez, explained the situation, the Fijians were unworried but the Tongans were 'profoundly distressed' because, they said, all Fijians bar the Lakebans 'were their enemies and would eat them'. For a week Dumont d'Urville struggled north-west through the Lau group, hoping in vain to land his passengers in

22 Dumont d'Urville 1830–33, IV: 400–401, 404, 412–413; Gaimard 1817–19: 429–435; 1832: 719–722.
23 Dumont d'Urville 1830–33, V: 158.
24 Dumont d'Urville 1830–33, IV: 400; Gaimard 1832: 720.
25 Dumont d'Urville 1830–33, IV: 401, 404–407; Gaimard 1832: 707–708, 721; Lottin 1832: 691–695.

Taveuni, and then sailed due south to Moala (Figure 6.6). Gaimard escorted them to the island, leaving Tubuanakoro and Toki well endowed with gifts. As a keen fieldworker, Gaimard was outraged that a strong rip and the crew's 'cowardice' prevented his realising his 'extreme desire' to go ashore: 'prudence', he railed, was doubtless 'very necessary during a voyage of discovery; but if, in turn and sometimes simultaneously, you fear reefs, storms, savages, illness, you are not fit for such expeditions'.[26]

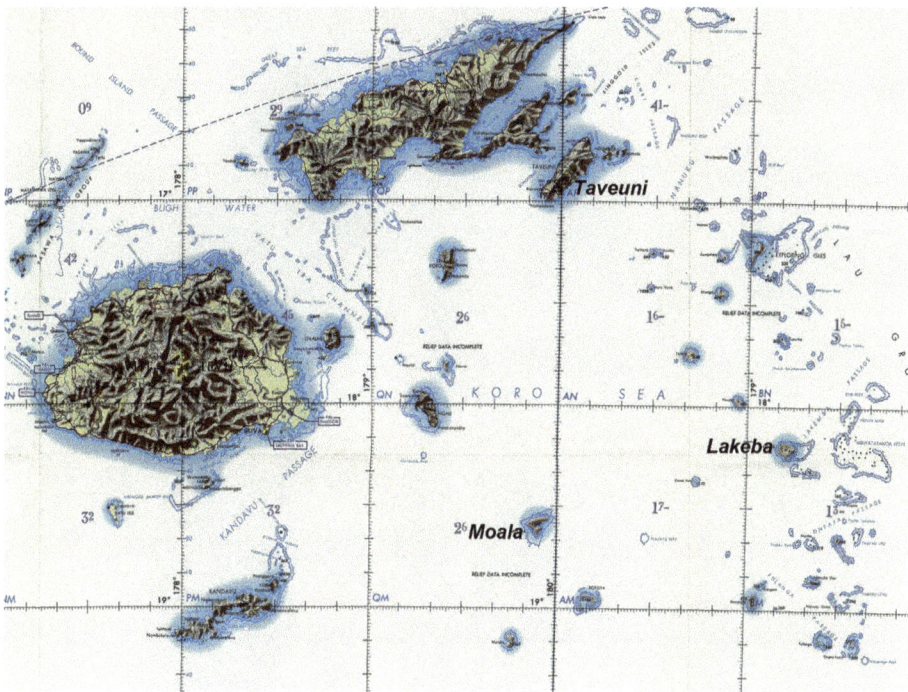

Figure 6.6 United States Air Force, 'Fiji Islands', 1968, lithograph, detail.

Source: Aeronautical Chart and Information Centre, US Air Force, St Louis, Perry-Castañeda Library Map Collection, Courtesy of the University of Texas Libraries, The University of Texas at Austin: www.lib. utexas.edu/maps/onc/txu-pclmaps-oclc-8322829_p_17.jpg, accessed 9 February 2014. Annotation B. Douglas.

---

26   Dumont d'Urville 1827; 1830–33, IV: 407, 409–410, 414–415, 423–425, 428–429; Gaimard 1832: 721–723.

Figure 6.7 Emmanuel-Adolphe Midy after Louis-Auguste Sainson, 'Archipel des Viti: Portrait en pied de Tounbouanokoro', 1833.

Lithograph, in Jules Dumont d'Urville, *Voyage de la corvette l'Astrolabe exécuté pendant les années 1826–1827–1828–1829 … Atlas historique*, J. Tastu, Paris: plate 98 (3).

Source: National Library of Australia, Canberra: nla.pic-an8264642.

All the French were extravagantly impressed by the 'remarkable intelligence and dignity' of Tubuanakoro whose portrayals by the artist Louis-Auguste de Sainson are lithographed in the *Atlas* of Dumont d'Urville's voyage (Figures 6.7, 6.10).[27] Ratu Loaloadravu Tubuanakoro was a son of Ratu Tanoa Visawaqa who, on the death of his powerful older brother Ratu Naulivou Ramatenikutu in 1829, became the fifth Vunivalu (warlord, political leader) of the island polity of Bau. Tubuanakoro, killed in an internecine conflict at Bau in 1832, was the older half-brother of Ratu Epenisa Seru Cakobau, who became the sixth Vunivalu in 1852 and was Tui Viti ('King of Fiji') in 1871–74.[28] The French voyagers in 1827 heard that Tubuanakoro was a 'nephew' (brother's son) of Naulivou whom Dumont d'Urville understood to be 'sovereign of <u>Embao</u> [Bau] leading chief of the large island <u>Viti-levou</u> [Viti Levu] and who claims a kind of sovereignty over most of the small islands to the E. of his residence'.[29] Tubuanakoro served Naulivou as 'agent' collecting tribute in the Lau Islands and elsewhere. In consequence, as he and Toki acknowledged, he was 'accustomed to travel' and unusually well informed. Since 'everything he said' seemed trustworthy, Gaimard saw him as a 'mine' of information to be 'carefully exploited' through Guttierez. In Sainson's whimsical phrase, Gaimard conducted 'long sessions' of 'severe assaults on the imperturbable amiability of the Fijian taxation officer'. In the process, he learned Fijian and Tongan names and population estimates for 109 islands or islets and 'a wealth of ideas on the manners, customs, and usages of the peoples of Fiji'. Dumont d'Urville invited Tubuanakoro to his cabin where he obtained 'the nomenclature of every island we saw' and 'discovered the existence of several others unmarked on the maps'. Both Frenchmen admired Tubuanakoro's precise reading of the 'position', 'direction' and 'names' of all the islands marked on Krusenstern's vestigial map of Fiji (Figure 6.4).[30] Gaimard also amassed a Fijian vocabulary of nearly 300 words, which Dumont d'Urville published and the modern linguist Albert Schütz deemed 'surprisingly accurate', given its circuitous acquisition from Tubuanakoro via the tacit agency of the interpreters.[31]

---

27   Sainson 1832: 726.
28   Routledge 1985: 42–96, 126–129, 208–210. See also World of Royalty 2001–14 for a genealogy of the Vunivalu of Bau.
29   Dumont d'Urville 1827 (original emphasis).
30   Dumont d'Urville 1827; 1830–33, IV: 413, 415, 423, 426–427; Gaimard 1832: 698, 700–701, 708–713, 717, 722; Sainson 1832: 727.
31   Dumont d'Urville 1834: 137–142; Schütz 1974: 450.

Figure 6.8 Jacques Arago after Louis-Auguste de Sainson, 'Enlèvement du canot de l'Astrolabe par les naturels de Tonga-Tabou (Iles des Amis)', 1833.

Lithograph, in Jules Dumont d'Urville, *Voyage de la corvette l'Astrolabe exécuté pendant les années 1826–1827–1828–1829 … Atlas historique*, J. Tastu, Paris: plate 87.

Source: National Library of Australia, Canberra: PIC Volume 577 #U1796 NK3340.

The French texts apply an extraordinary stream of positive epithets to Tubuanakoro: 'of very remarkable sagacity, intelligence, and kindness'; 'courage', 'sang-froid'; 'a very remarkable man, superior in his country'; 'the most knowledgeable of them'; a 'noble, mild, happy physiognomy'; 'courtesy', 'steadfastness'; 'noble affability'; and the encomium taken from widely travelled Dumont d'Urville's published narrative – 'a man of mild manners, attractive physique, and obliging character, he showed himself to be much superior, in my eyes, to all the savages I had seen thus far'.[32] All these words are overt signs of personal indigenous agency as processed in European perceptions. But the euphoria of French 'good opinion' of Tubuanakoro and its partial projection on to Fijians generally are also countersigns of these voyagers' relief at approved indigenous conduct, given the perennial insecurity of Oceanic voyaging under sail and the vulnerability of sailors to unpredictable local behaviour. Such relief typically generated positive depictions or softened negative ones, even in the

---

32   Dumont d'Urville 1827; 1830–33, IV: 424, 426–427; Gaimard 1832: 698, 709, 718; Sainson 1832: 726–728.

face of prejudiced aversion to physical appearance. The reverse was also the case. Less than a fortnight before the expedition reached Fijian waters, one of the *Astrolabe*'s boats had suddenly been attacked in Tongatapu and its crew seized by 'a compact mass of savages' more than 500 strong. Sainson depicted the scene (Figure 6.8). Dumont d'Urville was initially charmed by Tongans, their 'agreeable' physiognomies, 'comparable' to those seen in Europe, and their 'generous, obliging, hospitable' character. He ranked them 'above' other segments of 'the Polynesian race' for the quality of their agriculture and – despite proximity to Fiji – for showing fewer traces of physical 'mixing' with the 'black race' ('height stunted, nose flat, hair frizzy or curly, and very dark brown skin'). However, their unexpected, violent conduct provoked an about-face and led him to denounce them as 'barbarians' – 'perfidious', 'versatile', 'treacherous', 'covetous, audacious, and above all profoundly hypocritical'.[33] These words are indigenous countersigns.

In practice, Fijian appearance, 'conduct' and polity defied the emergent racial dichotomy of the (admired) 'copper-coloured or Polynesian race' and the (despised) 'black Oceanian or Melanesian race'. The French observers concurred a priori that 'the Fijians' did not belong to 'the *yellow race*' but were 'evidently part of the *black race*'.[34] They classed Toki of Lakeba behind only Tubuanakoro in intelligence and demeanour. Yet at first sight, referring to Sainson's portrait (Figure 6.9), Dumont d'Urville had 'instantly' seen in 'his colour, features, attitude and manners … the true type of the black Oceanian race' that he had previously observed in New Ireland, New Guinea and New Holland. In most respects, the excellent Tubuanakoro struck them otherwise: his 'aquiline nose', 'the cut and the feature of his face, his simply suntanned complexion, his appearance and his figure' brought to mind 'the Arab type', though they noted that his 'ample, curly hairdo' was close to 'that of the Papuans and the Melanesians generally' (Figure 6.10).[35]

---

33 Dumont d'Urville 1827; 1830–33, IV: 80, 129–133, 166, 221, 228–229, 231.

34 Dumont d'Urville 1830–33, IV: 414, 427, 447, 453; Gaimard 1832: 718, original emphasis; Quoy 1830–32, IV: 696.

35 Dumont d'Urville 1830–33, IV: 408, 427; Gaimard 1832: 714, 718; Sainson 1832: 728.

Figure 6.9 Emmanuel-Adolphe Midy after Louis-Auguste Sainson, 'Archipel des Viti: Toki frère du chef de Lakemba', 1833.

Lithograph, in Jules Dumont d'Urville, *Voyage de la corvette l'Astrolabe exécuté pendant les années 1826–1827–1828–1829 … Atlas historique*, J. Tastu, Paris: plate 98 (2).

Source: National Library of Australia, Canberra: nla.pic-an8264642.

Figure 6.10 Emmanuel-Adolphe Midy after Louis-Auguste Sainson, 'Archipel des Viti: Tounbouanokoro', 1833.

Lithograph, in Jules Dumont d'Urville, *Voyage de la corvette l'Astrolabe exécuté pendant les années 1826–1827–1828–1829 … Atlas historique*, J. Tastu, Paris: plate 98 (5).

Source: National Library of Australia, Canberra: nla.pic-an8264642.

In the relatively immediate genres of journal and narrative, racial typology was stymied by twin existential paradoxes: that a 'black race' combining such hair with 'black skin verging on chocolate', 'flattened face, squashed nose' and 'thick lips' should also be generally 'very handsome men', 'remarkable in stature and strength', with 'fine' physiques; and that they should practise pottery-making, unknown in Polynesia.[36] In his abstract racial taxonomy of Oceania, Dumont d'Urville resolved the conundrum by reconstituting 'the blacks of Fiji' as the 'first rank' of the Melanesian race. He attributed their 'advantages' of 'laws', 'arts', government, and 'a dose of intelligence and judgement very remarkable for savages' not to their own agency but to their proximity to the Tongans and 'frequent communications' with 'the Polynesian race'.[37] He historicised and further racialised this judgement in a passage in his narrative:

> these Islanders, forming the last link of the black Oceanian race in the east, would undoubtedly have opposed the progress of the yellow or Polynesian race towards the west. After a long era of warfare, they forged friendly relations; the Tongans are admitted as traders and even colonists to several Fijian islands; frequent alliances occur between the two races, and from their mixing results an intermediary race which, in a century or two, will perhaps constitute the main population of this archipelago.[38]

Echoes of this enduring racial ranking are encrusted in the heavily Polynesian bias of the historiography of Oceanic voyaging and − until recently − in its omission or elision of indigenous agency apart from that of a handful of Polynesians. So, in a generally meticulous overview of Dumont d'Urville's passage through the Fiji Islands, Helen Rosenman alluded to Tubuanakoro only in passing as 'one of *Astrolabe*'s ex-passengers'. John Dunmore, decorated historian of French Pacific exploration, mentioned him not at all. Yet both devoted some detail to the Tongan Mouki, despite his lesser contribution to the expedition and its textual legacy.[39]

Two dominant strands in positive French evaluations of their Fijian experience are utility and affect or emotion. The inestimable practical value of the navigational aid provided by Mouki and Tubuanakoro, implicitly mediated by the interpreters, is patent. But it evoked little more overt appreciation than Dumont d'Urville's reiterated phrase 'very useful' − an appropriate expression for a terse, male, military discourse.[40] Yet the crux of Tubuanakoro's appeal to the French was emotion − or its apparent absence. Affect has recently become an acceptable, even required theme in historical scholarship, undermining the relentless rationalism of conventional positivist historiography. Cases in point with respect to Oceanic voyaging are Vanessa Smith's *Intimate Strangers* and my own recent work.[41] Writing about indigenous intermediaries, Harry Liebersohn

---

36   Dumont d'Urville 1830–33, IV: 445–446; Gaimard 1832: 718–719; Quoy 1830–32, IV: 696–697; Sainson 1832: 727.

37   Dumont d'Urville 1832: 12–13.

38   Dumont d'Urville 1830–33, IV: 450–451.

39   Dunmore 1969: 202–206; Rosenman 1987, I: 127–133. See also Douglas 2014a: 26–33 for a critique of Oceanic voyage historiography.

40   Dumont d'Urville 1827; 1830–33, IV: 400.

41   Douglas 2014a; Smith 2010.

characterised their relationships with and representations by voyagers as an ambivalent 'mixture of interest and feeling'.[42] Every French observer I have cited applauded the 'perfectly calm' 'courage' and 'noble tranquillity' with which Tubuanakoro confronted the prospect of exile from his homeland while deploring the bitter wailing of the Tongans and eventually Toki.[43] In a passage saturated by affective countersigns of indigenous agency, Dumont d'Urville summed up the emotional value placed by naval officers on the virtues of stoicism and restraint:

> His conduct always presented a happy union of gravity, courtesy, reserve and stability of spirit; never did he abandon himself, as did his companions, to uncontrolled transports of joy or grief, rage or satisfaction, according to the influence of circumstances.[44]

I conclude by briefly discussing a different, far more elusive nexus of interest, utility, feeling and agency implied in stories about two indigenous women. The first is a Tahitian who evidently taught her English lover, the illiterate marine private Samuel Gibson, to speak Tahitian during Cook's first visit to the island in 1769. Gibson tried to desert, was forcibly retaken to the ship and flogged, but returned to Tahiti in 1773 as a corporal on the *Resolution*. On this occasion, he served as Cook's regular interpreter because he 'spoke the language tolerable well'.[45] The second woman is a young Tasmanian, one of two female transcontinental travellers encountered by Dumont d'Urville's expedition in 1826 at King George's Sound in south-western Australia where they were living and working with a party of sealers.[46] Unnamed by the French, they were later identified as Mooney and Dinah.[47] Sainson depicted them sympathetically (Figure 6.11) but in their shipboard zoological journal, Gaimard and his colleague Jean-René Constant Quoy animalised these women's 'thick, protuberant lips, lengthening into a kind of snout [*museau*]'.[48] In their formal *Zoologie*, they used Sainson's portraits as evidence to render this exaggerated personal facial feature, seen on *two* women and depicted by Sainson on only one, as the defining characteristic of a 'distinct race' in Van Diemen's Land.[49] This generic sequence from contemporary journal to scientific treatise epitomises the counterfeit logical trajectory on which the science of race depended – a priori typification with intellectual slippage from particular to type.

---

42   Liebersohn 2006: 140.
43   Dumont d'Urville 1830–33, IV: 415, 423–424; Gaimard 1832: 699, 722; Sainson 1832: 727.
44   Dumont d'Urville 1830–33, IV: 427.
45   Cook 1955–67, I: 114–115, 140; II: 233.
46   The lithograph caption assigns the women to Kangaroo Island where Tasmanian women had reportedly lived with sealers from the 1810s (Taylor 2002).
47   Amery 1998: 52–53; Clarke 1998: 31, 33.
48   The term *museau* ('muzzle', 'snout') referred specifically to 'the dog and some other animals' and was sometimes 'popularly' extended to people, 'but only with contempt or in jest' (Institut de France 1835, II: 247).
49   Quoy and Gaimard 1830a: 198–199; 1830b: 45–46.

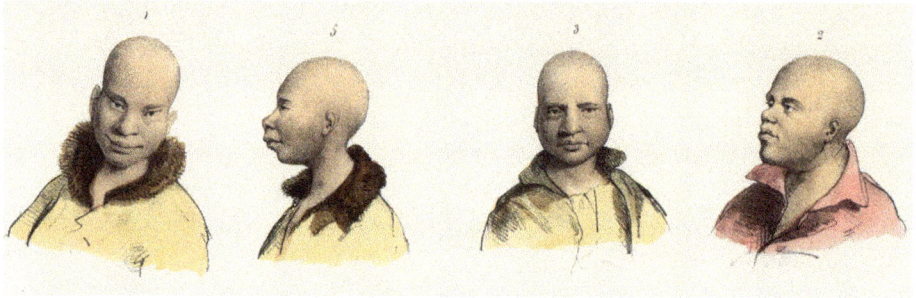

Figure 6.11 Hippolyte-Louis Garnier after Louis-Auguste de Sainson, 'N^{lle}. Hollande: Ile des Kanguroos: femmes de l'île', 1833.

Lithographs, composite, in Jules Dumont d'Urville, *Voyage de la corvette l'Astrolabe exécuté pendant les années 1826–1827–1828–1829 … Atlas historique*, J. Tastu, Paris: plate 12 (1), (2), (3), (5).

Source: National Library of Australia, Canberra: nla.pic-an8133372.

Yet here, too, signs and countersigns of indigenous agency perturb racial system. Quoy and Gaimard reported the sealers' open acknowledgement that they depended on their indigenous wives for food and 'that without them they would probably have died of misery'. Quoy also recognised the naturalists' own debt to the 'skill and industry' of these women in procuring natural history specimens – oysters, other shells and large lizards.[50] Much later, in an 'erotic biography' of his colleague, Quoy recalled sardonically that Gaimard – gregarious and lascivious – quickly made friends with the sealers and 'especially with their wives'.[51] Dumont d'Urville equivocally acknowledged one of the Tasmanian women as having a 'kind of intelligence' despite corresponding 'in the highest degree to her racial type'. She gave Gaimard a list of about 100 words of the language of Port Dalrymple (Launceston) which Dumont d'Urville published, hoping it was 'exact' since her English lover had served as interpreter.[52] The word list is at once a rare public sign of female agency in an encounter with Europeans and a countersign of the tangled skein of agency in such transactions. The list includes the terms arse, breast, penis, testicle and vulva – likely countersigns of the woman's sexual liaisons with her lover and perhaps with Gaimard. Like the Tahitian, Mooney and Dinah represent the almost invisible multitude of indigenous women who tutored their foreign sexual partners in local language and manners or otherwise purveyed knowledge and assistance to strangers.

In conversation with Tubuanakoro, Gaimard gathered that the Fijians divided humanity into 'three races of men or three different peoples': *Kaï-Viti* (themselves); *Kaï Tonga* (the Tongans); and *Kaï Papalan-hi* [*papalagi*]

---

50   Quoy 1830–32, I: 206; Quoy and Gaimard 1830a: 198; 1830b: 44–45.
51   Quoy n.d.: 12–13.
52   Dumont d'Urville 1830–33, I: 105–106; 1834: 9–10.

(foreigners).[53] Condescending, he saw this tripartite classification as a token of their limited geographical knowledge. From another perspective, however, it is a sharp reminder of the Fijians' rapidly expanding world view and the kaleidoscopic multinational activity already under way in a part of the world still almost unknown to European science and cartography. To a greater or lesser extent, Enrique, the Malay pilots, Tumai, Pedro, Ahutoru, the Tahitian woman, Tupaia, Ma'i, Mahine, Kadu, Mouki, Tubuanakoro, Toki, Samuel Gibson, José Mediola, Guttierez and his companions, the sealers, Dinah, and Mooney were participants in a mobile global undertow which arrogant naval voyagers elided, despised, but were often forced to enlist and depend on.

Acknowledgements

I gratefully acknowledge research support from the Australian Research Council (project numbers DP0665356 and DP1094562) and the National Library of Australia which awarded me a Harold White Fellowship in 2010 and gave generous permission for the reproduction of images and maps.

References

Amery, Rob 1998, 'Sally and Harry: insights into early Kaurna contact history', in *History in Portraits: Biographies of Nineteenth Century South Australian Aboriginal People*, Jane Simpson and Louise Hercus (eds), Aboriginal History Inc., Canberra, 49–87.

Banks, Joseph 1962, *The* Endeavour *Journal of Joseph Banks 1768–1771*, J.C. Beaglehole (ed.), Public Library of New South Wales and Angus and Robertson, Sydney, 2 vols.

Bougainville, Louis-Antoine de 1771, *Voyage autour du monde … en 1766, 1767, 1768 & 1769*, Saillant & Nyon, Paris.

——1977, 'Journal de Bougainville commandant de la *Boudeuse*', in *Bougainville et ses compagnons autour du monde 1766–1769*, Etienne Taillemite (ed.), Imprimerie nationale, Paris, vol. 1: 141–497.

Bravo, Michael T. 1996a, 'The accuracy of ethnoscience: a study of Inuit cartography and cross-cultural commensurability', *Manchester Papers in Social Anthropology* 2: 1–36.

---

53   Gaimard 1832: 699; see also Dumont d'Urville 1830–33, IV: 426.

——1996b, 'Ethnological encounters', in *Cultures of Natural History*, Nicholas Jardine, James A. Secord and Emma C. Spary (eds), Cambridge University Press, Cambridge: 338–357.

——1999, 'Ethnographic navigation and the geographical gift', in *Geography and Enlightenment*, David N. Livingstone and Charles W.J. Withers (eds), University of Chicago Press, Chicago and London: 199–235.

Burnett, D. Graham 2002, '"It is impossible to make a step without the Indians": nineteenth-century geographical exploration and the Amerindians of British Guiana', *Ethnohistory* 49: 3–40.

Caldwall, James, after William Hodges 1777, 'Omai', engraving, in James Cook, *A Voyage Towards the South Pole and Round the World … in the Years 1772, 1773, 1774, and 1775 …*, W. Strahan and T. Cadell, London, vol. 1, plate 57, facing p. 168, David Rumsey Map Collection, www.davidrumsey.com/luna/servlet/detail/RUMSEY~8~1~24038~870082, accessed 9 February 2014.

Carter, Harold B. 1998, 'Notes on the drawings by an unknown artist from the voyage of HMS *Endeavour*', in *Science and Exploration in the Pacific: European Voyages to the Southern Oceans in the Eighteenth Century*, Margarette Lincoln (ed.), Boydell Press and National Maritime Museum, Woodbridge, Suffolk, 133–134.

Chamisso, Adelbert von 1821, 'Bemerkungen und Ansichten von dem Naturforscher der Expedition', in Otto von Kotzebue, *Entdeckungs-Reise in die Süd-See und nach der Berings-Straße … unternommen in den Jahren 1815, 1816, 1817 und 1818 …*, Gebrüdern Hoffmann, Weimar, vol. 3: 3–179.

Chappell, David 1997, *Double Ghosts: Oceanian Voyagers on Euroamerican Ships*, ME Sharpe, Armonk, NY, and London.

Choris, Louis 1822, *Voyage pittoresque autour du monde, avec des portraits de sauvages d'Amérique, d'Asie, d'Afrique, et des îles du Grand Océan …*, [J.B.B. Eyriès] (tr.), Firmin Didot, Paris.

Clarke, Philip A. 1998, 'The Aboriginal presence on Kangaroo Island, South Australia', in *History in Portraits: Biographies of Nineteenth Century South Australian Aboriginal People*, Jane Simpson and Louise Hercus (eds), Aboriginal History Inc., Canberra, 14–48.

Cook, James 1955–67, *The Journals of Captain James Cook on his Voyages of Discovery*, J.C. Beaglehole (ed.), Hakluyt Society, Cambridge, 3 vols.

Douglas, Bronwen 2013, 'Philosophers, naturalists, and antipodean encounters, 1748–1803', *Intellectual History Review* 23: 387–409.

——2014a, *Science, Voyagers, and Encounters in Oceania 1511–1850*, Palgrave Macmillan, Basingstoke and New York.

——2014b, 'Naming places: voyagers, toponyms, and local presence in the fifth part of the world, 1500–1700', *Journal of Historical Geography* 45: 12–24.

Driver, Felix and Lowri Jones 2009, *Hidden Histories of Exploration: Researching the RGS-IBG Collections*, Royal Holloway, University of London, and RGS-IBG, London.

Dumont d'Urville, Jules 1827, 'Rapport à S.E. le Ministre de la Marine et des Colonies sur les operations de la corvette l'Astrolabe, depuis son départ du Port-Jackson, le 19 décembre 1826, jusqu'à son arrivée à Amboine, en Sept. ᵇʳᵉ 1827 …, Amboine, 7 octobre 1827', manuscript, Archives centrales de la Marine, Service historique de la Défense, Vincennes: BB⁴ 1002.

——1830–33, *Voyage de la corvette l'Astrolabe exécuté … pendant les années 1826–1827–1828–1829 … Histoire du voyage*, J Tastu, Paris, 5 vols.

——1832, 'Sur les îles du grand Océan', *Bulletin de la Société de Géographie* 17: 1–21.

——1834, *Voyage de découvertes de l'Astrolabe exécuté … pendant les années 1826–1827–1828–1829 … Philologie*, Ministère de la Marine, Paris, vol. 2.

Dunmore, John 1969, *French Explorers in the Pacific: The Nineteenth Century*, Clarendon Press, Oxford.

Forster, Georg 1777, *A Voyage Round the World in His Britannic Majesty's Sloop, Resolution …*, Benjamin White et al., London, 2 vols.

Forster, Johann Reinhold 1778, *Observations Made during a Voyage Round the World, on Physical Geography, Natural History, and Ethic Philosophy*, G. Robinson, London.

Gaimard, Joseph-Paul 1817–19, 'Voyage physique dans l'hémisphère austral, et autour du monde, exécuté successivement sur la corvette du Roi l'Uranie et la corvette de S.M. la Physicienne, commandées par Mʳ. Louis de Freycinet … pendant les années 1817, 1818, 1819 et 1820: Journal historique, vol. 1', manuscript, State Library of Western Australia, Perth: MN 1188 purl.slwa. wa.gov.au/slwa_b1745716_001, accessed 21 May 2014.

——1832, 'Extrait du journal', in Jules Dumont d'Urville, *Voyage de la corvette l'Astrolabe exécuté … pendant les années 1826–1827–1828–1829 … Histoire du voyage*, J. Tastu, Paris, vol. 4: 698–726.

Guest, Harriet 2004, 'Ornament and use: Mai and Cook in London', in *A New Imperial History: Culture, Identity and Modernity in Britain and the Empire, 1660–1840*, Kathleen Wilson (ed.), Cambridge University Press, Cambridge, 317–344.

Hervé, Georges 1914, 'Aotourou ou le Taitien à Paris', *Revue anthropologique* 24: 209–219.

Hetherington, Michelle (ed.) 2001, *Cook & Omai: The Cult of the South Seas*, National Library of Australia, Canberra.

Hodges, William [c. 1775], *Omai, a Polynesian*, oil, Royal College of Surgeons of England, London: RCSSC/P 241. BBC Your Paintings www.bbc.co.uk/arts/yourpaintings/paintings/omai-a-polynesian, accessed 9 February 2014.

Institut de France 1835, *Dictionnaire de l'Académie française*, sixth edition, Firmin Didot frères, Paris, 2 vols.

Kotzebue, Otto von 1821, *Entdeckungs-Reise in die Süd-See und nach der Berings-Straße … unternommen in den Jahren 1815, 1816, 1817 und 1818 …*, Gebrüdern Hoffmann, Weimar, 3 vols.

Krusenstern, Adam Johann von 1824a, *Atlas de l'Océan pacifique*, par ordre de Sa Majesté impériale, St Petersbourg, vol. 1.

——1824b, *Recueil de mémoires hydrographiques, pour servir d'analyse et d'explication à l'Atlas de l'Océan Pacifique*, Imprimerie du Département de l'Instruction publique, Saint-Pétersbourg, vol. 1.

Lewis, David 1994 [1972], *We the Navigators: The Ancient Art of Landfinding in the Pacific*, second edition, University of Hawai'i Press, Honolulu.

Liebersohn, Harry 2006, *The Travelers' World: Europe to the Pacific*, Harvard University Press, Cambridge, MA.

Lottin, Victor-Charles 1832, 'Extrait du journal', in Jules Dumont d'Urville, *Voyage de la corvette l'Astrolabe exécuté … pendant les années 1826–1827–1828–1829 … Histoire du voyage*, J. Tastu, Paris, vol. 4: 691–695.

Munilla, Martin de 1963, 'Relaçion del descubrim[ien]to de la parte Austral y incognita del Sur y de n[uest]ros frayles', in *Austrialia franciscana*, Celsus Kelly (ed.), Franciscan Historical Studies (Australia) and Archivo Ibero-Americano (Madrid), Madrid, vol. 1: 21–94.

Newell, Jenny 2005, 'Pacific travelers: the Islanders who voyaged with Cook', *Common-place* 5(2), www.common-place.org/vol-05/no-02/newell/index.shtml; www.common-place.org/vol-05/no-02/, accessed 8 February 2014.

Parsonson, G.S. 1966, 'The Problem of Pouro and Manicolo', in *La Austrialia del Espíritu Santo* …, Celsus Kelly (tr. and ed.), Hakluyt Society, Cambridge, vol. 2, Appendix 2: 377–379.

Pereire, Jacob-Rodrigue 1771, 'Observations sur l'articulation de l'insulaire de la mer du Sud, que M. de Bougainville a amené de l'île Taiti, & sur le vocabulaire qu'il a fait du langage de cette île', in Louis-Antoine de Bougainville, *Voyage autour du monde … en 1766, 1767, 1768 & 1769*, Saillant & Nyon, Paris, 403–407.

Pigafetta, Antonio [c. 1525], 'Navigation et descouurement de la Inde superieure et isles de Malucque ou naissent les cloux de girofle … commanceant en lan Mil V^{cc}. et xix', Yale University Library, New Haven: Beinecke MS 351, brbl-dl.library.yale.edu/vufind/Record/3438401, accessed 8 February 2014.——1906 [1525?], *Magellan's Voyage around the World: the Original Text of the Ambrosian MS., with English Translation* …, James Alexander Robertson (tr. and ed.), Arthur H. Clark Co., Cleveland, 3 vols.

Quirós, Pedro Fernández de 1973a [c. 1609], [Memorial número 8 … presentado al Rey Felipe III], in *Australia su descubrimiento y denominación* …, Carlos Sanz (ed.), Dirección General de Relaciones Culturales, Ministerio de Asuntos Exteriores, Madrid, 23–26.

——1973b [1609], *Copia de unos avisos muy notables dados a la S.C. y Real Magestad del Rey Don Felipe nuestro Señor* …, Gabriel Graells y Giraldo Dotil, Barcelona, in *Australia su descubrimiento y denominación* …, Carlos Sanz (ed.), Dirección General de Relaciones Culturales, Ministerio de Asuntos Exteriores, Madrid, 29–32.

——2000, *Descubrimiento de las regiones australes*, Roberto Ferrando Pérez (ed.), Dastin, Madrid.

Quirós, Pedro Fernández de and Jeronimo de Valera 1963, 'Memorial de Quirós al Arzobispo de Lima … sobre las dudas propuestas por Quirós [Lima, 1605]', in *Austrialia franciscana*, Celsus Kelly (ed.), Franciscan Historical Studies (Australia) and Archivo Ibero-Americano (Madrid), Madrid, vol. 1: 12–16.

Quoy, Jean-René Constant 1830–32, 'Extrait du journal', in Jules Dumont d'Urville, *Voyage de la corvette l'Astrolabe exécuté … pendant les années 1826–1827–1828–1829 … Histoire du voyage*, J. Tastu, Paris, vol. 1: 200–212; vol. 4: 696–698.

——n.d., 'Paul Gaimard', manuscript, Médiathèque Michel-Crépeau, La Rochelle: MS 2508.

Quoy, Jean-René Constant and Joseph-Paul Gaimard 1830a, 'Extrait du journal zoologique', in Jules Dumont d'Urville, *Voyage de la corvette l'Astrolabe exécuté … pendant les années 1826–1827–1828–1829 … Histoire du voyage*, J. Tastu, Paris, vol. 1: 192–199.

——1830b, 'De l'homme', in *Voyage de découvertes de l'Astrolabe exécuté … pendant les années 1826–1827–1828–1829 … Zoologie*, J. Tastu, Paris, vol. 1: 15–59.Raj, Kapil 2010 [2007], *Relocating Modern Science: Circulation and the Construction of Knowledge in South Asia and Europe, 1650–1900*, Palgrave Macmillan, Basingstoke and New York.

Rensch, Karl H. 2000, *The Language of the Noble Savage: The Linguistic Fieldwork of Reinhold and George Forster in Polynesia on Cook's Second Voyage to the Pacific 1772–1775*, Archipelago Press, Canberra.

Rosenman, Helen (tr. and ed.) 1987, *An Account in Two Volumes of Two Voyages to the South Seas …*, Melbourne University Press, Carlton, 2 vols.

Routledge, David 1985, *Matanitu: The Struggle for Power in Early Fiji*, Institute of Pacific Studies, University of the South Pacific, Suva.

Safier, Neil 2008, *Measuring the New World: Enlightenment Science and South America*, University of Chicago Press, Chicago and London.

——2010, 'Global knowledge on the move: itineraries, Amerindian narratives, and deep histories of science', *Isis* 101: 133–145.

Sainson, Louis-Auguste de 1832, 'Extrait du journal', in Jules Dumont d'Urville, *Voyage de la corvette l'Astrolabe exécuté … pendant les années 1826–1827–1828–1829 … Histoire du voyage*, J. Tastu, Paris, vol. 4: 726–728.

Salmond, Anne 2003, *The Trial of the Cannibal Dog: Captain Cook in the South Seas*, Allen Lane, London.

——2008, 'Voyaging exchanges: Tahitian pilots and European navigators', in *Canoes of the Grand Ocean*, Anne Di Piazza and Erik Pearthree (eds), Archaeopress, Oxford, 23–46.

Schaffer, Simon, Lissa Roberts, Kapil Raj and James Delbourgo (eds) 2009, *The Brokered World: Go-betweens and Global Intelligence, 1770–1820*, Science History Publications, Sagamore Beach, MA.

Schütz, Albert J. 1974, 'The forerunners of the Fijian dictionary', *Journal of the Polynesian Society* 83: 443–457.

Short, John Rennie 2009, *Cartographic Encounters: Indigenous Peoples and the Exploration of the New World*, Reaktion Books, London.

Smith, Vanessa 2010, *Intimate Strangers: Friendship, Exchange and Pacific Encounters*, Cambridge University Press, Cambridge.

Staum, Martin S. 1996, *Minerva's Message: Stabilizing the French Revolution*, McGill-Queen's University Press, Montreal and Kingston.

Taylor, Rebe 2002, *Unearthed: the Aboriginal Tasmanians of Kangaroo Island*, Wakefield Press, Kent Town, SA.

Thomas, Nicholas 1997, 'Introduction: Tupaia's map', in *In Oceania: Visions, Artifacts, Histories*, Duke University Press, Durham, NC, and London, 1–20.

Torres, Luis Váez de 1878, [Carta de Luis Váez de Torres, escribió á Don Felipe III desde Manila, … en 12 de Julio de 1607], in Justo Zaragoza, 'Descubrimientos de los Españoles en el Mar del Sur y en las costas de la Nueva-Guinea', *Boletín de la Sociedad Geográfica de Madrid* 4: 12–27.

Turnbull, David 1998, 'Cook and Tupaia, a tale of cartographic *méconnaissance?*', in *Science and Exploration in the Pacific: European Voyages to the Southern Oceans in the Eighteenth Century*, Margarette Lincoln (ed.), Boydell Press and National Maritime Museum, Woodbridge, Suffolk, 117–131.

Wagoner, Phillip B. 2003, 'Precolonial intellectuals and the production of colonial knowledge', *Comparative Studies in Society and History* 45: 783–814.

Williams, Glyndwr 2003, 'Tupaia: Polynesian warrior, navigator, high priest – and artist', in *The Global Eighteenth Century*, Felicity A. Nussbaum (ed.), Johns Hopkins University Press, Baltimore, 38–51.

World of Royalty 2001–14, 'Vunivalu of Bau (title)', members.iinet.net.au/~royalty/states/fiji/vunivalu.html, accessed 10 February 2014.

7

Cross-cultural knowledge exchange in the age of the Enlightenment[1]

John Gascoigne

Introduction

One of the most characteristic features of European exploration of the Pacific was the extent to which it was linked with the Enlightenment-linked goals of promoting the acquisition of knowledge. This was often closely associated with the quest for imperial advantage or the search for wealth since knowledge brought with it the possibility of finding new sources of wealth. As the extent of trade around the world increased so, too, were habits of mind stimulated which formed a natural parallel with those required to accumulate the systematic bodies of knowledge on which science was based. The keeping of ledgers, the insistence on accuracy and the building up of networks which spanned more and more of the globe created a culture which was congruent with the values of science.[2] The habits of mind promoted by the accumulation of wealth also

---

1   This chapter has drawn upon material from Gascoigne 2014 with the permission of the publisher, Cambridge University Press.
2   Cook 2007: 57, 58, 225, 410.

helped to shape the mentality of science and the preservation of knowledge more generally. Like science, successful commerce depends on records, on first-hand information and a critical and even sceptical attitude in the use of the available data. Establishing reliable inventories of information, which transformed the fleeting and contingent into manipulable data sets, was basic to both commerce and science. Increasingly, too, with the development of more sophisticated systems of accounting European capitalism promoted a quantifying spirit that became a way of viewing and understanding the world more generally.[3]

Knowledge, however, could also be an end in itself: the product of curiosity, a need to make sense of the world or to give greater dignity to intrusion on other lands and peoples. More subtly, too, it could be a way of reshaping a view of the world that reflected the outlook of a dominant culture. For empires are in part imagined constructions that give privileged status to the way in which the imperial power sees the world and to the knowledge systems that are built on such assumptions.[4] Thus, as European science incorporated more of the world into its systems of classification and analysis, it took on a universalising aspect as local forms of knowledge from around the globe were translated into terms familiar to Europeans and amenable to European exploitation. The increasing dominance of the scientific world view from the late eighteenth century was, indeed, to be one of the most notable instances of the growing convergence of humankind.

Human divergence was, however, reflected in the multiplicity of forms of knowledge around the globe. Understandings of the way in which the world worked were linked to local needs and conditions giving rise to a great variety of knowledge systems. Knowledge was, for example, basic to Aboriginal society, which placed much less emphasis on possessions than Europeans. Survival was linked to knowledge of the local sources of water and food, along with the ritual forms that helped to sustain these.[5] The need to identify and pass on knowledge about what types of plants and animals could sustain human life prompted the growth of systems of classification with particularly important types of animals being subdivided into forms which went beyond the boundaries of Western definitions of a particular species. Globalisation expanded the number and diversity of such 'contact zones' (as Mary Louise Pratt terms them), areas in which different cultures came into contact and, for all their differences, could share their forms of knowledge with each other.[6]

3   Cook 2004: 100–101, 118.
4   Gascoigne 2006: 107.
5   Hallam 1987: 73.
6   Pratt 1992: 6–7.

Natural history

Across the globe many such interactions between indigenous and Western systems of knowledge took place – though the effect tended to be to subsume the local in more generalised systems of knowledge. Natural history provided a way of drawing together such a vast range of information from around the world into forms familiar to Western culture.[7] Natural history, then, extended beyond European charting of the world's surface to mapping the nature and extent of its flora, fauna, minerals and human population. The drawing together of diverse local knowledges into the generalising categories of natural history happened both at the global level and within Europe itself as folk knowledge was absorbed into learned discourse.[8] This could mean that objects lost some of their cultural resonance as they were lifted out of the traditional frameworks of meaning with which they had been associated by particular localities or peoples.[9] Loss of cultural specificity was countered by Western universalising which drew such diverse materials from around the world into forms of knowledge that were meant to be applicable for all peoples and places.

Natural history came to assume a growing importance and centrality in Western travellers' accounts, rising to particular prominence in the late eighteenth century when the Pacific came under close European scrutiny. As such systems waxed in authority, European openness to other systems of knowledge tended to wane. Such scientific self-confidence tended to parallel the rise of greater European imperial control over the globe, which brought with it less of an inclination to treat other cultures as having their own value as potential sources of new knowledge.

Generally speaking, Europe was more inclined to value knowledge from other parts of the globe in the earlier stages of the rise of science to the dominant system of intellectual authority that it became over the course of the eighteenth century. Following its foundation in 1660, the early Royal Society was very active in promoting the accumulation of knowledge from around the globe from whatever source. This was also true on the European Continent. In his address to Frederick II of Prussia of 1752, which set out the benefits of greater exploration of the globe in general and the South Seas in particular, the French scientist Pierre-Louis Maupertuis paid tribute to the advantages to be gained from studying other cultures' forms of knowledge, displaying particular admiration for Japanese medicine.[10] Though Linnaeus's system of classification did much

---

7   Pratt 1992: 38; Smith and Findlen 2002: 18.
8   Drayton 2001: 237.
9   Raj 2004: 253; Chaplin 2001: 197–198.
10   Maupertuis 1756, II: 414.

to promote attitudes of Western scientific superiority, Linnaeus himself was very conscious of the benefits of drawing on local systems of knowledge (as he himself did in Lapland) so that new forms of understanding could be produced from the mediation between the localised and the general.

Natural history focused particularly on indigenous knowledges of local products that might be useful to Europeans. When Cook set off on his *Endeavour* voyage, the president of the Royal Society, the earl of Morton, instructed him, for example, to observe of the people he encountered how they used plants: 'Their powers in Medicine, whether Salutary or noxious' and 'Particularly, such as give vivid or lasting colours for dyeing'.[11] Banks took such injunctions seriously and made extensive enquiries on these points, especially among the Tahitians with whom he spent three months. He also took a close interest in their many medicinal herbs and admired their surgical techniques. Contact with the Australian Aborigines was much more limited, but Banks evidently sought out their names for local flora since he noted that 'they had a knowledge of plants as we plainly could perceive by their having names for them'.[12] Other European explorers also ventured into this 'contact zone' between cultures which made sharing of knowledge possible. While in Tahiti, Bougainville's naturalist, Philibert Commerson, immersed himself in ethnobotany, remarking that 'all their plants are known and distinguished with names that even indicate their affinities'.[13]

The European quest for knowledge of and from the Pacific depended, however, on the cooperation of those on the other side of the beach to share information with the explorers and others who came in their wake. The willingness of indigenous peoples to give information about the world in which they lived differed with time and circumstance. In parts of Polynesia, lengthy sojourns by European visitors built up enough linguistic and cultural familiarity to provide at least some basis for communication. This generally led to a two-way exchange, the Polynesians being as curious about the Europeans as they were about them. Contacts with other societies such as the Australian Aborigines were, in the early stages, generally much more fleeting, though as Australia came under British rule contact inevitably became more extensive.

Establishing such 'contact zones' where Europeans and Indigenous peoples might exchange information required a good deal of mutual trust and understanding, which could take time to establish. On the *Investigator* voyage, Robert Brown seems to have been able to draw on some elements of Aboriginal knowledge of the local flora and fauna no doubt because he had two Aboriginal intermediaries,

---

11   Cook 1955–69, I: 517.
12   Banks 1962, I: 353, 375–376; II: 116.
13   Taillemite 1977, II: 507.

Bungaree and Nanbaree, on board. It was very likely through their ability to establish rapport with the different Aboriginal groups encountered that Brown derived such knowledge as the native names for plants that he recorded in north Australia in 1803.[14] A few days later, on 8 February, Peter Good, the gardener on board, wrote of the people of the Gulf of Carpentaria islands that '[i]t appears they have some knowledge of Botany and distinguish the different Trees & vegetables by distinct names'.[15] In Sydney, Brown appears to have built up a rapport with an Aboriginal by the name of Bagra since one of his notebooks includes 'Native names of Plants & c. taken down from Bagra a very intelligent native of Broken Bay' along with lists of Aboriginal names for other plants and animals from elsewhere.[16] Reliance on Aboriginal intermediaries was to continue. The naturalist, George Caley, who was dispatched to New South Wales by Joseph Banks, was, as he told Banks, dependent on an Aboriginal assistant who could 'trace anything so well in the woods'. One such collector, Moowattin, accompanied Caley back to London in 1810, spending a year there at the expense of Joseph Banks.[17] When collecting botanical specimens from Western Australia in the early 1840s, Georgiana Molloy relied closely on an Aboriginal named Calgood.[18] Given that the study of natural history extended to the human world, it is not surprising that some of Brown's natural history notebooks also include records of Aboriginal vocabularies. His 'New Holland plants notebook', for example, gives a list of some Aboriginal words for parts of the body as well as for plants.[19]

Knowledge of indigenous languages and customs could only come with protracted exposure to them and few had greater opportunities for such intensive immersion than the missionaries. Apart from the Spanish on the Marianas, these did not arrive in the South Seas until the last decade of the eighteenth century. The Protestant London Missionary Society missionaries were sent off to Tahiti with a formidable scientific agenda drawn up by the virtual founder of the society, Thomas Haweis (very likely at the behest of Joseph Banks). Special attention was to be paid to potential items of trade such as sandalwood or coconut oil. To obtain the latter effectively required the special skills the Tahitians had developed and so a report was requested on their 'art of breaking it [a coconut] with facility and dispatch'.[20]

---

14   Vallance et al. 2001: 417.
15   Edwards 1981: 115.
16   Brown, papers, Natural History Museum, Vol. II, item 2, 44–51.
17   Clark 2008: 63, 66–67.
18   Lines 1994: 297, 301, 309.
19   Brown, papers, Vol. V, item 5, 61–3, 67; see also Brown, 'List …', Natural History Museum.
20   Haweis et al., Collection of papers 1795–1802, Mitchell Library, MSS 4190X: Vol. 1, 18–20.

Cartography and navigation

In their quest to map the largely unknown Pacific, Westerners were particularly eager to glean local geographical information even though localised forms of cartography often meshed awkwardly with Western conceptions of how to depict the world – something which was borne out in Captain Cook's lack of comprehension of the map of the Polynesian islands drawn up by the Tahitian navigator, Tupaia, on the *Endeavour* voyage.[21] When, in 1596, Quirõs encountered the Santa Cruz archipelago (now a part of the Solomon Islands) he elicited from the indigenous people 'the names of all the islands, pointing out the bearings with their hands'. To get some sense of the distances, the Spanish also asked 'the number of days it took to go to each one'. Like most people, these informants expected some return for this knowledge, which, they hoped, would take the form of the Spanish using their firepower to attack their enemies whom they sought to blacken in Spanish eyes by describing as 'cannibals'.[22] With the aid of the two Vanuatuans whom he brought back with him to New Spain from his last voyage to the Pacific of 1605–06, Quirõs compiled a guide to some of the islands of Vanuatu and how to get to them.[23]

Early eighteenth-century Jesuit missionaries to the Micronesian Palau Islands recorded how the Paluans, using small stones, indicated the position of the different islands 'and marked out, as well as they could, the Name of each, its Extent and Distance from the others'. The Jesuits were so impressed with the resulting map that it was published in the *Philosophical Transactions of the Royal Society* in 1708–09.[24] Soon afterwards another Jesuit missionary, Father Juan Cantova, drew on local reports to compile a map of the Micronesian Caroline Islands, which was accurate enough to be used by Otto von Kotzebue, navigator on the 1803–06 Russian circumnavigation of the earth under Ivan von Krusenstern. As part of his cartographical enquiries, Cantova also gained some information on Micronesian navigation techniques including the use of a 12-point compass.[25]

As the scale of European intrusion into the Pacific expanded there were more and more encounters with the seagoing techniques of the indigenous peoples of the Pacific, and particularly those of the Micronesians and Polynesians. Micronesian boat-building skills were greatly admired by European visitors. The French Lieutenant Crozet called in at Guam when returning from Marion

---

21 Turnbull 1998.
22 Quirós 1904, II: 360.
23 Burney 1803–17, II: 480.
24 Claine 1707–9: 197.
25 Hezel and Del Valle 1972: 41.

du Fresne's ill-fated voyage and thought that when it came to the construction of vessels 'they had nothing new to learn'.[26] Cook was similarly admiring of Polynesian boats.

Using such craft, as the European explorers came increasingly to appreciate, the Micronesian and Polynesian people, too, to a remarkable degree had overcome the 'tyranny of distance' dictated by the immensity of the Pacific. Navigational knowledge in Polynesian culture was sacred and the arts of the navigator were closely linked with those of the priest. Indeed, Tupaia, who accompanied Cook on his first voyage, combined both roles using his skills to bring Cook through the sea of islands surrounding Tahiti where Tupaia joined the *Endeavour*. As Banks wrote, what made Tupaia's presence on board 'more than anything else desirable is his experience in the navigation of these people and knowledge of the Islands in these seas; he has told us the names of above 70, the most of which he has himself been at.'[27] Other Tahitians, on occasions, also passed on their geographical knowledge to Europeans. When the Tahitian Pautu accompanied the Spanish Domingo de Bonechea on his 1772–73 voyage through the Tuamotu Archipelago, Pautu revealed that he had visited most of these islands. Having got to know the Spanish Tahitian-speaking Maximo Rodríguez well, Pautu later passed on details of Polynesian navigational techniques along with a list of some 42 islands.[28] By the time that William Portlock arrived in the Micronesian Mariana Islands in 1788, the extent of contact with European vessels was such that he engaged a local indigenous pilot (who was chosen from a number of other possible contenders) to guide him to Macao.[29] There Portlock sold the furs he had traded in the Pacific north-west.

Often, however, such hard-won navigational knowledge was treated with greater reticence. Another Tahitian on board one of Cook's ships, Mahine, who accompanied Cook for much of his second voyage before returning to Tahiti, told George Forster that few knew all the secrets of navigation – for these were sacred lore passed on only to an elite. A similar select knowledge economy prevailed in the Micronesian Marshall Islands.[30] Indigenous navigational knowledge was the outcome of generations of close observation of the Pacific and its moods with the behaviour of all aspects of the environment, whether animate or inanimate, being minutely scrutinised for clues as to position and direction. Like European sailors, Polynesians looked to the stars as direction finders. After a three-month immersion in Tahitian society, Joseph Banks wrote of their observation of the stars that 'they know also the time of their annual appearing and disappearing

---

26 Crozet 1891: 94.
27 Banks 1962, I: 312.
28 Salmond 2006: 60.
29 Nicol 1822: 94.
30 D'Arcy 2006: 89.

to a great nicety, far greater than would be easily believed by an European astronomer'. Their close study of the sky, thought Banks, was also apparent in their ability to predict the weather – a skill in which he found them 'far more clever than Europaeans'.[31]

As an aid to remembering the position of the stars, apprentice navigators in the Carolines were taught with maps of the sky made from objects such as coral, coconut leaves and banana fibres on mats.[32] On board Cook's second voyage, George Forster encountered another such system of representation and memorisation when he noticed the way in which the Tahitian Mahine collected in New Zealand a number of small, slender twigs. These 'he carefully tied in a bundle, and made use of instead of journals'. Each island they visited was then represented by one of these twigs. The result, wrote Forster admiringly, was that 'he remembered the names perfectly well in the same order as we had seen them'.[33] Another such device was the use of leaves to represent islands, something that Surgeon Anderson struck at Tonga. When he inquired the number of islands in that archipelago the Tongans 'reckon'd upwards of a hundred and fifty to us by bits of leaves'.[34]

Such pictorial devices designed to preserve cartographical knowledge provided the bases for forms of maps. On occasions these were used in encounters between Europeans and the peoples of the Pacific to transmit knowledge across the cultural divide, providing what Michael Bravo calls a 'geographical gift'.[35] Such maps had been a part of cross-cultural contact since the days of Columbus. Indeed Columbus himself wrote that he had taken an Amerindian on board 'since the savage could draw a sort of chart of the coasts'.[36] The most widely disseminated such Pacific geographical gift was the map of the Polynesian sea of islands (with the exclusion of the distant points of the Polynesian triangle at Hawai'i, New Zealand and Easter Island) drawn up by Tupaia while on the *Endeavour* – though the chart that was eventually printed was a redrawing by Cook and Johann Reinhold Forster. Polynesian seafaring traditions were also evident in the maps of New Zealand provided by Māoris. On Cook's *Endeavour* voyage, Māori chiefs drew up, at Cook's request, a map of much of the east coast of the north island of New Zealand by making a charcoal sketch on the deck of the ship. At Cook's bidding, too, they provided many place names. A still

31   Banks 1962, I: 368.
32   Lewis 2007, I: 367.
33   Forster 2000, I: 287.
34   Cook 1955–67, III: 957.
35   Bravo 1999.
36   De Vorsey 1978.

more expansive map of the whole of New Zealand (excluding Stewart Island) was provided by the Māori Tuki in 1793 after he was kidnapped and taken to Norfolk Island to help establish a flax-growing industry there.[37]

Tuki's map (and possibly, too, the original one by Tupaia) was, in contrast to the map drawn in charcoal, put in a form that could be transported around the world. When La Pérouse arrived at the large island of Sakhalin in the Kuril chain off China, he encountered both transitory and more abiding forms of indigenous cartography. When questioned as to whether Sakhalin was an island or a peninsula, an elder drew a map showing that it was indeed an island while also sketching in the accompanying coastline of China with the strait in between. The map was drawn on the sand and met local needs, which were based on accumulated knowledge that did not require being recorded in more permanent forms. Interestingly, however, as La Pérouse wrote, another Sakhalin local seeing that the map was soon going to be washed away by the tide took 'one of our pencils with some paper; [and] he drew his island'.[38] Such familiarity with representations on paper may well have owed something to the proximity of the highly literate culture of China. As Bruno Latour has stressed, the transformation from a fugitive sketch on a tide-washed beach to an image that could be taken back to Paris to be reworked into maps of the globe brought with it the possibility of reconstructing the island of Sakhalin back at the Parisian 'centres of calculation'. The outcome of such a transformation in turn could provide the knowledge on which could be built global networks reaching from Paris to Sakhalin.[39]

Conclusion

As the human web expanded across the Pacific so, too, did the intersection of different forms of knowledge. Indigenous, locally based knowledge was drawn into Western-derived but increasingly universalising forms of classification, which could mask its origin. Central to the European scientific expeditions was the collecting impulse, which was given form and coherence through the pliable and plastic body of knowledge known as natural history with its systems of classification. Such systems were, however, well removed from the way in which indigenous people made sense of the world around them, employing classificatory categories which corresponded to their own needs and experience. For the people of the west coast of Vancouver Island, for example, the most basic divide in their taxonomy was between the animals of the sea and those of

---

37   Barton 1988.
38   Dunmore 1994–5, II: 290.
39   Latour 1987: 215–237.

the land.[40] Placing whales, sea otters and seals with land mammals as Western systems of classification did was, then, to translate their sense of the world into a quite different language. From a Western perspective, the increasingly scientific character of natural history had been linked with the passage away from medieval and early modern forms of an emblematic world view where plants and animals had potent symbolic significance.[41] Yet for many indigenous societies, such as the Australian Aborigines, such talismanic understandings of the natural world were at the core of their cosmology.[42]

Natural history, with its reliance on a vast haul of specimens from all corners of the globe, was rooted in the local, but this was largely disguised by the forms in which it was conveyed and the systems used to give it order and intelligibility. As natural history evolved (an appropriate word) towards a more theoretically based and even more generalised history of nature with its culmination in theories of biological evolution, the focus was less and less on the particular and more on the general. The individual and local characteristics of a specimen were of less interest than the extent to which it fitted into a larger pattern that could extend well beyond the immediate locality. This growing global context of knowledge was made possible by the systems of recording, classification and storage that both promoted and were a response to the scientific voyaging to the Pacific and other parts of the globe.

Transmuting vast and confusing mounds of specimens into abstractions that could be manipulated in manageable ways provided a route to the growing level of generalisation characteristic of science. The most obvious form of abstraction was the recording of a new plant or animal by transfixing it with the neatness of a Latin binomial classificatory definition. The ingrained habit of recording information was reinforced forcibly by the habits of commerce and, as navigation grew more sophisticated, the discipline of shipboard life with its figure-filled journals. Much of this knowledge had come from indigenous sources, and the participation of investigators on both sides of the frontier in a common pursuit had engendered some fellow-feeling and a sense of a shared recognition of common goals.[43] Nonetheless, the knowledge that was taken back to the Western repositories was transmuted into new and often unfamiliar forms.

Convergence between different peoples in the Pacific brought with it, then, a strong tendency to merge the local in the general. This was linked to the generalising impulse of Western science and its assumption that, wherever one was in the world, there could be only one truth – even if it was subject to

---

40   Moan 1978: 74–76.
41   Ashworth 1990.
42   Sutton 1988.
43   Cook 2012: 132.

constant revision. The Christian missionaries also believed that there was one truth though, in practice, the symbolic language of religion and its variant ritual practices did lend itself to some forms of cultural pluralism. Science, however, was not so readily rendered plural though its view of the world and methods were, at least in theory, open to all. The science that was shaped by exploration of the globe and the convergence between peoples became itself a human web that both disguised and transcended its local origins. 'Once forged out of global experiences', writes Jacob, 'after the mid eighteenth century European knowledge systems became global.'[44]

Science provided a world language that gradually spread beyond its European origins. Though still retaining strong links with the European thought-world out of which it had developed, it has proved accessible by humanity as whole.[45] Potent though it was, it was and is but one form of knowledge and one particular way of understanding the world. Contact with indigenous cultures was and is a reminder that there are other systems of knowledge in which the symbolic and affinities between the human and the natural world provide other ways of understanding the place of human beings in a complex and still bewildering universe.

References

Ashworth, William B. 1990, 'Natural history and the emblematic world view', in *Reappraisals of the Scientific Revolution*, David C. Lindberg and Robert S. Westman (eds), Cambridge University Press, Cambridge, 303–332.

Banks, Joseph 1962, *The Endeavour journal of Joseph Banks 1768–1771*, J.C. Beaglehole (ed.), Public Library of New South Wales, Sydney, 2 vols.

Barton, Phillip 1988, 'Maori cartography and the European encounter', in *Cartography in the Traditional African, American, Arctic, Australian, and Pacific Societies*, David Woodward and G. Malcolm Lewis (eds), Vol. 2, Book 3 of *History of Cartography*, J.B. Harley and David Woodward (eds), University of Chicago Press, Chicago, 493–536.

Bravo, Michael 1999, 'Ethnographic navigation and the geographical gift', in *Enlightenment and geography*, D. Livingstone and C. Withers (eds), University of Chicago Press, Chicago, 199–235.

---

44 Jacob 2008: 342.
45 Pyenson 1990: 77–78.

Brown, Robert, 'List of Aboriginal words, North Australia', Robert Brown papers, Misc. MSS, Box 2, Botany Library, Natural History Museum, London (microfilm, A[ustralian] J[oint] C[opying] Project M2495).

——papers, Misc. MSS, New Holland Plants (2 boxes), Botany Library, Natural History Museum (typescript transcript of Aboriginal natural history vocabulary, Mitchell Library, Ab 88/2).

Burney, James 1803–17, *A chronological history of the discoveries in the South Sea or Pacific Ocean*, Luke Hansard & Sons, London, 5 vols.

Chaplin, Joyce 2001, *Subject Matter: Technology, the Body, and Science on the Anglo-American Frontier, 1500–1676*, Harvard University Press Cambridge, MA.

Claine, Paul 1707–9, 'An extract of two letters from the missionary Jesuits, concerning the discovery of the new Philippine-Islands, with a map of the same', *Philosophical Transactions of the Royal Society* 26: 189–199.

Clark, Philip 2008, *Aboriginal Plant Collectors: Botanists and Australian Aboriginal People in the Nineteenth Century*, Rosenburg Publishing, Sydney.

Cook, Harold J. 2004, 'Global economies and local knowledge in the East Indies: Jacobus Bontius learns the facts of nature', in *Colonial Botany: Science, Commerce, and Politics*, Londa Schiebinger and Claudia Swan (eds), University of Pennsylvania Press, Philadelphia, 100–118.

——2007, *Matters of Exchange: Commerce, Medicine, and Science in the Dutch Golden Age*, Yale University Press, New Haven.

——2012, 'Moving about and finding things out: economies and science in the period of the Scientific Revolution', *Osiris* 27: 101–132.

Cook, James 1955–69, *The journals of Captain James Cook on his voyages of Discovery*, J.C. Beaglehole (ed.), Hakluyt Society, Cambridge, 3 vols in 4.

Crozet, Julien Marie 1891, *Crozet's voyage to Tasmania, New Zealand and the Ladrone Islands and the Philippines in the years 1771–2*, H. Ling Roth (trans.), Truslove and Shirley, London.

D'Arcy, Paul 2006, *People of the Sea: Environment, Identity and History*, University of Hawai'i Press, Honolulu.

De Vorsey, Louis 1978, 'Amerindian contributions to the mapping of North America: a preliminary view', *Imago Mundi* 30: 71–78.

Drayton, Richard 2001, 'Knowledge and empire', *The Oxford History of the British Empire*, Wm. Roger Louis (ed.), vol. 2, *The Eighteenth Century*, P.J. Marshall (ed.), Oxford University Press, Oxford, 231–252.

Dunmore, John (ed.) 1994–5, *The journal of Jean-François de Galaup de la Pérouse, 1785–1788*, Hakluyt Society, London, 2 vols.

Edwards, Phyllis I. 1981, *The Journal of Peter Good: Gardener on Matthew Flinders Voyage to Terra Australis 1801–03*, British Museum (Natural History), London.

Forster, George 2000, *A Voyage round the World*, Nicholas Thomas and Oliver Berghof (eds) assisted by Jennifer Newell, University of Hawai'i Press, Honolulu, 2 vols.

Gascoigne, John 1996, 'The ordering of nature and the ordering of empire: a commentary', *Visions of Empire: Voyages, Botany and Representations of Nature*, David Philip Miller and Peter Hanns Reill (eds), Cambridge University Press, Cambridge, 107–113.

——2014, *Encountering the Pacific in the Age of the Enlightenment*, Cambridge University Press, Cambridge.

Hallam, Sylvia 1987, 'Changing landscapes and societies: 15 000 to 6000 years ago', in *Australians to 1788*, D.J. Mulvaney and J. Peter White (eds), Fairfax, Syme & Weldon, Sydney, 47–73.

Haweis, Rev. Thomas and others, Collection of papers relating to early missions to the South Seas, 1795–1802, Mitchell Library, State Library of New South Wales, MSS 4190X.

Hezel, Francis X. and Maria Teresa Del Valle 1972, 'Early European contact with the Western Carolines, 1525–1750', *Journal of Pacific History* 7(1): 26–44.

Jacob, M.C. 2008, 'Afterward', in *Science and Empire in the Atlantic World*, James Delbourgo and Nicholas Dew (eds), Routledge, New York, 333–344.

Latour, Bruno 1987, *Science in Action: How to Follow Scientists and Engineers through Society*, Harvard University Press, Cambridge, MA.

Lewis, G. Malcolm 2007, 'Cartography: an overview, indigenous cartography, and speculative cartography', in *Oxford Encyclopedia of Maritime History*, John B. Hattendorf (ed.), Oxford University Press, Oxford, 4 vols, I: 366–369.

Lines, William 1994, *An all Consuming Passion: Origins, Modernity, and the Australian Life of Georgiana Molloy*, Allen & Unwin, Sydney.

Maupertuis, Pierre 1756, *Lettre sur le progès des sciences* in his *Oeuvres*, Lyon, 4 vols, II: 375–431.

Moan, Barbara 1978, 'Vanished companions: the changing relationship of the West Coast People to the animal world', *Sound Heritage* 7(1): 71–7.

Nicol, John 1822, *The Life and Adventures of John Nicol, Mariner*, William Blackwood, Edinburgh.

Pratt, Mary Louise 1992, *Imperial Eyes: Travel Writing and Transculturation*, Routledge, London.

Pyenson, Lewis 1990, 'Why science may serve political ends: cultural imperialism and the mission to civilize', *Berichte zur Wissenchaftesgeschichte* 13: 69–81.

Quirós, Pedro Fernandez de 1904, *The voyages of Pedro Fernandez de Quiros, 1590 to 1606*, Sir Clements Markham (ed.), Hakluyt Society, London, 2 vols.

Raj, Kapil 2004, 'Surgeons, fakirs, merchants, and craftspeople: making l'empereur's jardin in early modern South Asia', in *Colonial Botany: Science, Commerce, and Politics*, Londa Schiebinger and Claudia Swan (eds), University of Pennsylvania Press, Philadelphia, 252–269.

Salmond, Anne 2006, 'Cross-cultural voyaging: the first Spanish visits to Tahiti, 1772–1776', *Spain's Legacy in the Pacific, Mains'l Haul. A Journal of Pacific Maritime History* 42: 54–65.

Smith, Pamela H. and Paula Findlen 2002, 'Commerce and the representation of nature in art and science', in *Merchants and Marvels: Commerce, Science and Art in Early Modern Europe*, Pamela H. Smith and Paula Findlen (eds), Routledge, New York, 1–25.

Sutton, Peter 1988, 'Icons of country: topographical representations in classical Aboriginal traditions', in *Cartography in the Traditional African, American, Arctic, Australian, and Pacific Societies*, David Woodward and G. Malcolm Lewis (eds), Vol. 2, Book 3 of *History of Cartography*, J.B. Harley and David Woodward (eds), University of Chicago Press, Chicago, 353–386.

Taillemite, Étienne (ed.) 1977, *Bougainville et ses compagnons autour du monde 1766–9*, Imprimerie nationale, Paris, 2 vols.

Turnbull, David 1998, 'Cook and Tupaia, a tale of cartographic *méconnaissance*', in *Science and Exploration in the Pacific: European Voyages in the Southern Oceans in the Eighteenth Century,* Margarette Lincoln (ed.), Boydell Press, Woodbridge, Suffolk, 117–132.

Vallance, T.G., D.T. Moore and Eric W. Groves 2001, *Nature's Investigator: The Diary of Robert Brown in Australia 1801–1805*, Australian Biological Resources Study, Canberra.

8

British–Tahitian collaborative drawing strategies on Cook's *Endeavour* voyage

Harriet Parsons

This chapter comes out of an enquiry into the intellectual atmosphere and social dynamics of first contact in the Pacific on Captain Cook's *Endeavour* voyage. The common impression of the *Endeavour* is of a highly segregated community in which sailors and civilians were separated by class, rank, and in their first encounters with the people of the Pacific, by early concepts of race. In the *Art of Captain Cook's Voyages,* Bernard Smith and Rüdiger Joppien represent Cook and Joseph Banks as embarked upon a 'civilising mission'.[1] The 'myth model' formulated by Gananath Obeyesekere in the *Apotheosis of Captain Cook* of 'the redoubtable person coming from Europe to a savage land' influences much of the commentary on the relationship between Cook and Tupaia as discussed in this chapter.[2] But the *Endeavour* drawings, I argue, tell a different story in which Pacific people were working in creative collaboration with the British on this physical and intellectual voyage of exploration. By reconstructing the *Endeavour* drawing sessions – who was present, how many took part, where

---

1   Smith and Joppien 1985: 56.
2   Obeyesekere 1992: 11.

they took place and the drawing conventions in use – I propose to build a social picture of this ship and, in particular, of the British relationship with Tupaia who joined the *Endeavour* in Tahiti and became one of its artists.

The approach I have taken to art history treats creative production as a problem-solving strategy rather than hard evidence of an artist's particular attitudes or beliefs. Many of the questions raised require further investigation, particularly in relation to Polynesian history and culture, but in this first phase of my doctoral research I have been deliberately Anglo-centric because my broader argument is that a failure to appreciate the wider context of Georgian civilian and naval culture in relation to the *Endeavour*, particularly in these radical years preceding the American Revolution, has produced an unnecessarily constrained account of the capacity of both Britain and Polynesia for creative engagement in the pre-colonial Pacific.

Cultural perception and cultural practice

In *European Vision and the South Pacific,* Bernard Smith attributed to British artists in the Pacific an empirical 'objectivity', which he argued was itself a cultural artefact of the European Enlightenment. One of most important innovations of the *Endeavour* voyage was the introduction of visual documentation into scientific exploration. Smith and Joppien, in the catalogues of the *Art of Captain Cook's Voyages* and the *Charts and Coastal Views*, see both the *Endeavour*'s 'art' and 'charts and coastal views' as scientific modes of drawing. The *Endeavour*'s artists and cartographers worked across both genres, and so any analysis of the *Endeavour*'s art necessarily also entails consideration of its charts and coastal views. In this context, the distinction between amateur and professional artists also becomes ambiguous. However, Smith and Joppien's division of the *Endeavour* archive into two volumes, distinguishing the art of Cook's voyages from the naval drawings, inadvertently reinforces the impression of a segregated shipboard community. These works are most productive when regarded, not as the definitive observations of 'professional' eyes, but the trial-and-error experiments in representation of draughtsmen of all kinds. As such, this chapter approaches these late eighteenth-century images in a manner more usual to contemporary art: as the products of a visual culture examined through its drawing processes. In this context, the development of Tupaia's artistic practice becomes the instrument through which the British perception of the Pacific is mediated.

A reorientation of the *Endeavour*'s art history from cultural perception to cultural practice provides the prerequisites for an 'intellectual history', a history which, to paraphrase Quentin Skinner, aspires to a plausible account of what these artists, in drawing at the time they did, for the audience they addressed, could in practice have been intending to communicate.[3]

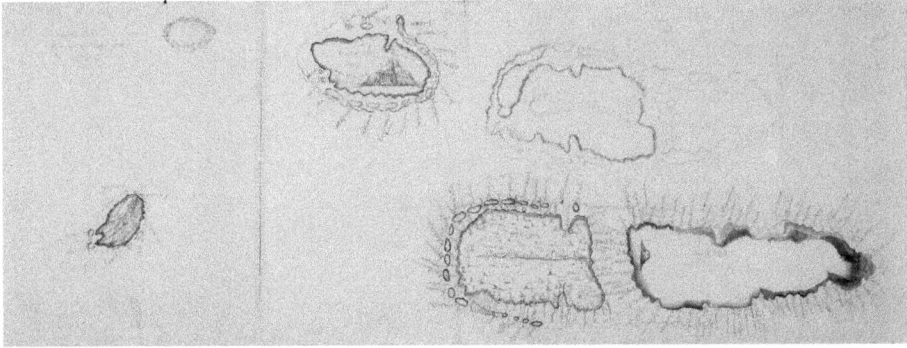

Figure 8.1 'Chart of the Society Islands', attributed to Joseph Banks.
Source: British Library, BL Add Ms. 15508 f.16, © British Library Board.

The sketch, 'Society Isles discovered by Lieut. J. Cook in 1769', held in the British Library (Figure 8.1), is a rough sketch in pencil, ink and wash. Its most striking feature is the level of detail contained in the words crowded around the island coastlines in Joseph Banks's handwriting. Smith and Joppien noted these were most likely 'derived from Tupaia and it is therefore probable that Banks drew this chart to preserve these names'.[4] Their use of the word 'preserve' implies Banks, in making this chart, was anticipating the loss of Polynesian culture; certainly, as already noted, Smith and Joppien considered Cook and Banks to be embarked upon a 'civilising mission'.[5]

In terms of the drawing process, this construction of British perception as inherently colonial is notable, not so much for what is included as for what is excluded from its consideration. Smith and Joppien recognised the relationship between the artist and the sitter (or in this case, the artist and his informant) *in situ* as distinct from the ultimate effects of European contact, but as Smith explains in *Imagining the Pacific,* his purpose as an historian was not to observe the inconsistencies between the artist's immediate experience and history but their continuity.[6] Within such a framework, the erratic exchanges of trial and error that comprise the creative process – and the meaning a drawing was actually made to communicate at the time – can be subsumed in the awareness

---

3   Skinner 1969: 49.
4   Smith and Joppien 1988: xlii.
5   Smith and Joppien 1985: 56.
6   Smith 1992: ix.

of subsequent colonisation. But if the sketch is approached as a working drawing, these 'redundant' negotiations of first contact may be retrieved from the *Endeavour*'s visual notes.

Tupaia's Chart

Tupaia is best known for the chart of 74 islands he made with Captain Cook, commonly called 'Tupaia's Chart', which survives as a copy in Cook's hand. Attempts have been made to decipher it since it was first published as an engraving by Johann Forster, a member of Cook's second voyage, in 1778. Cook left no account of Polynesian navigation in his journals and this has become pivotal negative evidence in the European interpretation of British–Polynesian relations. The silence is often taken for an absence of conversation. David Turnbull, for example, writes 'Cook appears never to have asked any of his informants how they navigated. What is especially interesting is that he did not ask Tupaia, or at least made no reference to asking him in any of his writings'.[7] Paul Adam goes further when he writes, 'Tupaia's chart and what it meant to Cook illustrates perfectly the incomprehension of the Europeans when faced with the nautical culture of the Polynesians';[8] while European resistance to Polynesian knowledge is also implicit in Anne di Piazza and Erik Pearthree's proposition that Tupaia 'succeeded in convincing Cook of his geographical knowledge', that Cook 'had occasions to convince himself' of Tupaia's expertise, and by their use of the subheading: 'Tupaia, Novice Cartographer'.[9]

Yet the chart itself demonstrably required a considerable investment of Cook's time, both in the process of its development and in the making of the fair copy. The integration of European and Polynesian concepts of space, distance and orientation testifies to a complex conversation; and indeed the notes marked by small ships are transcriptions of Tupaia's comments in Cook's pidgin Tahitian: 'In the time of the ancestors of Tupaia a friendly ship [arrived]' and so forth (Figure 8.3).[10] If we consider for a moment Skinner's criterion of what these artists, in drawing at the time they did for the audience they intended to address, could in practice have been intending to communicate, the choice of language dictates this chart was not designed for use at the home of the Admiralty's English-speaking officials but rather in the Pacific by its unique cohort of Tahitian-speaking Britons and their Polynesian counterparts.

---

7   Turnbull 2000: 59.
8   Adam cited in Turnbull 2000: 68.
9   Di Piazza and Pearthree 2007: 322.
10   Langdon 1980: 227.

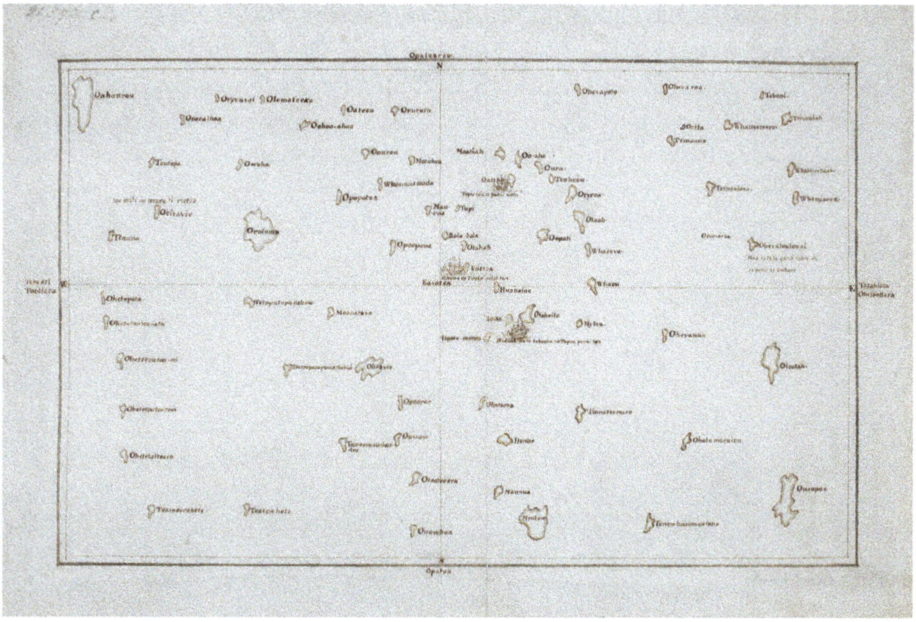

Figure 8.2 'Tupaia's Chart'.
Source: British Library, BL Add Ms 215193 (c), © British Library Board.

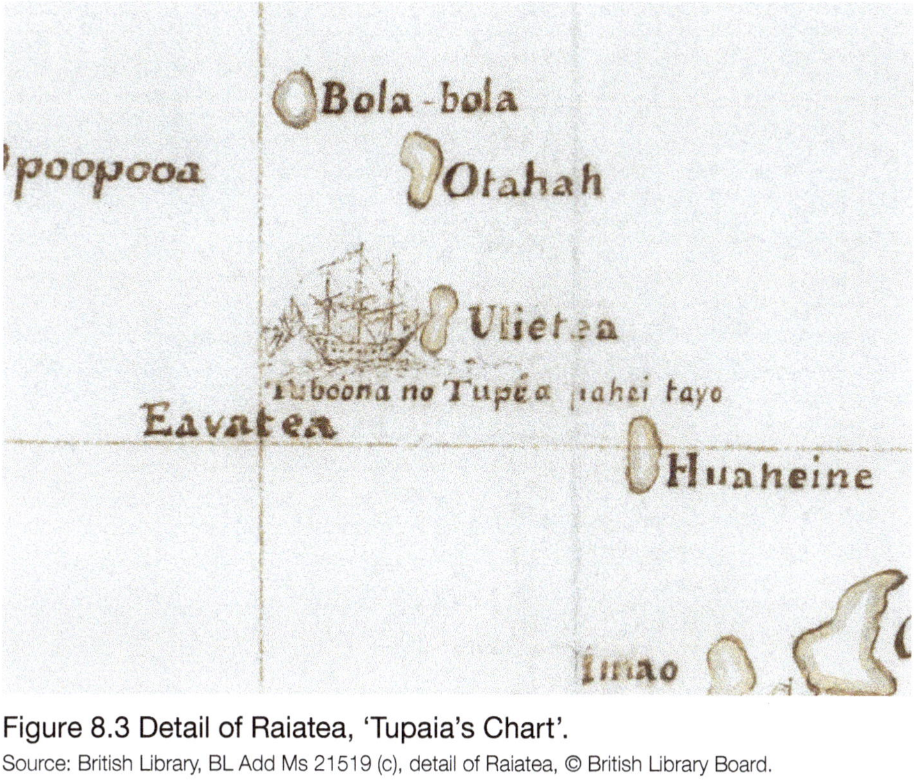

Figure 8.3 Detail of Raiatea, 'Tupaia's Chart'.
Source: British Library, BL Add Ms 21519 (c), detail of Raiatea, © British Library Board.

Nicholas Thomas singles out Tupaia's Chart as a rare example of concepts merging between the European and Oceanic imaginations, but he sees its cross-cultural fusion as compromised by what he calls in passing the 'moralising cartography of the Enlightenment'.[11] The association between Cook's cartography and a closed mind would seem to scuttle the possibility of cross-cultural collaboration, but it is difficult to conceive how the imaginative integration of European and Polynesian concepts Thomas observes could have been achieved without the free exchange of ideas.

Such a prescriptive approach to empirical observation seems more in tune with early nineteenth-century concepts of positivism than the eclectic iconoclasm that characterises the late eighteenth century in which the *Endeavour* voyage took place. In *European Vision*, Bernard Smith argued that the Linnaean taxonomy used by Banks represented a pivotal moment in the transition from neoclassical to empirical modes of scientific thought. The versatility it allowed for the classification of plants as well as clouds, animals and minerals caused multiple fields of natural history to suddenly merge into a single hierarchy. 'Landscape' was transformed from an expression of mood into a 'scientific' vision of 'typical' ecologies.[12]

Carl von Linné's system was indeed essential to Banks's research on Cook's first Pacific voyage, but it was only on the second that Johann Forster started applying the classificatory system to people when he defined the 'varieties' of the human species.[13] In *Imagining the Pacific,* Smith describes Banks's systematic expansion of knowledge in natural history as 'analogous' to Cook's systematic approach to navigation and cartography.[14] Thomas stops short of attributing Forster's experiments in classification on the second voyage to the artists on the first, but, in agreement with Smith, he seems to regard Forster's ethnography as nevertheless having imposed a dogmatic or moralistic framework on Cook and Tupaia's creative relationship.

Irrespective of the separate traditions to which cartography and natural history belong, the mode of perception von Linné's *Species Plantarum* engendered on the *Endeavour,* only 15 years after its first publication, has to be regarded as excitingly new not, as Thomas would seem to suggest, pervasive or habitual. Cook and Tupaia's cartography, by contrast, drew upon much older traditions.

11   Thomas 1997: 4.
12   Smith 1960: 6.
13   See Forster 1996.
14   Smith 1992: 42.

Thomas argues that natural history constrained the Polynesian voice by imposing 'Linnaean universals over indigenous classificatory schemes'.[15] However, such constraints, if they were already active on the first voyage, cannot be extrapolated from the silence in the journals. Equating silence in the writing with silence in speech treats the written word as impartial, but the *Endeavour* journals are not indiscriminate or necessarily candid records of the thoughts and conversations that took place on the voyage. If silence in the *Endeavour* journals is to be interpreted as a cultural phenomenon, it must be according to Georgian conventions of the written word, not the concepts it may be hiding.

Georgian silence

Little mention is made of Tupaia in the *Endeavour* journals, but many members of the expedition received similar treatment. Banks's friend and colleague Daniel Solander and his secretary Herman Spöring are rarely mentioned, while the artist Charles Praval would be unknown but for the muster list.

These journals were not necessarily the open-hearted records of their authors' innermost thoughts the modern reader might imagine. On his voyage around Newfoundland in 1766, Banks kept his notes on pieces of paper so that his journal would not be open to 'Every Petty officer who chose to peruse it'.[16] The *Endeavour* has a reputation as a remarkably happy ship and this must be attributed on a voyage of three years in no small part to the capacity of its members for discretion.

But the stakes were much higher than personal sensitivities. Greg Dening argues that on these ships, where the crowded conditions made physical solitude almost impossible, it was language, not architecture, that separated public from private life:

> Distance in naval command is something acted out, sometimes in so small a thing as a term of address, an invitation to dinner. Distance could be blurred by countervailing signs of relationships other than military. Ominously, there were many signs of spaces and relationships other than military on the *Bounty*.[17]

These 'other relationships' were the lines of patronage that governed naval hierarchy. Discipline is considered the keystone of modern naval command but, as N.A.M. Rodger writes in the *Wooden World*, Britain's Georgian Navy lacked even a single word for this concept in the modern sense:

---

15   Thomas 1997: 4.
16   O'Brian 1997: 49.
17   Dening 1992: 20.

This observation is of more than linguistic significance, for when men lack a word for something it is safe to assume they do not often think and talk about it. If eighteenth century sea officers had worried about discipline in their service, they would certainly have developed at least one word or phrase to express it.[18]

It was obligation and the pursuit of personal advantage that underpinned a system legendary for its stability and efficiency, not arbitrary power. In this context, suppression of independent thought was seen as undermining. Admiral George B. Rodney wrote, in the margin of a plan to instill strict obedience in a naval charity school, 'Those who are put over us if they act their part right, we ought to reverence. If they do not I say *no*. None of your passive obedience and non resistance, especially among seamen.'[19] Rodger argues the generation to which the *Endeavour*'s crew belonged was the last for whom the class structure was also the 'natural' order of things. Complaint and resistance to the details of authority were tolerated, even admirable in the eyes of Rodney, because they carried no implications for the basic stability of the social hierarchy as a whole.

Authority in the Navy operated on two principles: the intelligent cooperation demanded by the ship as a machine on which all lives depended, and the influence of personal 'interest'. Promotion was gained not through impartial measures of merit but the influence of patronage, frequently exerted by family members higher up. The perception of personal influence as sycophantic, as Rodger points out, is characteristically Victorian.

Interest was a normal feature of late eighteenth-century civil society, almost regarded as a form of currency that could be exchanged to mutual benefit. In the Navy, power accrued through liability. Promotion bound a man to his benefactor as a 'follower', and his sphere of influence continued to expand as his protégé in turn accrued further obligations through the use of his influence to promote others. The more successful or even famous a follower became, the more power accrued to his benefactor within a network of mutual obligation.

Whereas in civilian government a letter of reference openly acknowledging that the applicant's 'natural constitutional indolence governed him with irresistible sway' was no obstacle to promotion, in the Navy competence was a matter of survival.[20] Civilian political influence was strenuously resisted because it was recognised that the effect of any form of civilian advancement upon the power of officers to choose and promote their followers would be systemic. Any officer seen to bow to interests other than naval quickly lost influence, and without the

---

18   Rodger 1986: 205.
19   Rodger 1986: 210.
20   Rodger 1986: 332.

power to promote he lost the power of command over his followers because they lost their incentive to obey. It was on these vertical ties of mutual dependence and obligation that captains relied for their authority in the Georgian Navy.

Within the *Endeavour*'s wooden world, this paramount consideration placed Cook on an equal footing with the aristocratic Banks; and it was in this context that the Machiavellian figure of Tupaia, at the centre of a Tahitian political crisis, nurtured his own convivial relations with the British through their drawing sessions.

Tupaia's chart of the Society Islands

Tupaia's reasons for joining the *Endeavour* are not recorded but in 1769 he was in an uncomfortable position, both in Tahiti and his home island of Raiatea. He had lost his lands some 20 years before in an invasion of Raiatea by the neighbouring Boraborans, and now in Tahiti found himself on the wrong side of a war in which he had been a key political adviser.[21] Joining the British on their expedition provided an opportunity for a strategic withdrawal and, it could be speculated, to return later from a position of strength as their intermediary in the Pacific.

Smith and Joppien interpret the words Banks recorded on the chart he made with Tupaia as 'coastal features', which Anne Salmond describes more narrowly as the 'place names of islets, passages and settlements'.[22] However, John Olstad identifies them as the estates of the landholders.[23]

Anita Smith explains in 'The Cultural Landscapes of the Pacific Islands' that the landholding system typical of Polynesian high islands distributes environmental resources by dividing the island like a cake from the central volcanic peak to the ocean. In the case of the chart of the Society Islands each 'coastal feature' would represent the seaside boundary of one of these segments. Cook's map of Tahiti shows a similar segmentation of the island into its regions of governance.

This reading has important implications for the nature of Banks's interest in this chart because, as Anita Smith explains:

> The Pacific Island land tenure systems are intimately tied to traditional systems of governance and social structures which in turn are reflected in the ways in which people organize themselves in the landscape … From a cultural heritage

---

21 See Salmond 2004, 2009.
22 Salmond 2009: 205.
23 I am indebted to John Olstad, PhD candidate in Linguistics at Newcastle University, for interpreting this map.

perspective, they are an inseparable component of many Pacific Island cultures and their traditional knowledge, customs and language. For example, as is common in the region, the Cook Island word *vaka* means both a social and a territorial unit …[24]

Banks's investment of time in this extensive list of landholdings suggests dispossession was not on his mind when he was making this chart. He was Tupaia's *taio*, or ceremonial friend, and Salmond argues it was this relationship which made it possible for Tupaia, a 'high-priest navigator', to share sacred navigational information with him and his people.[25] Banks was not a sailor and these landholdings have little navigational value to European cartography, but within the context of Banks's Georgian culture, the chart might be interpreted politically as a diagram of Polynesian 'interests' in the region and, as such, Tupaia and his British collaborators might be regarded as each inducting the other into the knowledge systems of his culture through these cartographic drawing sessions.

This mode of creative learning was not foreign to Cook, who began his education in cartography under similar circumstances, through a chance meeting on a beach in Canada. Major Samuel Holland was a military engineer who was making a survey where Cook's ship the *Pembroke* was anchored when, Holland writes, Cook became 'particularly attentive to my operations; and as he expressed an ardent Desire to be instructed in the use of the Plane Table; (the Instrument I was then using) I appointed the next Day in order to make him acquainted with the whole process'.[26] Holland met with Cook and 'two Young Gentlemen' (officers from Cook's ship) to teach them the skill of hydrography and drawing then continued in the Great Cabin which, 'Dedicated to scientific purposes and mostly taken up with a Drawing Table, furnished no room for Idlers'. Cook and Holland used this time to compile the materials for a newly accurate chart of the Gulf and River St Lawrence, Newfoundland.

Dening describes the Great Cabin as the main social space: a place where Cook 'could work at his drawings, write his journals, be the "experimental gentleman", and make a table for his quarterdeck'.[27] This description paints a picture of quiet retreat from the commotion of shipboard life, but the workspace suggested by Holland's letter is a more active place shared by cartographers working cooperatively in the manner of Cook and Holland and, on the *Endeavour*, with Banks and his party of scientists. The drawing table normally in constant use by the officers on the *Endeavour* was also in demand by the scientists for the preservation and classification of specimens as well as for writing journals,

---

24 Smith 2007: 41–43.
25 Salmond 2009: 203, 204.
26 Smith and Joppien 1988: 64.
27 Dening 1992: 20.

for painting and drawing and, of course, for meals. The Banks–Tupaia chart contains a variety of drawing styles and their identification gives an indication of the number of people who may have been present in this drawing session, as participants or observers.

Smith and Joppien identified the sketch as a drawing by Banks but di Piazza and Pearthree argue the chart was drawn by Tupaia with the variation in style demonstrating his apprenticeship in European cartography. Salmond includes Cook in the creative group who produced this chart, but like di Piazza and Pearthree attributes the drawing as a whole, which is 'drawn without perspective (like his sketches of *marae*)', to a single draughtsman, Tupaia.[28] However Holland's description of the making of the Newfoundland chart shows Cook working as part of a group and this points to an unexplored alternative: that the different styles are not imitations but the original contributions of other draughtsmen.

Di Piazza and Pearthree observe that the 'inked outlines of [some islands] are ragged, and that of Ulieatea (Raiatea) is highlighted in various styles as if it were a practice exercise. The rough pen hatching imitates Cook's style, and the ink washes the style of [the master's mate, Richard] Pickersgill or [the master, Robert] Molyneux.'[29]

The 'rough pen hatching' is typical of Cook's surveys. For example, four charts held in the British Library (a sketch of part of the Bay of Rio de Janeiro, two surveys of parts of New Zealand, and a chart of the north-east coast of New Zealand from Table Cape to Cape Runaway) show this cross-hatching.[30] However, while these points of similarity argue strongly in favour of Cook's participation in this drawing session, they are not definitive. Smith and Joppien attributed all the Cook charts, except his original surveys, jointly to him and Isaac Smith, an Able Seaman who, as Cook wrote in a letter, 'was of great use to me in assisting to make surveys, Plans, Drawings &c^a in which he is very expert'.[31] Smith and Joppien noted that the only drawing that could be securely attributed to Isaac Smith was a drawing of an iceberg in the log he kept on Cook's second voyage, held in the Public Records Office, London.[32] Isaac Smith was a cousin of Cook's wife, and had first joined Cook on the *Grenville* at the age of 13 on his Newfoundland voyage. A draft for a chart of the Harbour of Croque held in the State Library of New South Wales, and which has been attributed to Cook,

28   Salmond 2009: 205.

29   di Piazza and Pearthree 2007: 322.

30   British Library, BL 31360 f.28, BL 31360 f.52 and BL 31360 f.54, and BL 31360 f.53; see Smith and Joppien 1988, I: plates 11, 207, 232, 180.

31   Smith and Joppien 1985: 55.

32   Smith and Joppien 1985: 55; Admiralty records, PRO Adm 55/105 f.66v, Public Records Office, London; see Smith and Joppien 1988, II: plate 12.

clearly shows the writing of a child in the heading – the 'N' in 'Plan' and at the end of 'Newfoundland' are backwards – while Cook's adult hand is identifiable in the faintly legible 'Scale of one mile'.[33] This chart provides a genuine example of an apprenticeship in cartography. While elements such as the cross-hatching may be described as typical of Cook, they are not necessarily evidence of his 'hand'. They are also part of Smith's style and represent what might be termed a 'micro-school' of draughtsmanship in which Cook's influence is apparent.

The combination of wash and cross-hatching, which can be seen on the top left coast of 'Ulieateah' (Raiatea), can also be seen in Robert Molyneux's chart of New Zealand.[34] Richard Pickersgill's use of ink wash shows no distinctive characteristics which would argue either for or against his participation in this drawing session, but given that Johann Forster acquired his copy of Tupaia's Chart from him, which he then amalgamated with a copy owned by Banks to make his engraving, Pickersgill had strong reason to take an interest.[35] Pickersgill's chart has been lost, but the differences between Forster's engraving and the surviving chart made by Cook indicate significant variation arguing that Pickersgill engaged in a similar collaboration with Tupaia. The relationship with Tupaia is further supported by the notes on his chart of 'Ohetiruah' (Hiti-roa or Rurutu),[36] which refer to Tupaia by name: 'Tobiea a Native of Otihite Describes 9 Others lying to the westward not far distant some of which are very large and all of them beginning their Names with oheti as this does.'[37] Smith and Joppien also compare the most striking feature of this chart, the peaks of 'Bolabola' (Borabora), with Sydney Parkinson's drawing.

Learning to draw by copying was a standard mode of teaching in the eighteenth century, and while it is difficult to positively identify the participation of any particular draughtsman by direct examination of the chart alone, a strong case for Cook's active contribution to this drawing session can be made, based on the working methods he employed in other charts.

33 Cook, James, A plan for the Harbour at Croque in Newfoundland, SAFE/PXD11 a156008, State Library of New South Wales, Sydney.
34 New Zealand: North Island and South Island, including Stewart Island and Cooks Streight (Cook Strait), 1770, ADM 352/386 [formerly 458 shelf 69], The National Archives, Kew.
35 Suarez 2004: 148.
36 Richard Pickersgill (?), French Polynesia: Austral Islands: Ohetiruah (Rurutu or Oheteroah), 1769, ADM 352/469 [formerly 497/4 shelf Hf], The National Archives, Kew; see Smith and Joppien 1988, I: plate 160.
37 Smith and Joppien 1988:155.

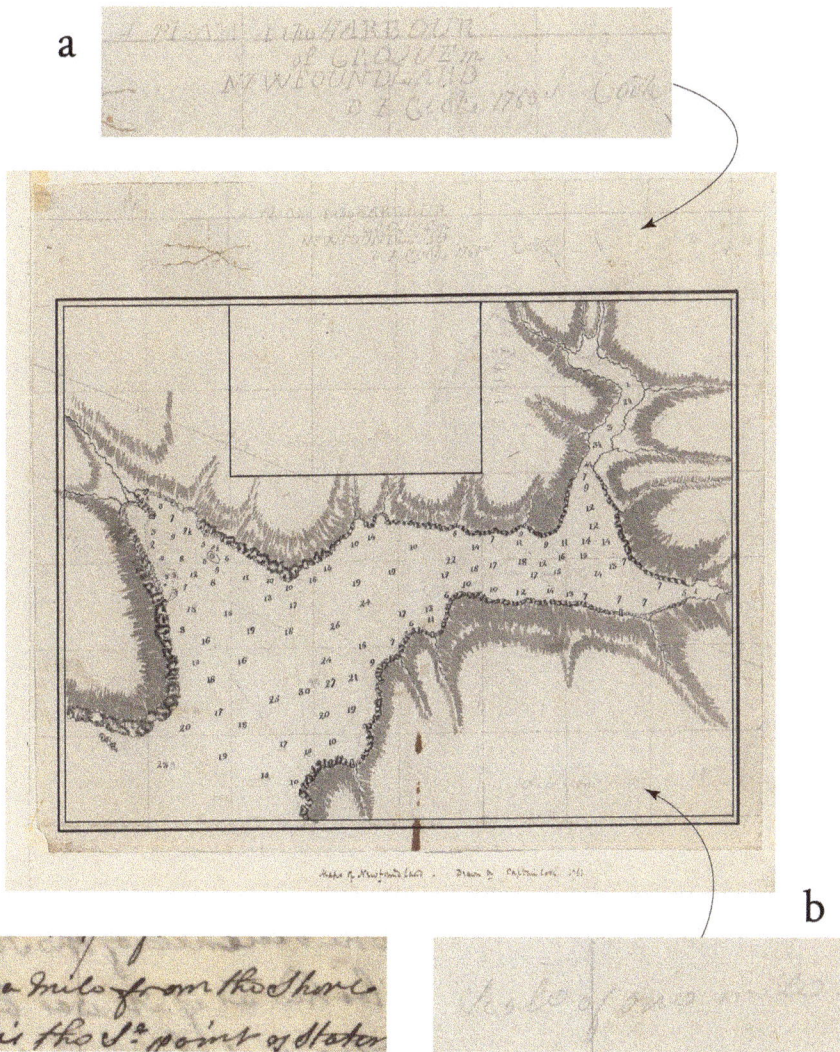

Figure 8.4a 'A Plan of the Harbour of Croque in Newfoundland by J Cook, 1763'. The 'n' in 'Plan' and at the end of 'Newfoundland' are written backwards.

Source: Collection of Admiral Isaac Smith, SAFE/PXD11 a156008, State Library of New South Wales, Sydney.

Figure 8.4b 'A Plan of the Harbour of Croque in Newfoundland by J Cook, 1763' (detail). In the body of the chart, 'Scale of one mile' has been written in a more sophisticated hand.

Source: Collection of Admiral Isaac Smith, SAFE/PXD11 a156008, State Library of New South Wales, Sydney.

Figure 8.4c Sample of James Cook's handwriting.

Source: Journal of HMS *Endeavour*, 1768–1771, holograph, National Library of Australia, nla.gov.au/nla.ms-ms1-s27v-e-cd.

Cook is noted for the accuracy of his cartography and where he was able to make his own survey, comparison with the modern map shows this is also true of his chart of the Society Islands. But Richard Pickersgill's chart of Raiatea shows large parts of the island were not surveyed and from the ship's track it is clear both Bola Bola (Borabora) and Maurua (Maupiti) were only seen from a distance.[38] Nevertheless, they are complete on Cook's chart, suggesting the missing parts were extrapolated from Tupaia's sketch and verbal descriptions.

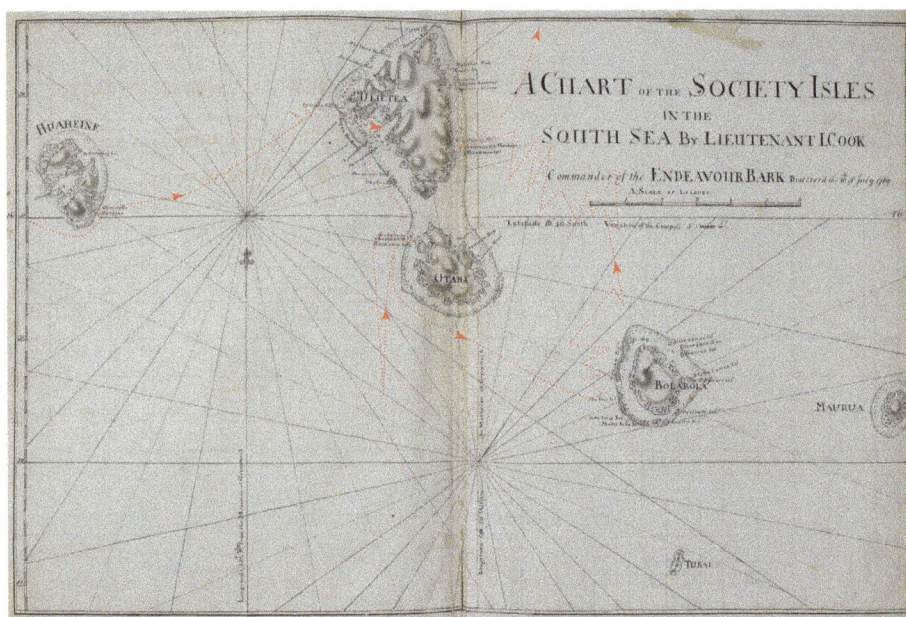

Figure 8.5 James Cook, 'A Chart of the Society Isles in the South Sea' with the ship's track superimposed. Although the *Endeavour* did not make a complete survey of the islands of Raiatea (Ulietea), Bola Bola (Borabora) and Maupiti (Maurua), they are complete on his chart.
Source: British Library, BL Add Ms 7085 f.11, © British Library Board.

This practice of working from information, by eye and experience, or 'Lead, Lookout and Local Knowledge' as David Turnbull puts it, was not alien to Cook.[39] Coastal sailing requires the skills of a pilot rather than a navigator and it is on this level that Tupaia's chart of the Society Islands operates.

---

38   Richard Pickersgill, A Plan of the Islands Uliateah [Raiatea] and Ottahau [Tahaa] discover'd July the 16th 1769 in His Majesty's Ship Endeavour Lieutenant James Cook, Commander, 1769, ADM 352/471 [formerly 497/7 shelf Hf], The National Archives, Kew; see Smith and Joppien 1988, I: plate 145.
39   Turnbull 2000: 60.

Cook spent the early years of his military career from 1763 to 1767 surveying the Newfoundland coastline, and his chart of part of the south coast, which he published with a commentary, can be used to illustrate how the information contained in this chart of the Society Islands is qualitatively different from the more famous 'Tupaia's Chart'.

Andrew David describes in his introduction to the *Charts and Coastal Views of Captain Cook's Voyages* the use of the 'running survey', made from a moving ship, and the more accurate method of triangulation, made from fixed points of observation.[40] In Newfoundland, Cook learned how to base small parts of his chart on triangulated calculations while improvising the remainder from a running survey. His book, *DIRECTIONS For Navigating on Part of the South Coast of Newfoundland ...*, provides a valuable insight into his working process. Implicit within its repetitive structure are questions and answers that take a captain on an imaginative tour through the approach to each of these bays: What is the depth? What is the bottom? Are there rocks? Is it sheltered? What are the landmarks? Is there wood? Is there water?

> One League and a half to the Northward of St. John's Head is the Great Bay de Leau, wherein is good Anchorage in various depths of Water, sheltered from all Winds. The best Passage in is on the East-side of the Island laying in the Mouth of it; nothing can enter in on the West-side but small Vessels and Shallops.
>
> To the Westward of Bay de Leau, 3 Miles NNW. from St. John's Head is Little Bay Barrysway, on the West-side of which is good Anchorage for large Ships in 7, 8, or 10 Fathom Water; here is good Fishing Conveniencies, with plenty of Wood and Water.[41]

These 'questions and answers' are very similar to what Salmond describes as the 'basic information taught to star navigators' which were learned as lists of recitations:

> These lists included a brief description of each island – its name; size; whether it was low or high; whether or not it had a reef; the location of good harbours; the main foodstuffs produced there; whether or not it was inhabited; whether or not the people were friendly and the name of its *ari'i* or high chief.[42]

Johann Forster described the same process in his account of the making of Tupaia's Chart:

> Tupaya ... when on board the Endeavour, gave an account of his navigations and mentioned the names of more than eighty isles which he knew, together with their size and situation, the greater part of which he had visited, and ... gave

---

40   David 1988: xxv.
41   Cook 1766: 12.
42   Salmond 2009: 203–204.

directions for making one according to his account, and always pointed to that part of the heavens, where each isle was situated, mentioning at the same time that it was either larger or smaller than Taheitee, and likewise whether it was high or low, whether it was peopled or not, adding now and then some curious accounts relative to some of them.[43]

There are a number of similarities between Cook's chart of Newfoundland and Tupaia's chart of the Society Islands. The symbol for an anchorage in the key to Newfoundland appears in the harbours of Opoa and Fa'aroa. The depth in fathoms indicated by an encircled figure in the Newfoundland chart is represented in Tupaia's Society Islands chart in shades of ink wash. Cook describes Opua in his *Journal* on the upper side of 'Ulieatea' as 'good anchorage between or just within the 2 Islands in 28 fathom, soft ground'. He wrote 'There are more harbours at the south end of this Island as I am inform'd but these were not examind by us'.[44] These harbours, which appear out of proportion but in detail on his own chart, correspond to the wash around the right side of 'Ulieatea' in Tupaia's version. In addition, Salmond remarks, 'Sometimes the navigators also sketched the sailing courses between islands in the sand on a beach, along with the coastlines, reefs, passages and harbours of these places'. On Tupaia's chart of the Society Islands, a faint pencil line shows the outline of the reef with its openings into the harbour. Even though the islands are not in the relationship conventionally used in European charts, a dotted line corresponds to the *Endeavour*'s route from Huahine to Raiatea, sailing into the harbour at Opoa [Oopoa], marked by a small anchor, and then north-west, within the reef, to exit via the channel at Fa'aroa [Wharoa], also marked by an anchor as a harbour.

This chart does for Cook what he was doing in his book for the captains of Newfoundland: it tells the way through unknown waters. It describes the complex discussion that Cook and Tupaia were able to carry out with limited vocabulary because they shared the common language of pilots. Much emphasis is placed upon Cook's skill in mathematical calculations, but in this chart we see him using a narrative tradition in which British and Polynesian concepts of space, distance and orientation converge.

---

43   Forster 1996: 310.
44   Cook 1768–1771: 40.

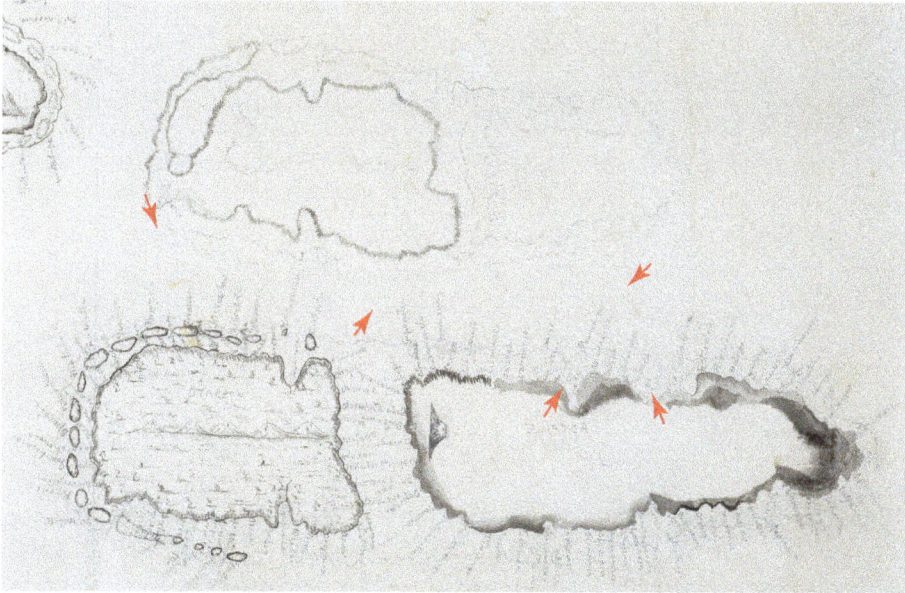

Figure 8.6 James Cook, 'A Chart of the Society Isles in the South Sea' (detail). The chart shows the openings in the reef to the harbours of Opua (Oopoa) and Fa'aroa (Wharoa) marked by small anchors and the line marking the *Endeavour*'s route from Huahine to Raiatea.
Source: British Library, BL Add Ms. 15508 f.16, © British Library Board.

Transmission and translation

Smith and Joppien say only that the words in Banks's handwriting on the chart of the Society Islands were 'derived' from Tupaia, but this summation gives no hint of the complexity of the process of cultural assimilation it required to arrive at the point of transcription. Cook struggled to reconcile the navigational references that were recited to him as lists in an oral tradition, with the coordinates of longitude and latitude he needed to make a chart. He wrote as the *Endeavour* was preparing for its departure from Tahiti: 'I have before hinted that these people have an extensive knowlidge of the Islands situated in these seas – Tupia as well as several others hath given us an account of upwards of seventy'.[45] The passage shows Cook thinking as he writes. It begins as the sketch of a plan for a chart made from local knowledge but it has been revised mid-sentence:

---

45   Cook 1768–1771: 35.

their names are as follows of them Tupia says he himself hath been at and thosr mark'd with an obelist — but as the account they have given of their situation is so vague and uncertain I shall refar giving a list of them untill I have learnt from Tupia the situation of each Island with a little more certainty — [46]

Cook gives some idea of the challenges he was facing when he writes 'the Accounts taken by and from different people differ ... sencibly one from a nother both in names and Number'.[47] Salmond's analysis of the lists transcribed by Cook and Molyneux shows they contain only 39 islands in common, 'indicating that during his conversations with these two men, the high priest-navigator shared different fragments of his navigational knowledge'.[48] But she also notes that a number of the islands are mythological: 'for instance Tumu-papa, a name that refers to the creator Tumu (Ta'aroa's phallus) and Papa, the Earth; and those names beginning with Hiti-, evidently drawn from the story of the ancestral voyager Rata (Hiti-teare, Hiti-tautaureva, Hiti-tautaumai, Hiti-poto, Hiti-te-tamaruire etc.).'[49] The British also had difficulty assimilating Tahitian place names for 'want of rightly knowing how to pronounce the names of the Islands after them' and this created spelling variations making it difficult to compare notes.[50]

Transcription represents only one facet of the complex problem-solving this drawing session demanded. The second component, essential to cartography, is a common unit of measurement. John Olstad agrees with di Piazza and Pearthree on the Polynesian character of the geography of the Society Islands chart. In addition to the islands' segmentation, he identifies a number of features, particularly the shape of the islands. Just as, as Salmond notes, the distance between islands was measured by sailing time from a known point of departure,[51] the distance on land, Olstad suggests, has been measured by time of travel, causing mountainous areas to appear wider on the page while level areas appear narrower.

Although Banks's landholdings may engage different concepts of space, direction and orientation from the islands Cook was attempting to chart, the Society Islands chart makes the first successful attempt to transform a list transcribed from a chanted recitation into a recognisable, European-style chart.

---

46   Cook 1768–1771: 35.
47   Cook 1768–1771: 74.
48   Salmond 2009: 204.
49   Salmond 2009: 204.
50   Cook 1768–1771: 77.
51   Salmond 2009: 204.

Conclusion

The British voyagers' impression of Tupaia is largely unrecorded in the *Endeavour* journals. The nature of their conversations, the impact upon British perception of the concepts he introduced, and the scope of their plans for the future have survived only in fragments. Recourse to speculation is unavoidable in the reconstruction of history, but whether the British were critical or simply critically engaged with Polynesian culture is an open question. Silence in writing does not necessarily correspond to indifference in the course of a process of problem-solving. Problems are often puzzled out in drawing before they are committed to writing, and the problems Tupaia and the British were facing were multifarious, simultaneously engaging language, concept and the diplomatic relations of first contact. Reconstructing these conversations relies upon the nature of the active culture. Increasingly, the culture and political atmosphere of late eighteenth-century Tahiti is coming to light, but the intellectual atmosphere on the *Endeavour* belongs to a particularly tumultuous period in British history. Cook's own voyages were contributing to radical transformations in scientific and philosophical thought so that attitudes that may have become prevalent by the second and third voyages were not necessarily influences on the first. First contact in the Pacific was undeniably violent but critical or disparaging comments, or equally expressions of admiration, while obviously important when recorded in writing are not necessarily reliable gauges of the intellectual atmosphere of the voyage as a whole. The *Endeavour*'s visual archive offers an opportunity to test how these attitudes played out in practice. By examining who was working with whom in these drawing sessions, surprising alliances emerge and a wide variety of imaginative strategies for communicating and reconciling divergent concepts illuminate the discrete silences of the journals.

References

Cook, James 1766, *DIRECTIONS For Navigating on Part of the South Coast of Newfoundland, WITH A CHART thereof, Including the ISLANDS of St. PETER's and MIQUELON, And a particular ACCOUNT of the Bays, Harbours, Rocks, Land-Marks, Depths of Water, Latitudes, Bearings, and Distances from Place to Place, the Setting of the Currents, and Flowing of the Tides, &c. From an actual SURVEY, taken by Order of Commodore PALLISSER, Governor of Newfoundland, Labradore, &c., Printed for the AUTHOR, and Sold by J. MOUNT and T. PAGE on Tower-Hill*, London, available at www.gutenberg.org/ebooks/21915 and nla.gov.au/nla.map-rm423.

——Journal of HMS *Endeavour*, 1768–1771, holograph, available at www.nla.gov.au.

David, Andrew 1988, 'Introduction', in Bernard Smith and Rüdiger Joppien, *The Charts and Coastal Views of Captain Cook's Voyages, Volume I: The Voyage of the Endeavour, 1768–1771,* Andrew David (ed.), Melbourne University Press in association with the Australian Academy of Humanities, Melbourne.

Dening, Greg 1992, *Mr Bligh's Bad Language: Passion, Power and Theatre on the Bounty*, Cambridge University Press, Melbourne.

Di Piazza, Anne and Erik Pearthree 2007, 'A new reading of Tupaia's Chart', *Journal of Pacific Studies* 116(3): 321–340.

Forster, Johann 1996, *Observations made during a voyage round the world, on physical geography, natural history, and ethnic philosophy,* Nicholas Thomas, Harriet Guest and Michael Dettelbach (eds), University of Hawai'i Press, Honolulu.

Langdon, Robert 1980, 'The European ships of Tupaia's Chart: an essay in identification', *Journal of Pacific History* 15(4): 225–232.

O'Brian, Patrick 1997, *Joseph Banks,* Collins Harvill, London.

Obeyesekere, Gananath 1992, *The Apotheosis of Captain Cook: European Mythmaking in the Pacific,* Princeton University Press, Bishop Museum Press, Oxford, New Jersey, Honolulu.

Rodger, N.A.M. 1986, *The Wooden World: An Anatomy of the Georgian Navy,* Collins, London.

Salmond, Anne 2004, *The Trial of the Cannibal Dog: Captain Cook in the South Seas,* Penguin, London.

——2009, *Aphrodite's Island: The European Discovery of Tahiti,* University of California Press, Berkeley and Los Angeles.

Skinner, Quentin 1969, 'Meaning and understanding in the history of ideas', *History and Theory* 8(1): 3–53.

Smith, Anita 2007, 'The cultural landscapes of the Pacific islands', in *Cultural Landscapes of the Pacific Islands: ICOMOS Thematic Study, Interim Report, June 2007*, Anita Smith and Kevin L. Jones, UNESCO, available at www.unesco.org.

Smith, Bernard 1960, *European Vision and the South Pacific, 1768–1850: A Study in the History of Art and Ideas,* Oxford University Press, Melbourne.

——1992, *Imagining the Pacific: In the Wake of the Cook Voyages,* Melbourne University Press, Miegunyah, Melbourne.

Smith, Bernard and Rüdiger Joppien 1985, *The Art of Captain Cook's Voyages,* Vol. I: *The Voyage of the* Endeavour *1768–1771,* Oxford University Press in association with the Australian Academy of Humanities, Melbourne.

——1988, *The Charts and Coastal Views of Captain Cook's Voyages,* Vol. I: *The Voyage of the* Endeavour, *1768–1771,* Vol. II: *The voyage of the* Resolution *and* Adventure, *1772–1775,* Andrew David (ed.), Hakluyt Society in association with the Australian Academy of Humanities, Melbourne.

Suarez, Thomas 2004, *Early Mapping of the Pacific: The Epic Story of Seafarers, Adventurers and Cartographers Who Mapped the Earth's Greatest Ocean,* Periplus, Singapore.

Thomas, Nicholas 1997, 'Introduction: Tupaia's Map', in *In Oceania: Visions, Artifacts, Histories,* Duke University Press, Durham and London, 1–20.

Turnbull, David 2000, '(En)-countering knowledge traditions: the story of Cook and Tupaia', *Humanities Research* 1: 55–76.

9

Encounters and the photographic record in British New Guinea

Antje Lübcke

The intricacies of encounters between photographers and their subjects need to be examined more closely, especially in the colonial context, as it has too often been taken for granted that the photographer was solely responsible for the resulting image or the only agent in the photographic encounter. The cameras that were used and the associated materials and chemicals needed for photography in the late nineteenth century meant that setting up a shot and developing a photograph were neither simple nor quick tasks. European photographers who travelled to the newly acquired territories of empire relied on local carriers and interpreters to assist them in their work; and when it came to photographing the indigenous people of these lands, the photographic encounter was shaped to varying degrees by their willingness to be photographed. Just as Felix Driver and Lowri Jones assert that 'exploration was a joint project of work' and a 'shared experience',[1] I argue that the practice of photographing foreign lands and indigenous peoples was similarly dependent on local expertise and participation for its success.

In this chapter I examine a series of photographic encounters in south-east New Guinea in the late nineteenth century – in 1885 to be precise. These encounters were between the Melbourne-based professional photographer

---

1   Driver and Jones 2009: 11, 5.

John William Lindt and the Papuans of British New Guinea. In particular, I am interested in how the Papuans Lindt photographed influenced the nature of the encounter and the resulting image, and in the mediating role played by the missionary Reverend William G. Lawes of the London Missionary Society (LMS). Further, I argue that Lindt's camera can also be understood as an historical actor or agent in photographic encounters. The cultural and social values and meanings attached to the camera in the late nineteenth century and its mere physical presence, often significantly influenced the interactions that took place. Both sides of the photographic encounter are investigated, and while my analysis relies primarily on the visual and textual documents created by Lindt and other Europeans, by critically examining these sources and considering the concomitant conditions that shaped these particular encounters, a more nuanced picture emerges that allows the uncovering of indigenous people's agency.

Lindt in New Guinea

Johannes Wilhelm Lindt came to Australia from Germany in 1862 at the age of 17.[2] A romantic, middle-class, educated youth, he had run away to sea and worked his passage to Australia aboard a Dutch ship. After a time spent travelling in Australia, tuning and repairing pianos, Lindt settled in Grafton on the Clarence River in New South Wales, where he took up work as an apprentice for the artist and photographer Conrad Wagner in his photographic studio. There he received his photographic training, and after taking over the running of the studio in 1870 made his living producing *carte-de-visite* portraits and photographing subjects as diverse as horses and cattle, landscape views, and the local architecture. He also regularly undertook fieldtrips, lugging the cumbersome and fragile photographic equipment (including a portable darkroom) with him to visit outlying hamlets. On these trips he photographed local Australian Aboriginal people, capturing them on glass-plate negatives, and in 1873–74 he produced his famous series of around 60 tableaux portraits titled *Australian Aboriginals*.[3] Lindt won several medals for his photographs in international exhibitions and following this success he moved to Melbourne in 1876 with his wife Anna (nee Wagner – the daughter of Lindt's former boss). It was not long before he opened his own studio on Collins Street, where he continued to sell his Clarence River portraits and views but also added to his catalogue by photographing the city that was now his home.[4]

---

2   Lindt became a naturalised British subject in 1869.

3   For discussions of Lindt's photographs, see Cato 1955: 70–75; Jones 1985; Newton 1988: passim; Orchard 1999; Poignant 1992: 56; Quanchi 2007: passim; Quartermaine 1992; Willis 1988: 86–90.

4   Jones 1985: 3–6.

In early 1885 when, as Lindt writes, 'rumours of annexation [of south-east New Guinea] became rife',[5] Reverend Lawes visited Melbourne while on deputation in the country and the two men discussed Lindt's dream of visiting the Pacific island that he had first sighted in 1868, on his return voyage from a visit to Europe.[6] It seems little further encouragement was needed for Lindt to set about turning his dream into a reality. He persuaded an influential friend and client, Sir Frederick Sargood, to introduce him to Sir Peter Scratchley. Scratchley was the first Special Commissioner of British New Guinea, which had been declared a Protectorate in a series of flag-hoisting ceremonies performed by Commodore John Elphinstone Erskine and the Australian Squadron in villages along the south-east coast in November 1884. Lindt convinced the Special Commissioner to allow him to join his expedition to New Guinea as its official photographer, and even secured darkroom facilities on board SS *Governor Blackall* for developing his glass-plate negatives.[7] Undoubtedly, Lindt's reputation as a talented photographer of landscapes and cityscapes as well as his celebrated series of tableaux portraits of Australian Aboriginal subjects influenced the Commissioner's decision to allow Lindt to join the expedition.

Lindt arrived in Port Moresby at the end of August 1885 and remained in New Guinea for six weeks. (He was originally meant to stay for the full three months of the official expedition, but his wife took ill.) He returned to Melbourne at the end of October with approximately 128 exposed glass-plate negatives and subsequently made available for sale 124 of these (as prints) through his Collins Street studio.[8] The complete set of 'Picturesque New Guinea' photographs was presented in five albums, and customers who visited Lindt's studio could select the images they preferred in a number of formats. Lindt chose to enlarge seven of the photographs to 48 x 36 inches for the explicit purpose of display in 'Libraries, Museums and Halls', and these could also be purchased, in oak frames, through his studio.[9]

---

5   Lindt 1887: ix.
6   Lindt 1887: viii.
7   Jones 1985: 11.
8   There are four views of Brisbane and Cooktown included in the 'Picturesque New Guinea' series.
9   Lindt 1888: 8. A complete set of Lindt's 'Picturesque New Guinea' albums is held at the State Library of Victoria (SLV) in Melbourne (LTA 156 – LTA 160, Pictures Collection). The Cambridge University Museum of Archaeology and Anthropology in the UK also has a complete set (G.2.1, A.1. – A.5. LDT, PNG), while individual albums containing a selection of images from the series are held at the SLV (H2009.46/1–12, Pictures Collection, SLV), the Mitchell Library in the State Library of New South Wales in Sydney (PXB 420), and the National Gallery of Australia in Canberra (acc. no.: 84.1484.1–25). The Mitchell Library also holds a complete set of the display-size prints (ML611), though these were taken out of their frames in July 1933, and the National Museum of Victoria (Museum Victoria) also has five carbon print enlargements of Lindt's New Guinea photographs, as well as two from his 'Picturesque New Hebrides' (1890) series, in its collections. Individual prints from the 'Picturesque New Guinea' series can be found in collections in the UK, Australia, New Zealand, Germany, the USA, and Switzerland. There are almost certainly more 'Picturesque New Guinea' prints in both public and private collections the world over.

Taking advantage of the public interest generated in England and Australia around the acquisition of a new territory, Lindt dedicated his 'Picturesque New Guinea' series and the book of his travels that he wrote on his return to Melbourne to Queen Victoria. The book was also titled *Picturesque New Guinea* and contains 50 autotype reproductions of Lindt's New Guinea photographs. Further, Lindt enlarged, framed and put on display a selection of the images in colonial exhibitions in London (1886) and Melbourne (1888), where they were seen by the many visitors who attended these spectacles of empire. Around 5.5 million people visited the Colonial and Indian Exhibition in 1886, where photographs from England's far-flung territories were put on display alongside 'curios' and the marketable natural and cultural products of each country.[10]

It is clear that Lindt's image of New Guinea was conceived long before leaving Australian shores. Along with his preconceptions of what New Guinea must be like, based on his reading and encounters with the Italian naturalist-explorer Luigi Maria D'Albertis and Reverend Lawes, the fact that Lindt only had a set amount of time in New Guinea meant he likely had in mind a catalogue of views and subjects he wanted to capture. The subjects that appealed to Lindt, or at least those he selected for his 'Picturesque New Guinea' series, are diverse. They range from posed group portraits of 'native teachers', to more relaxed shots of expedition parties setting out from Port Moresby – though these are only seemingly 'relaxed', as the exposure times in early photography meant the subjects often had to remain motionless for long periods (depending on light conditions). Lindt also photographed the local landscapes and flora, including views of scrub, bush tracks, coconut groves, bays, beaches, and rivers, as well as the campsites of the expedition parties, village scenes and dwellings, material culture, stuffed birds of paradise, rituals and ritual structures, boats associated with the expedition and the mission, and the local sea craft. Jack Cato notes that it was Lindt's 'self-imposed task ... eventually to provide the British people with a magnificent panorama of life and conditions in this, the newest of Britain's protectorates'.[11] While many of the subjects Lindt photographed were likely dictated by the requirements of the official expedition, it is certainly an impressive list and shows Lindt's versatility in the field. Viewed as a whole, the 'Picturesque New Guinea' series represents a clear visual agenda on the part of the photographer.[12]

---

10   Barringer 1998: 23.

11   Cato 1952: 402.

12   Lindt was not the first professional photographer to travel to south-east New Guinea. Augustine Dyer accompanied Commodore Erskine's official expedition in 1884 in order to document the proclamation of the British Protectorate. John Paine also sold proclamation prints through his Sydney studio, though his photographs were taken by two petty officers on board HMS *Espiegle* (see Newton 1988: 58; Barker 2010: 99, 135).

Aside from fulfilling the photographer's aesthetic and commercial requirements, the 'Picturesque New Guinea' series was intended to serve the purposes of the political and scientific expedition of which Lindt was a part. Lindt's motto had long been 'Truth – but Truth in a pleasant form' and, indeed, a key underlying narrative of Lindt's book is that of the professional artist-photographer as a valuable asset to the expedition.[13] This is not surprising as the camera was employed in the service of science soon after its invention in 1839. It was believed it could faithfully record the countries and peoples that were being 'discovered' by European explorers. In the opening lines of the preface to Lindt's book he writes of his disappointment that, in the past, exploring expeditions had not chosen their artists and photographers with as much care as they selected the scientific staff, which acted to underscore the importance, at least in Lindt's mind, of his accompanying the 1885 expedition:

> For years past, when perusing the account of exploring expeditions setting out for some country comparatively unknown, I always noticed with a pang of disappointment that, however carefully the scientific staff was chosen, it was, as a rule, considered sufficient to supply one of the members with a mahogany camera, lens, and chemicals to take pictures, the dealer furnishing these articles generally initiating the purchaser for a couple or three hours' time into the secrets and tricks of the 'dark art', or when funds were limited to purchase instruments, it was taken for granted that enough talent existed among the members to make rough sketches, which would afterwards be 'worked up' for the purpose of illustrating perhaps a very important report.[14]

Lindt was convinced he had succeeded in capturing scenes straight from 'savage real life' during his time in New Guinea.[15] However, the 'reality' committed to the glass-plate negatives was mediated through the European photographer's perspective and preconceptions, and enhanced through the developing and printing processes employed in Lindt's studio, and the framing devices used in the subsequent display and reproduction of the images. The visual archive, like all archives, is partial. But this archive can also be read against the grain and alongside the textual archive to uncover the agency of local actors.

Local agency in photographic encounters

While Lindt left behind an archive of texts and images from which his perceptions and motivations may be inferred, such an archive does not exist for the other side of this cross-cultural encounter to the same degree. Polynesian and Papuan

---

13   Lindt 1883: 3. See also Lindt 1888: 5.
14   Lindt 1887: vii.
15   Lindt 1887: 44.

teachers who worked for the LMS occasionally wrote letters to the organisation, and several travelled to Australia and England where they were presented to curious audiences. But how they and other Papuans might have perceived the encounters with European photographers in New Guinea must be inferred from the writings and images produced by Lindt and others at the time, as well as from an understanding of the surrounding contexts. In approaching the question of how Papuans might have perceived the photographic encounters with Lindt, it is worth considering Felix Driver's suggestion that the process of imaging places such as New Guinea might best be conceived of 'in terms of transactions rather than projections'.[16] While Driver analyses sketches, approaching the photographic encounter as a 'transaction' or an exchange, in which all parties are invested to varying degrees, opens the way for understanding the process of the individual photograph's production as 'negotiated in various ways'.[17] This can lead to the uncovering of indigenous agency in the photographic encounter and in encounters more generally. Some evidence for the negotiations involved in Lindt's photographs are provided by Lindt himself, both in the text in *Picturesque New Guinea* as well as in some of the images.

Lindt introduces the sections in his book where he writes about his photographic sojourns in the villages of south-east New Guinea in a casual manner – he always 'sallies' forth to photograph – but he clearly relied on carriers, interpreters and assistants in order to carry and set up his bulky and heavy equipment and to get subjects to pose for his camera.[18] What is interesting in Lindt's book is that he frequently mentions the aid he received, and he also photographed these helpers. For example, in a campsite scene photographed by Lindt on his first inland trek, at Badeba Creek, the Papuan carriers/guides/interpreters can be seen resting alongside the two European explorers in the image (Figure 9.1). These carriers and helpers were not always local or, indeed, Papuan. The explorer H.O. Forbes employed Malay servants and Amboynese hunters for his expeditions and Lindt writes that Forbes spoke to him 'very highly of these dusky retainers as being faithful and affectionate', and then notes, 'This testimony I am able to corroborate from my own experience; I have found both the Malays and the Sundanese as servants industrious and obedient.'[19] Despite the omission of names, the mere mentioning of this help received from Papuans, Malays and others, and Lindt's photographing of these men, is remarkable, as local help was seldom acknowledged in early travelogues in order to magnify the heroism and bravery of the male European 'hero-explorer'.[20]

---

16   Driver 2004: 3.
17   Driver 2004: 3.
18   Lindt 1887: 30.
19   Lindt 1887: 20.
20   Driver and Jones 2009: 11.

Figure 9.1 J.W. Lindt, 'The Camp at Badeba Creek', 1885.

Albumen silver, 15 x 20.5 cm.

Source: 'Picturesque New Guinea', vol. 2, acc. no. H42424, plate 25, Pictures Collection, State Library of Victoria, Melbourne.

What is clear from Lindt's narrative in *Picturesque New Guinea* is that when these helpers were not present, the exchanges and encounters with the local villagers were often awkward and drawn out. In many cases, the European expedition members had to use gestures and mime in order to acquire information from the locals and to get their cooperation in posing for Lindt's camera. On Heath Island, Lindt recounts in detail how he and Mr Smart (a conchologist) were reduced to acting out a cannibal feast, with Mr Smart as the main course, in order to ascertain whether some 'flagged places' they came across were associated with cannibalism.[21] In another instance, in Kamali village, Lindt writes how he decided to stay on longer than the other expedition members, due to it being 'more attractive than the village we had just quitted', and while at first he had misgivings about getting sitters, to Lindt's astonishment all the inhabitants eventually turned out, and he writes that this was 'evidently with the object of being photographed'.[22] What this episode makes clear is that the Papuans of the south-east coast were often willing, though also at times hesitant, participants in the photographic encounter.

---

21   Lindt 1887: 87.

22   Lindt 1887: 65–66.

Even with the help of interpreters, Lindt sometimes struggled or did not get to take the photographs he wanted. In Moapa, for instance, he set about attempting to photograph a ceremonial structure in the centre of the village that had ornamented human skulls hanging from it. However, due to the strong wind blowing that day he was concerned the skulls would be reduced to blurred traces on the negative. Lindt writes that he offered 'almost any price (in tobacco) to induce the natives to go up and steady the skulls while the picture was being taken', but he was ultimately unable to convince them and was reluctantly 'compelled to trust to the pen, unaided by the camera'.[23] In Kapa Kapa, where Lindt met a couple in mourning for their three children, he found it took 'a good deal of persuasion' by their interpreter to get them to pose in a group portrait for him.[24] What these encounters, or failed encounters, in Moapa and Kapa Kapa make clear is that the Papuans Lindt wanted to photograph sometimes refused to participate. Paradoxically, then, it is the absence of certain scenes in the photographic record that speaks volumes in terms of indigenous agency in many early encounters.

The tactless incidents in Moapa and Kapa Kapa aside, Lindt was aware of etiquette and clearly had been briefed on how to behave in certain situations in order to ensure the goodwill of the Papuans – this, of course, being due to the fact he was connected with an official expedition sent out to New Guinea to establish and maintain good relations with the indigenous islanders. On one occasion ,Lindt writes that he would never enter a dwelling without first obtaining the owner's permission, it being 'absolutely necessary to observe a certain amount of etiquette to avoid giving offense'.[25] In another display of his adherence to local customs and rules of etiquette, Lindt participated in a local ceremony in Sadara Makara, a Koiari village inland from Port Moresby. After shaking hands with one of the chiefs, Lohio-bada, Lindt was invited to exchange names with him and was thereby given the name Misi Lolo (meaning 'maker of pictures' in the Koiari language).[26] This display of goodwill and willingness to participate in local traditions no doubt helped Lindt obtain subjects for his photographs the following day, when he 'sallied' into the village with his camera:

> The native population, men, women, and children, gathered round Misi Lolo with a childlike curiosity to watch my proceedings, and readily obeyed all instructions. They stood in groups, took the proper attitudes, and even posed picturesquely, as conscious that they were being immortalized in picture.[27]

---

23   Lindt 1887: 75.
24   Lindt 1887: 60–61.
25   Lindt 1887: 87.
26   Lindt 1887: 40.
27   Lindt 1887: 44.

Aside from the fact Lindt had been introduced to the Koiari people the previous day as 'an artist who had come to take pictures of the village', and also that he came to New Guinea in the company of the 'Great White Chief' (as Sir Peter Scratchley was introduced to many Papuans),[28] there was another factor that likely contributed to this 'easy' and automatic performance of the photographic encounter: the mediating presence of the LMS missionary, Reverend William G. Lawes.

Missionary as mediator

Reverend Lawes and his camera were well known to the residents of the villages in the Port Moresby mission district as Lawes had been working in this region of New Guinea since 1874. In his memoir of his time spent living and working in New Guinea, the natural history collector Andrew Goldie recounts that Lawes's name was 'sufficient as a passport'.[29] By simply shouting 'Misi Lao' (as Lawes was called by the Papuans) the guides who accompanied Lawes on his regular tours of the territory surrounding Port Moresby would warn their 'countrymen of the arrival of Mr Lawes and thus the intelligence was carried from mountain to mountain'.[30] Though Lawes did not accompany the expedition to Sadara Makara, the Koiari people knew what was expected of them in front of the camera as a result of his earlier visits and readily assumed the poses Lindt suggested. What Lindt witnessed was a 'scripted' performance.

This performance for the photographer was also likely prompted by the fact that Lindt's expedition party had with it tobacco and tomahawks for trading and payment. For many Papuans, being party to the 'performance of [the photograph's] creation'[31] was a curiosity, and sitters frequently benefitted in material terms. As Helen Gardner and Jude Philp note in relation to Reverend George Brown's photographic practices on New Britain, the subjects of his photographs were often paid with trade goods in order to sit still before the missionary's camera.[32] Frequently there are signs of this practice in missionaries' and other travellers' photographs from the Pacific. For example, a subject might be holding the knife, tomahawk, or tobacco given them for their time and cooperation. Tobacco was widely used as an item of trade in the Pacific, and it is known that Lawes was a major importer to New Guinea.[33]

---

28 Lindt 1887: 40.
29 Goldie 2012: 72.
30 Goldie 2012: 72.
31 Gardner and Philp 2006: 190.
32 Gardner and Philp 2006: 178.
33 Hays 1991: 96, 98.

The mission station in Port Moresby was the first port of call for many European visitors who came to New Guinea. In the early years of the mission, Lawes played host to the occasional exploration party led by scientists such as the ethnographer Octavius C. Stone, but by the late 1870s the number of arrivals drastically increased. This was a result of the short-lived gold rush on the Laloki River in 1878 and the increasing interest aroused in Australia around the question of annexation. As Robert Holden writes, the annexation of New Guinea fuelled 'Australia-wide feelings of common interests and shared responsibility',[34] and in 1883 the *Age* and *Argus* newspapers dispatched journalists to report on the state of the land and its people following the ultimately unsanctioned annexation by Queensland of the south-eastern part of the island.[35] Lawes was an important intermediary for these men, as well as for the collectors, ethnographers and botanists who visited Port Moresby, as he knew the land and its people, and could speak the Motu language. However, he did not approve of the new 'breed' of explorer to land on New Guinea shores in 1883. In a letter to the LMS secretary, Lawes does not hide his contempt and writes:

> We have two parties of white men here at present representing two Melbourne papers, the 'Argus' and 'Age'. They are here for exploration or rather perhaps to make interesting letters for their papers – one we know, descriptive of country, was written and sent before they arrived here, or had even set a foot on New Guinea.[36]

When it was finally decided that the territory would officially become a British protectorate, Lawes declared 'Almost anything ... will be better than leaving the people and their lands at the mercy of lawless men and mad adventurers'.[37] Sir Peter Scratchley, sent to New Guinea in 1885 to establish good relations with the Papuans, was therefore a welcome guest.

As a missionary working for the LMS, Lawes did not have much time or money to spend on personal pastimes. While mission societies understood the power of pictures in mission work, there is no indication in the correspondence between Lawes and the LMS secretary that he was expected to supply photographs for them or that he was compensated for the cost of his photographic equipment and supplies. Indeed, Lawes threatened to leave the mission on a number of occasions, writing that the stipend he received 'never has been enough' to make ends meet.[38] Lawes therefore photographed the New Guinea villages, landscapes and people when the opportunity arose. The arrival of Sir Peter Scratchley's official expedition, with the professional photographer on board, presented just such an opportunity.

---

34   Holden 1988: 27.
35   See Souter 1963: 49–56.
36   Lawes to W. Whitehouse, 23 July 1883, p. 4, microform M93 LMS Papua Letters, National Library of Australia [hereafter NLA].
37   Lawes to Rev. R.W. Thompson, 30 October 1884, p. 2, microform M93 LMS Papua Letters, NLA.
38   Lawes to Rev. R.W. Thompson, 12 February 1884, p. 3, microform M93 LMS Papua Letters, NLA. See also Lawes to Rev. R.W. Thompson, 14 May 1886, p. 4, microform M94 LMS Papua Letters, NLA.

Figure 9.2 J.W. Lindt, 'Poling a Lakatoi to Windward, Port Moresby', 1885.

Albumen silver, 15 x 20.5 cm.

Source: 'Picturesque New Guinea', vol. 1, acc. no. H42423, plate 20, Pictures Collection, State Library of Victoria, Melbourne.

The photographic encounter between Lawes and Lindt resulted in a number of duplicates (or very similar subjects from slightly different angles) in the two men's photographic oeuvres. For example, their images of H.O. Forbes's expedition party setting out on an inland trek and the lakatoi (large Motu trading canoes) in the harbour of Port Moresby preparing for the annual westward voyage to trade the local pottery for sago and other products. In Lindt's lakatoi photograph, Lawes can be seen in the foreground of the image composing or exposing a photograph of a large lakatoi with another man assisting him or looking on (Figure 9.2), while in the photograph of Forbes's expedition party he is standing to the right of the image with three other European men (Figure 9.3).[39] It is not difficult to imagine that

---

39   Lawes's photographs of these scenes are in an album held at the School of Oriental and African Studies (SOAS) in London (CWM/LMS/Papua New Guinea/Photographs/Box 1, file 1). His New Guinea photographs are as widely dispersed as Lindt's, owing to the fact he gave, or most likely sold, a large selection of his negatives to the Sydney-based professional photographer Henry King in c. 1890–93. There is an album of Lawes's photographs compiled by King in the Mitchell Library in Sydney (PXE 720), and two further albums, as well as loose prints, are held in London at SOAS (CWM/LMS/Papua New Guinea/Photographs/Box 1, file 1; CWM/LMS/Papua New Guinea/Photographs/Box 3, file 4). The University of Southern California Library has digitised 130 Lawes prints held at SOAS and these are available to view online at digitallibrary.usc.edu. Further prints of Lawes's New Guinea pictures are held in collections in Australia, the UK, New Zealand, the USA and Germany.

Lawes enjoyed discussing the work of the expedition party as well as Lindt's work on these occasions, and he did not let the opportunity to photograph alongside the professional photographer pass him by. Virginia-Lee Webb has termed this phenomenon the 'tourist effect', which occurs when individuals in a group gather or line up to photograph the same scene, event or monument, for example – an experience familiar to many travellers today.[40] Lindt also took several photographs of the local Motu 'water carriers' during his time in Port Moresby, as did Lawes, and when Reverend Brown visited Port Moresby in 1890 it seems Lawes took him to photograph these women as well.[41] Perhaps Brown wanted to capture his own version of the subject made famous by Lindt five years earlier.

11. H. O. Forbes Esq., at Hanuabada, Port Moresby.—J. W. Lindt, Melbourne.

Figure 9.3 J.W. Lindt, 'H. O. Forbes Esq., at Hanuabada, Port Moresby', 1885.

Albumen silver, 15 x 20.5 cm.

Source: 'Picturesque New Guinea', vol. 1, acc. no. H42423, plate 11, Pictures Collection, State Library of Victoria, Melbourne.

---

40   Webb 2006: 60.

41   Rev. Brown's photograph of the Motu 'water carriers' is in an album of his New Guinea views held in the Mitchell Library at the State Library of New South Wales (Album of Papua New Guinea, Rev. George Brown, ca. 1890–1905, PXA 925, Mitchell Library, State Library of New South Wales, Sydney).

Figure 9.4 J.W. Lindt, 'The Chiefs of Garia & Saroa, on board S.S. Governor Blackall', 1885.

Albumen silver, 15 x 20.5 cm.

Source: 'Picturesque New Guinea', vol. 3, acc. no. H42425, plate 65, Pictures Collection, State Library of Victoria, Melbourne.

Lawes was not the only European to play host to the Special Commissioner and the expedition party during their time in New Guinea. The Reverend James Chalmers, who had worked alongside Lawes since 1877, also acted as host, guide and interpreter for the expedition on its southward journey along the coast. Lindt captured him in a photograph of an assemblage of chiefs from the villages of Garia and Saroa who had been invited on board the *Governor Blackall* to receive gifts in exchange for ceasing aggressions against the village of Kaele (Figure 9.4). The image is mentioned by Lindt in his narrative and he writes that these men presented 'perhaps the most curious human group ever assembled on the deck of a steamer, the chiefs making no objection, although none of them had ever seen a camera before, and they probably supposed the proceeding to be some mystical rite preliminary to the negotiations'.[42] Whether the claim that the chiefs had never seen a camera is true or not, by recounting the encounter

---

42 Lindt 1887: 62.

in this way, Lindt underscores the importance of the task he was employed to undertake during the expedition while at the same time adding a further layer of meaning and interest to the image.

The camera as historical actor

Photography in the nineteenth century was a mechanical, chemical, social and cultural process. Unlike most photography today, taking a photograph in the late nineteenth century was not a simple or quick undertaking. More often than not, the cameras used were large and cumbersome objects. As Susan Sontag writes, 'Picture-taking is an event in itself',[43] and when Lindt and others photographed south-east New Guinea it was, in fact, more a case of *making* photographs than taking them. The word 'taking' implies little effort on the photographer's part other than exposing the negative. We know the equipment Lindt used in New Guinea due to the sales catalogue he compiled in 1888 in which he makes special mention of the lenses employed for his 'Picturesque New Guinea' series. Lindt took six lenses with him on the expedition, all of which fitted the flange of his whole-plate camera, thereby giving him 'a wonderful facility of securing almost any kind of subject'.[44] The camera itself, though Lindt does not describe it, would have been made of wood and, as it could hold whole glass-plate negatives, was a conspicuous and cumbersome apparatus needing time and effort to transport and set up.

Lindt had the luxury of a darkroom on board the *Governor Blackall*, which meant he did not have to develop his glass negatives in the field. By 1885 he was also using gelatin dry plates – a much easier process than the wet and dry collodion plates he had used up until 1880.[45] However, he did not have the equipment or comforts of his Melbourne studio on hand and had to make do with whatever makeshift facilities he could rig up in order to change and store away the exposed plates. In one instance, Lindt stole away to the hut that was his accommodation for the night and used a lamp covered in red cloth, all the while hoping there would be no interruptions by the curious 'natives'.[46] He also had to transport his camera, lenses and glass-plate negatives whenever he ventured out to photograph in the villages and surrounding areas, or rather the hired carriers would transport these for him. In his narrative, Lindt writes that 'the impedimenta required for even a few nights of camping [are] both bulky and heavy' and he had great difficulty making up 'portable packages for the

---

43   Sontag 1979: 11.
44   Lindt 1888: 44.
45   Jones 1985: 8.
46   Lindt 1887: 43.

native carriers'.[47] When the expedition party finally reached the village, often after many hours of walking over steep or uneven terrain and after several river crossings, subjects had to be scouted out and, in the case of human subjects, convinced to sit for the photographer. Some may not have seen a camera before, or been photographed, and part of the photographer's and/or interpreter's task was to persuade them to take part. Once posed in front of the camera the negotiations that ensued were frequently dictated by the technology – most notably, the need to sit or stand still due to the sometimes long exposure times. In the case of Lindt's photograph of the Garia and Saroa chiefs, the subjects were brought to him and the camera was another novelty in an already alien situation. However, the chiefs still had to be active participants in the encounter in order to ensure that the resulting image was a success. The photographic encounter between Lindt and the chiefs was therefore a collaborative undertaking: the Papuans 'watched' and 'obeyed' while Lindt prepared the equipment and instructed them.

Critical reflections on the camera's materiality and impact in colonial encounters have drawn attention to its cumbersomeness for the early outdoor photographers and its equation with disease, colonial guns and European aggression in 'first' encounters.[48] Early encounters in the Port Moresby mission district were occasionally shaped by an element of fear, as some Papuans believed the camera was an object imbued with deadly or harmful powers. However, investigating beyond the Papuans' initial responses to the camera reveals the extent of the technology's influence on encounters in New Guinea. While visiting the village of Boera in January 1876, Lawes found he was able to take photographs of the teacher's house and the village unhindered, but on attempting to take some of the people 'they were afraid that it would cause their death!'[49] This early encounter between Lawes and the people of Boera influenced his approach to photographing and he subsequently changed his method of working. In a journal entry written on 9 August 1877, Lawes notes,

> I want to get some [views] of the natives but must disarm their suspicion first or they will think as the natives at Boera that the camera is a disease-making machine. I have shown them those I have printed of Anuapata and the natives and they are greatly taken with them.[50]

---

47 Lindt 1887: 30.
48 See, for example, Morris 2009: 1; Ryan 1997: 143–144; Sandweiss 2002: 223.
49 Lawes, journal entry, 12 January 1876, microfilm CY292, Mitchell Library, State Library of New South Wales [hereafter ML].
50 Lawes, journal entry, 9 August 1877, microfilm CY292, ML.

To what extent this is Lawes projecting his experience at Boera onto the Papuans in question is unclear, but this is an interesting episode as it highlights the different responses that cameras and photographs could elicit. It also illustrates the way in which Lawes consciously used photographs in his interactions with Papuans as a result of earlier reactions to the camera.

That the photographic encounter in New Guinea in the late nineteenth century was often not a spontaneous or natural encounter is further evidenced by the positioning of several of the human subjects in Lindt's photographs. The problems presented by long exposure times meant that several of his subjects are posed in an almost regimented manner. Indeed, in several of Lindt's images containing large groups of Papuans the people are seated, which supposedly was the pose in which they were less likely to move and thereby ruin the shot. Lawes also reported on the problems associated with long exposure times and recounts one instance in a diary entry for November 1877 that occurred in the village of Kerepuna:

> Took a few photographs today of houses and some of the natives yesterday and today. The people are anxious to be taken, but many of them can't remember to sit still, will turn around to speak to someone when the plate is half exposed and so on.[51]

The experience of being photographed was a curiosity to the people of Kerepuna and by acquiescing to their requests Lawes was engaging in a similar transaction to those of the Reverend Brown, who, as Gardner and Philp note, 'used the making of a photograph to form relationships with local people'.[52] As mentioned above, Lawes even took photographs back to the villages in which they were taken and reported that the local people of his district were 'very much interested in the photographs', and that chiefs would approach him to have their portraits taken.[53]

The regimenting of Papuan bodies, which takes its most extreme form in the anthropometric and type portraits done by several visitors to the region, was therefore also often dictated by the demands of the technology rather than solely by current trends in science. Lawes took many such portraits in the makeshift studio he set up at the mission house in Port Moresby, and while Lindt had intended to take such 'head shots' as well, his efforts were thwarted by the strong trade winds that blew him and his 'studio' across the porch.[54] Such portraits pose the most complex and interesting set of questions, as they

---

51   Lawes, journal entry, 29 November 1877, microfilm CY292, ML.
52   Gardner and Philp 2006: 178.
53   Lawes, journal entry, 10 August 1877, microfilm CY292, ML; Lawes, journal entry, 13 August 1877, microfilm CY292, ML.
54   Lindt 1887: 55–56.

encapsulate the distance in the photographic encounter. They produce a sense of unease in most viewers today – a cultural unease stimulated by our knowledge of the photographer's intentions and the ultimate use to which such photographs were put. We can assume that in the case of Lawes and Lindt their intentions were related to recording racial differences and otherness; but the minds of the subjects, their motivations, thoughts and feelings are less clear. How might these encounters have been perceived by the portrait sitters as they were seated against a white-sheet backdrop outside the mission house in Port Moresby, instructed to turn one way, then the other, and to hold still, the camera almost 'pinning' them to the spot? For those who were used to Lawes and his camera this may have seemed an extension of his *in situ* photography in their villages. But what of those who came from villages further afield, where there was no mission station or teacher? Did they enjoy the experience or feel pressured into it? Such questions are difficult or, indeed, impossible to answer, but they are important questions if we want to begin approaching the nuances of such photographic encounters.

Conclusion

That the local Papuans frequently determined the nature of the photographic encounter is evidenced in certain episodes in the text Lindt wrote for his book, as well as in images from his series that record the guides and/or interpreters who accompanied him. While Lindt may have framed his narrative in such a way as to place himself centre stage as the explorer-artist-photographer – 'sallying forth' to photograph the people and exotic landscapes of New Guinea – he nevertheless notes the vital assistance given to him by Papuan guides and interpreters, as well as European interpreters, Polynesian teachers working for the LMS, and traders with knowledge of the local people and their culture. One European, in particular, may be said to have directly influenced several of Lindt's encounters – the LMS missionary, Reverend Lawes – and by placing the photographic outputs of these two men side by side, more searching questions can be asked about the nature of each man's encounters with the Papuans of south-east New Guinea. Finally, focusing on photography as a technological and social process allows a space to be opened up in which the local people can be seen to act in, and impact on, this particular form of exchange – what becomes clear is that the photographic encounter was not, and seldom is, one-sided.

References

Barker, Geoffrey 2010, 'Refracted Vision: Nineteenth-Century Photography in the Pacific', Master's thesis, University of Sydney.

Barringer, Tim 1998, 'The South Kensington Museum and the colonial object', in *Colonialism and the Object: Empire, Material Culture and the Museum*, Tim Barringer and Tom Flynn (eds), Routledge, London and New York, 11–27.

Cato, Jack 1952, 'The Great Lindt', *The Australasian Photo-Review*, July: 396–497.

——1955, *The Story of the Camera in Australia*, Institute of Australian Photography, Melbourne.

Driver, Felix 2004, 'Imagining the tropics: views and visions of the tropical world', *Singapore Journal of Tropical Geography* 25(1): 1–17.

Driver, Felix and Lowri Jones 2009, *Hidden Histories of Exploration: Researching the RGS-IBG Collections*, exhibition catalogue, Royal Holloway, University of London, in association with the Royal Geographical Society, London.

Gardner, Helen and Jude Philp 2006, 'Photography and Christian mission: George Brown's images of the New Britain Mission 1875–80', *The Journal of Pacific History* 41(2): 175–190.

Goldie, Andrew 2012, 'Andrew Goldie's memoir: 1875–1879', reprinted in *Memoirs of the Queensland Museum Culture*, vol. 6, Clive Moore, Steve Mullins (eds), Queensland Museum, Brisbane, 39–127.

Hays, Terence E. 1991, '"No tobacco, no hallelujah": missions and the early history of tobacco in Eastern Papua', *Pacific Studies* 14(4): 91–112.

Holden, Robert 1988, *Photography in Colonial Australia: The Mechanical Eye and the Illustrated Book*, Hordern House, Sydney.

Jones, Shar 1985, *J. W. Lindt: Master Photographer*, Currey O'Neil Ross Pty Ltd, South Yarra, Victoria.

Lindt, J.W. 1883, *A Few Results of Modern Photography*, Welch & Whitelaw, Melbourne.

——1887, *Picturesque New Guinea*, Longman, Greens and Co., London.

——1888, *A Few Notes on Modern Photography*, McCarron, Bird and Co., Printers, Melbourne.

Morris, Rosalind C. 2009, 'Introduction', in *Photographies East: The Camera and Its Histories in East and Southeast Asia*, Duke University Press, Durham, NC, and London.

Newton, Gael 1988, *Shades of Light: Photography and Australia 1839–1988*, Australian National Gallery, Collins Australia with assistance from Kodak, Sydney.

Orchard, Ken 1999, 'J. W. Lindt's Australian Aboriginals (1873–74)', *History of Photography* 23(2): 163–170.

Poignant, Roslyn 1992, 'Surveying the field of view: the making of the RAI photographic collection', in *Anthropology and Photography 1860–1920*, Elizabeth Edwards (ed.), Yale University Press in association with The Royal Anthropological Institute, London, New Haven and London, 42–73.

Quanchi, Max 2007, *Photographing Papua: Representation, Colonial Encounters and Imaging in the Public Domain*, Cambridge Scholars Publishing, Newcastle.

Quartermaine, Peter 1992, 'Johannes Lindt: photographer of Australia and New Guinea', in *Representing Others: White Views of Indigenous Peoples*, Mick Gidley (ed.), University of Exeter Press, Exeter.

Ryan, James R. 1997, *Picturing Empire: Photography and the Visualization of the British Empire*, University of Chicago Press, Chicago.

Sandweiss, Martha A. 2002, *Print the Legend: Photography and the American West*, Yale University Press, New Haven and London.

Sontag, Susan 1979, *On Photography*, Penguin Books, London.

Souter, Gavin 1963, *New Guinea: The Last Unknown*, Angus and Robertson, Sydney.

Webb, Virginia-Lee 2006, 'In situ: photographs of art in the Papuan Gulf', in *Coaxing the Spirits to Dance: Art and Society in the Papuan Gulf of New Guinea*, Robert L. Welsch, Virginia-Lee Webb, Sebastian Haraha, exhibition catalogue, Hood Museum of Art, Dartmouth College, Hanover.

Willis, Anne-Marie 1988, *Picturing Australia: A History of Photography*, Angus and Robertson Publishers, North Ryde, NSW, and London.

10

Noongar and non-Aboriginal people going along together (*Ngulla wangkiny, ni, katitjin Noongar nyidyung koorliny, kura, yeye, boorda*)

Len Collard and Dave Palmer

Introductions

Len: *Kaya. Yeye. Nidja Ngunnawal boodjar ngulla nyinniny.*

Ngulla koort kwoppa koorliny Canberra 2013. *Ngulla wangkiny kura Noongar wam koorliny. Nidja* Dave. *Nyuny kwel Len. Ngulla koorliny birrit* or Perth. *Ngulla karleep Whadjuk Nyungar boodjar.*

Dave: Hullo, we start by acknowledging Ngunnawal as the bosses for country in Canberra. Our hearts were very happy to visit in 2013 and to meet people and talk about Noongar and others going along together in the past. Len and I are from Perth in Western Australia. Noongar country is where our home fires burn.

We acknowledge that we first presented the ideas for this paper in Ngunnawal country where their home fires burn. We thought about it and wrote it in Noongar country.

Len: The conference organisers were right to observe that the history of colonial interaction in this country has included many instances of various Indigenous intermediaries (guides, translators, cultural attaches, workers, entertainers, friends and hosts) acting to assist and support the lives of the 'newcomers'. For example, my *moort* (family) has an extended history of offering *katitjin* (Noongar knowledge) about our *boodjar* (country), offering local sources of *daartj wer mearniny* (food, both meat and vegetables), *kep* (water) *karla* (warmth), *mia* (shelter), *balyi* (protection from danger), *kwoppa wiern* (spiritual goodness) and *djooripin moort* (familial and emotional support).

Dave: In the early years of colonial exploration there was no shortage of instances where those who came to Noongar country were either cruel or openly hostile.[1] On the other hand, as Noongar accounts and Wedjela diaries, journals and other historical documents demonstrate, many had a deep reliance on Noongar hospitality, knowledge and labour.[2]

In this paper we want to do two things. We would like to revisit some of the historical accounts of life in early colonial south-west Australia, drawing out instances where Noongar took on 'centre stage' in development, shaping the cultures, language, enterprise and everyday experiences of others. We also want to extend the way in which these early texts are interpreted by 'talking back' to the old voices through the adoption of what we will call Noongar hermeneutic methods. Most scholars who turn their attention to intermediary contact on the colonial frontier rely exclusively on an interrogation of the archival material. Some have buttressed this with recognition of the oral accounts of later years. What we want to do is propose additional methods for entering into conversations with the past, inspired by how the 'old people' (Noongar elders who have passed down their practices) read the country, listen to it speak and make assessments about what has happened.

Len: As a consequence, the style and methods adopted are a little unconventional. We draw on the cultural experience and knowledge gained from *koorliny yirra Noongar* (growing up Noongar), *katitjin Noongar wangkiny* (learning to speak the language) and *katitjin Noongar* (interpreting the 'evidence' using Noongar ways of thinking). We have also used the oral accounts of other Noongar as well as material from the written historical record. Some Western-trained historians

---

1   Bates 1992; Moore 1974 [1884]; Green 1984.
2   Haebich 1988; Hodson 1993; Pope 1993.

might not always accept the evidentiary strength of this approach. What is important here is that we are trying to move in and out of these traditions, Noongar and non-Noongar history making.

Boorna wangkiny ni: Listening to what has been written

Dave: We should start by explaining where and whom we are talking about.

Len: Those who identify as Noongar call the south-west corner of Western Australia their *karla* (where their home fires burn). Noongar are those who have *moort* and cultural affiliations to the first people who have lived in the region for at least 40,000 years. Noongar *boodjar* runs from as far north as Geraldton, south-east to the small town of Noongar on the Great Eastern Highway all the way as far east as Esperance on the south coast. This area takes in much of the state of Western Australia's wheat belt, many hundreds of kilometres in coastline, the state capital, Perth, and the regional cities of Bunbury and Albany.[3]

The word '*Noongar*' is translated by many as 'people' and is consistently used by those with affiliations to 14 dialect groups across the greater cultural block of Noongar. To Noongar, *boodjar* is critically important. In the old days each family group had their own *kaleep* (or camping places), which had enormous importance for them. For Noongar their *moort* and *katitjin* is intricately tied up with *boodjar*. This relationship is made manifest in the way people maintain their obligations to each other, their place and people's conduct. In *kura* (the 'old days') all Noongar were born into a complex system of social groupings that ensured each was a member of a 'skin' or moiety group. As well as sharing a place in these groups with other humans, Noongar 'skin' includes flora, fauna, rocks, rivers and places. In this way, different parts of *boodjar* are *moort* related in the same way as brothers and sisters, uncles and aunties. For many Noongar their 'old people' (those who have passed away) have symbolically and literally moved back to dwelling amongst the rocks, the trees and animals. For many Noongar this means that to visit and care for *boodjar* is to visit and care for *moort* (the old people).[4]

Dave: We also know from the colonial record that Noongar life has changed dramatically since non-Aboriginal people first came to the area to live in 1829. Long-held traditions, practices and language have been under enormous pressure, particularly between the 1850s and 1940s when families were forced

---

3   Collard 2007b; Hallam 1979.
4   Collard 2007a, 2007b.

to relocate away from their *karla* (or homelands). Many continued to be removed from their *moort* through generations of government policy that involved forced family separation. These shifts in life have been recorded in oral traditions, song and dance traditions and in fine artwork such as the 'Carrolup style' of painting that emerged from the Carrolup Mission near Katanning.[5]

Len: However, Noongar connection to *boodjar, moort, katitjin* and *wangkiny* (language) has proved remarkably resilient, managing to maintain, reignite and renew itself.[6] Often this is most clearly expressed in Noongar forms of art, craft, music-making, theatre, film and language revival.[7] However, what many people don't realise is that these ways of being and thinking are still incredibly powerful in shaping the way that people do history and think about their relationship to the past.

Dave: So why are these Noongar ideas so important when thinking about history in the south-west? Surely they don't alter the facts do they?

Len: On the contrary, these ideas have everything to do with the facts. How can we expect to make any sense out of what has happened with, to and by Noongar if we have no idea of the fundamental concepts and 'epistemological' frames that make sense to Noongar?

Dave: Well then, let us have a look at some of these ideas by turning to the early history of Noongar dealing with outsiders.

Moort ni: Listening to this Noongar family and people's oral accounts

Len: I want to tell you a story from *kura* or a long time ago. Many Noongar remember this story and tell it in a number of ways. It might help to set the scene. The account is also on the colonial record.

When they first realised that the big ships carried people, Noongar thought the coastal explorers were *djanga* or returned spirits of their *noitj moort* or dead relatives coming home again. Some were happy, and they welcomed the white spirit beings as members of their family. Noongar would have known that they had important protocols to carry out. It was their responsibility to teach their *moort* all about Noongar *katitjin* of the *boodjar*, because they had obviously

---

5   Haebich 1988.
6   Collard 2007a, 2007b.
7   Collard and Palmer 2006.

forgotten everything when they had 'died'. Some were frightened and ran and hid. Others invited the *djanga* back into their country and into their worlds literally as their kin or *moort*. They invited them to relearn about their *boodjar*.

Clearly without Noongar *katitjin* or help the *djanga* were *dwangabert, meeowbert* and *kaat warra djanga*. They were blind, deaf and spirits without knowledge. *Barl bidiboort wah?* Or they stumbled about in the bush as if they were lost. Sometimes Noongar helped the newcomers, reminding them of where they were and how to stay safe. Noongar still tell this story today and elaborate on different parts.

Dave: The explorer and later governor of South Australia and New Zealand George Grey realised as early as December 1838 that Noongar understood the newcomers as returned relatives. This he claimed was a perfectly reasonable conclusion given they had such profound connections to their country and an enormous reticence to give up or leave their *karleep* (home camp) for long periods. He recorded that:

> They themselves never having an idea of quitting their own land, cannot imagine others doing it; – and thus when they see white people suddenly appearing in their country, and setting themselves down in particular spots, they imagine that they must have formed an attachment for this land in some other state of existence; and hence conclude the settlers were at one period black men, and their own relations.[8]

I remember when I first began to look at historical documents I was immediately struck by the extent to which Noongar seemed open and hospitable to outsiders. Indeed, Noongar seem to have an extended history of welcoming and offering hospitality to outsiders.[9] I was also struck by the richness of the accounts from these times in the stories of contemporary Noongar.[10] Immediately I was confronted with the question of why this might have been so. Len, do you have an explanation?

Len: Part of the reason lies in the fact that Noongar were well accustomed to regular visits from *wam* or 'outsiders'. Noongar regularly visited country that was controlled by others, sometimes travelling hundreds of miles. Unless you have an understanding of the Noongar idea of *moort*, you might be forgiven for thinking that people lacked a bit of order or simply meandered about the place in a state of child-like utopian bliss. However, this was not the case. My old Pop, Tom Bennell, used to talk about how Noongar would regularly visit others, partly out of obligation to their *moort*, partly to carry out ceremonial, social

---

8   Grey 1841: 302–303.
9   Grey 1841; Green 1984.
10   Bennell 1993; Walley 1995; Collard 2007a, 2007b.

and economic 'business' and partly to help out with the sustaining of *boodjar*. Along with this is the obvious importance of story, song and performance in the life of Noongar family. *Moort* is one of the centre pieces of Noongar life both as a way of setting up relationships so *wam* (strangers) are incorporated, and of recording and transmitted through oral means amongst family and across the generations.[11]

Dave: This is also well accounted in the colonial record. According to archaeologist Sylvia Hallam, before colonisation meetings between different Noongar groups were highly structured events, 'with elements of ceremonial preparedness for conflict, formal peace-making, reciprocal exchange of gifts, and sometimes actual conflict and resolution of conflict'.[12] Outsiders were given a place within Noongar kin structures, facilitating participation in such things as education and knowledge attainment, marriage and sexual relationships, involvement in important meetings, the gathering and distribution of food, economic and social reciprocity, attendance at funerals, intergroup conflict and indeed contact and avoidance of others.[13] These stories of *wam* were also critical in the songs, dances and narratives that have continued to filter down from generation to generation.[14]

Len: This practice of comparing the archival records with contemporary oral accounts is not particularly novel for historians.

Wangkiny nitja boodjar ni: Listening and talking back to this country

Len: As mentioned earlier, in contrast to Western ideas about country as inanimate Noongar see it as part of our *moort*. Before we were born our *wiern* or spirit dwells in country. Our 'old people', or those who have passed away, go back to *nyinniny* (sit down) in country. Part of the job of these *boordier* (bosses of country) is to watch over their *moort* and keep us safe. They do this in many ways, including communicating with us through the wind, animals, our *kanya* (feelings) or *koornda* (sense of shame) and various other signs.[15]

Dave: So are you saying that it is possible to draw upon the 'old people', those who are no longer with us, in our history work?

---

11   Collard 2005.
12   Hallam 1983: 134.
13   Green 1984; Haebich 1988.
14   Scott and Brown 2005.
15   Clark 1994: 3.

Len: *Ngulla boodjar ngulla boordier* (our country is our boss and guide). Noongar learn a great deal by talking to country, literally singing out to the 'old people' and listening for its response. My *konk Whadjuck/Balardong* (my Whadjuck and Balardong uncle) Sealin Garlett reminded one time about his own experiences about this very matter telling me that:

> my Grandma (Yurleen) used to say this was to be passed on to her children and her grannies ... there are places where you find serenity; where you find a sense of belonging ... that this is a part of our place, this is a part of our area, our culture. *Nitcha boodjar koonyarn nitcha koorl buranginy boodjar karluk maya koonyarn wah. Deman deman and maam wiern kia moort koonyarn. Deman and maam noonookurt, boodjar koonyarn karla koorliny. Koorlongka boorda gneenunyiny.* Those words say that this is my country where I belong. This is *deman* and *maam*, my grandmother and grandfather's land, this is their land where their spirits move now. *Boorda* or later on, this is going to be the responsibility of my children and my children's children, their home and this place will always be linked to their spirit.[16]

As I said before, Noongar are literally related to country. We talk with it, walk with it, feed it and get nourished by it. Country reveals things to us. Let me explain some more. Before you and I were born we dwelt within country as spirits. When we pass away we head back to this form. Each tree, animal, rock and piece of vegetation are *moort*. We have brothers and sisters that are certain trees, rocks that are my grandparents, animals that are my parents.

Dave: Anthropologist Deborah Bird Rose puts it beautifully when she says:

> In Aboriginal English, the word 'country' is both a common noun and a proper noun. People talk about country in the same way that they would talk about a person: they speak to country, sing to country, visit country, worry about country, grieve for country and long for country. People say that country knows, hears, smells, takes notice, takes care, and feels sorry or happy. Country is a living entity with a yesterday, a today and tomorrow, with consciousness, action, and a will toward life.[17]

Len: Rose observes that the process of moving on country not only involves the young and their living elders 'going along together', it also demands we go along together with elders and ancestors long passed away.[18] Important here is the conception that the dead are an integral part of the maintenance of life and the education and experience of the young and living. It involves 'paying dues' to the ancestors, respecting the cycle of life in death and death in life and

---

16   'Nidja Beeliar Boodjar Noonookurt Nyininy', Murdoch University, wwwmcc.murdoch.edu.au/ multimedia/nyungar/.

17   Rose 2002: 14.

18   Rose 2004.

learning about their obligations to pass this on to those who 'come behind'.[19] To do this we sing out, announcing our presence, recognising those who have passed and seeking guidance about how to keep ourselves safe. We also listen to what country has to say to us, using language and singing out. Through this the history of a place becomes revealed.

Dave: We could describe this as forming a kind of hermeneutic circle, an interpretive process that involves speaking out and listening for a response to language. According to philosopher Hans-Georg Gadamer, what is crucial in any interpretive exercise 'is the process of identifying and linking the alien with the familiar information, selectively focusing the interpreters' search for new perspectives'.[20] This depends on people's enthusiasm to be open to new possibilities.[21] Gadamer might say of our interest in this paper, we need to playfully enter into dialogue with what some consider being alien or unfamiliar sources (Noongar language, country and concepts), thus allowing us to talk back to the historical texts until new understanding emerges.[22]

Perhaps one way to illustrate this is to turn to the way you interpret country through speaking and listening back to the Noongar sound(s) of place names.

Len: A specific contribution of Noongar in the south-west of Western Australia has been through the naming of places. Indeed more than 60 per cent of place names in the south-west are of Noongar origin. Today, when we look around Western Australia many towns, suburbs, freeways and street signs use Noongar names. In this way country speaks to us about its history. So prolific is the penetration of Noongar into the type of English spoken in the south-west that one could read a street directory and learn a great deal about country. Of course this is only possible if we have an understanding of language. However, it is not always this simple. Various forms of spelling have been used to record place names. Sometimes this Europeanisation of places makes it hard to figure out what a place means.

Dave: You have taught me the practice of speaking aloud the name of a place, sounding it out so as to help aurally process what the words might be. This often works to magically illuminate what a word might mean despite the fact that it has been written in a strange way.

Len: One example is the place name Manjoordoordap which is the old name for the modern place we know as Mandurah. According to the claims made by historians, Mandurah means a place of trade and festivities. By speaking out

---

19   Muecke 1997, 2004.
20   Regan 2012: 293.
21   Gadamer 2004: 4.
22   Gadamer 2004: 269.

this word and listening to how it sounds its meaning has come to me. *Manda* is the word for gathering to exchange. *Djookoord* is a wife or a female lover. *Ap, up* or *p* is the location of a place. Taken together and spoken out loud a much richer meaning revealed itself to us. In this way, Manjoordoordap speaks to us as a source of its own history, outlining the importance of the area as a place for romantic interludes during times of trade and exchange and cultural festivities. Interestingly, this continues to be the case to this very day, as Mandurah is a place that attracts lovers to meet, enjoy time by the ocean and relax in each other's company.[23]

Dave: It is through speaking and listening that meaning can become clearer. In this way the process of interpreting history literally demands listening to the sounds of words to explore the multitude of possible Noongar meanings hidden behind the oral and written pronunciation. In this way you are literally having a conversation with country, using your voice in a process of call and response.

Gnarl koorliny katitjin baranginy ni: Sweat, moving and grasping hold of this thing

Len: Being on *boodjar* is also important because it helps invigorate and make the country safe, productive and responsive. To be on country includes the act of keeping stories for that country alive. To stay away from country is to risk these stories passing away.

Dave: So in this way the business of doing history makes it necessary to be on and around country?

Len: One set of concepts that is strongly connected to ideas about *boodjar* is what we would call *ngulla koorliny* (going along together). For as long as I can remember an important ethic for growing up was that individuals go along on country with others, particularly those that are older and know what they are doing. I remember being taught as kids that country does not look kindly on you wandering off on your own. We were instructed in no uncertain terms that if we were to go off somewhere we do it in twos and threes. If something goes wrong then there is always someone to look after you. If one person doesn't know something then there is more chance of you surviving if there are two or three of you and you were with someone with experience.

Dave: What has this got to do with interpreting history in the south-west?

---

23   Take a look at the Nyungar Place Names website: www.boodjar.sis.uwa.edu.au.

Len: To put it simply, unless you produce sweat on country you are not going to find out anything about that place. This old Noongar practice of going along on country to understand that country and its history is a useful elixir to problems that come from spending all our time in archives and in front of our computers. When on country we get to see things that would have been instrumental in shaping what went on. Through listening to birds, the shape and strength of wind, seeing the species and experiencing the climate we get a clearer idea of how that country was used and what would have happened. Going out on country also helps us to see the presence of Noongar influence a little more clearly. It is also a good way of understanding the geographical and climatic context that confronted people.

Dave: It's also a greater way to open up our imagination to what might have gone on. For example, I remember walking with you through places like the Pinjarra massacre site, various parts of the Swan River and King George's Sound to help us get a sense of how Noongar would have experienced first sightings of the colonists, where they may have been able to position themselves and take note from topographical signs. This, combined with your knowledge of seasons, prevailing winds and hunting practices, helped us get a great sense of what was likely to have happened. It also gave me a strong sense of how important Noongar would have been to those who did not know the country. It helped me see how it is that Noongar have such a deep history of being next to colonists at many points in the history of the south-west.

Len: Being on country with Noongar changed the relationship some early colonists had with Noongar. As soon as colonists started exploring country it became apparent that Noongar (particularly the young and fit) possessed very sophisticated knowledge of immense value. Noongar presence in an area became a sign that food, water, other valuable resources, and knowledgeable men and women were close to hand.[24] People like John Drummond, an early settler from York, came to realise that 'good land to the aborigines [sic] was good land for them'.[25] The most popular areas included King George's Sound, the Swan and Murray estuaries, the Avon Valley, Leschenault Inlet, the Vasse district, and the rich country around Pinjarra.[26]

Dave: The Western Australian writer Jesse E. Hammond records that *Wedjela* travellers, shepherds, merchants and explorers looked for well-marked Noongar *bidi* or foot-tracks 'like cattle-pads and just as plain'.[27] Indeed, a good deal of these tracks formed the basis many of today's main roads.[28]

---

24   Markey 1976: 9.
25   Wollaston cited in Hallam 1991: 48.
26   Markey 1976: 8.
27   Hammond 1933: 18.
28   Clarke 1996: 76.

For example, when surveyor Ensign Dale first travelled east from the Swan River through the rolling hills and into the Avon Valley, he commented on the potential for utilising country already worked by Noongar.[29] Likewise, John Bussell saw the potential for exploiting pasture around Talanup (today known as Augusta) which had been carefully tended by Noongar firestick hunting.[30] Patrick Armstrong argued that Noongar created a 'mosaic of plant communities' highly conducive to European systems of agriculture. He claimed that the complex environmental systems were due to 'variations in the manner and frequency of firing as much as to differences of soil, topography and water relations'.[31]

Len: In 1836 Lieutenant Henry William St Pierre Bunbury was stationed in the York, Pinjarra and Busselton districts, and over the course of the next 18 months undertook various exploratory excursions in the region.[32] Whilst in Noongar country he noted that:

> By these fires ... the country is kept comparatively free from underwood and other obstruction, having the character of an open forest through most parts of which one can ride freely; otherwise in all probability, it would soon become impenetrably thick, and ... the labour cost of clearing would be so greatly increased as to take away all the profit, and it would change the very nature of the country, depriving it of the grazing and pastoral advantages it now possesses ... It is true that we might ourselves burn the bush, but we could never do it with the same judgment and good effect of the Natives.[33]

This is neither hardly surprising nor terribly unique to exploration in the south-west of Australia. We see similar patterns in the attempts of early British colonial 'explorers' and administrators. Indeed, Captain Arthur Phillip, the first Governor-Designate to the colony of New South Wales, was instructed by his authorities to seek out signs of Aboriginal people so that their knowledge could be turned to the advantage of the newcomers.[34] Long has the West recognised the value that the East has to itself.[35]

---

29 Garden 1979.
30 Bussell 1833.
31 Armstrong 1978: 31.
32 Cammilleri 1966.
33 Markey 1976: 11.
34 Rolls 1998: 64.
35 Voltaire cited in Clarke 1997: 3.

Kanya koort weirn ni: Listening to this feeling in and of the heart and spirit

Dave: Len, the word intermediary has its roots in the medieval Latin *intermediatus*: 'lying between'. Likewise, the business of being intimate takes its meaning from the Latin *intimus* 'inmost' (adj.) or 'close friend' (n.). In the 1600s the idea of intimacy was often used as a euphemism for 'sexual intercourse'.[36] What about matters of the heart and soul?

Len: An idea that I have been raised with is the importance of *kanya koort*. Thinking and knowledge exchange works best when our *koort* (hearts) are *kanya* (in good spirit). Our capacity for understanding the past is very much tied up with our ability to use our spirit, what we often describe as our emotions and intuition.

Dave: My friends from the Kimberley talk about the importance of the *liyarn*, a part of the human body where the spirit sits, in knowledge. Without a healthy *liyarn* one cannot understand country, history and culture. Conversely, an unhealthy *liyarn* can lead us to make mistakes, get confused and misjudge where we are.

Len: Yes, that is like our *kanya* or *wiern*, our spirit. Healthy *kanya* and *koordan* comes from being on country, being with our family and singing on and for country. You rely on it and it becomes stronger and more illuminating. If we try and go about finding things out about country without our old people and without listening to our *kanya* and *koordan* then we will become *kaat wara*, we will get confused.

I have no doubt Noongar *kanya* and *koordan* have been important to non-Noongar. In the early days they were often physically and socially isolated from contact with others. It is true that this isolation was not good for their spirit. It drove many to fear Noongar. As a result many came to rely on Noongar for friendship, comfort and sexual intimacy.

Dave: There are many examples of this. Noongar like Tommy Windich rode at the head of many important exploration parties led by people like the Forrest brothers.[37] He would have combined his keen observation and navigation skills with this approach of 'intuiting' and reading the country's many signs.

---

36   Etymoline 2014.
37   Wilson 1981: 115.

Len: This is right: 'feeling' our way around country and around history is much more important than we often admit. Indeed, we use metaphors that reveal our reliance on *kanya* and *koordan*. Historians 'follow leads', 'track down' the truth, head down a particular 'path', 'pick up' clues and 'dig up' the facts. Perhaps we need to be a bit more honest, take some clues from Noongar and get out on country as a way of doing history.

Kura, yeye, boorda: From the past, until today and into the future: Conclusion

Len: Let me read to you what the early Quaker traveller James Backhouse observed about the influence of Noongar:

> A few of the boys assimilate themselves, in some degree, with the servants and the Settlers, and the little Blacks are often the playfellows of the white children; but even, under these circumstances, the Blacks are growing up in much the same state of barbarism as their ancestors; and it is a question, whether the white children do not learn more of barbarism from the Blacks, than the Blacks acquire of civilisation from the Whites.[38]

Dave: If early colonial historians were to have embraced contemporary terminology, they may well have described some Noongar as expert consultants, cultural attachés, diplomatic peacekeepers or historians. During very early colonial life in the south-west, many non-Aboriginal people, many parties of 'explorers', and many government officials were assisted in some way by Noongar guides and cultural experts. Indeed, as historian Ian Clark reminds us, those exploration parties which eschewed advice and help from Aboriginal people, such as the ill-fated Burke and Wills expedition, failed.[39]

Len: Noongar acting as guides set up the pattern for many later engagements which saw distinctly Noongar knowledge and expertise become important for people living in the south-west of Australia.[40] We could also say that they offered insights to those of interested in talking about this history. We might say:

> *Noonook 'kura boordier'. Noonoook koorliny bulla. Noonook boorna wangkiny ni, moort ni, boodjar ni, wangkiny ni, geenunginy boordier ni, koorliny katitjin baranginy ni, wiern kanya and koordan koort.*

---

38   Backhouse 1843: 539–540.
39   Clark 1994: 21.
40   Richards 1993: 56.

Dave: Yes, what you say is 'later on whitefella gain much knowledge because they followed along behind Noongar, being taken in as family, taught language and introduced to country, becoming strong in knowledge and spirit'. Noongar have a long involvement in offering their methods of coming to 'know' about things. Non-Noongar have a long involvement in drawing upon this intelligence and helping it to open up knowledge. If we want to better understand the past surely we could do well to draw upon Noongar methods and combine listening to the written sources, listening to family accounts, listening to country, speaking and listening out loud to country, making some sweat and getting out of the archives, listening and looking for signs of Noongar agency and using our spirit and heart to see.

Len: *Kia, boorda ngulla kwoppa Noongar wangkiny, ni, katitjin – kura, yeye, boorda. Boorda noonarkoort geeninginy nitja wah?*

Later on then we will be able to speak, listen and think wisely about the connections between yesterday, today and the future. Later on you will see, eh?

References

Armstrong, Patrick H. 1978, 'The Aboriginal practice of firing the bush: the evidence of early newspapers', *Journal and Proceedings of the Royal Western Australian Historical Society* 8(2): 31–34.

Backhouse, James 1843, *A Narrative of a Visit to the Australian Colonies*. Hamilton, Adams and Co., London.

Bates, Daisy 1992, *Aboriginal Perth: Bibbulmun Biographies and Legends*, Peter J. Bridge (ed.), Hesperian Press, Carlisle.

Bennell, Tom 1993, *Kura*, revised edition, Glenys Collard (ed. and comp.), Nyungar Language Centre, Bunbury.

Bussell, J. 1833, 'Report of an expedition to the northward from Augusta by Mr J. C. Bussell', in *Journals of Several Expeditions Made in Western Australia During the Years 1829, 1830, 1831 and 1832: Under the Sanction of the Governor General Sir James Stirling, Containing the Latest Authentic Information Relative to that Country, Accompanied by a Map*, Joseph Cross (ed.), Facsimile, University of Western Australia Press, Nedlands, 178–185.

Cammilleri, Cara 1966, 'Bunbury, Henry William St Pierre (1812–1875)', *Australian Dictionary of Biography*, National Centre of Biography, The Australian National University, adb.anu.edu.au/biography/bunbury-henry-william-st-pierre-1846/text2137, accessed 28 July 2014.

Clark, Ian D. 1994, *Sharing History: A Sense for All Australians of a Shared Ownership of Their History*, Australian Government Publishing Service, Canberra.

Clarke, John James 1997, *Oriental Enlightenment: The Encounter between Asian and Western Thought*, Routledge, London.

Clarke, Peter 1996, 'Adelaide as an Aboriginal landscape', in *Terrible Hard Biscuits: A Reader in Aboriginal History*, Valerie Chapman and Peter Read (eds), Allen and Unwin, St Leonards, 69–93.

Collard, Len 2005, 'Nidja beeliar boodjar noonookurt nyininy: A Nyungar interpretive history of the use of boodjar (country) in the vicinity of Murdoch University, Perth, Western Australia', wwwmcc.murdoch.edu.au/multimedia/nyungar.

——2007a, 'Wangkiny ngulluck Nyungar nyittiny, boodjar, moort and katitjin: talking about creation, country, family and knowledge of the Nyungar of south-western Australia', in *Speaking From the Heart: Stories of Life, Family and Country*, Sally Morgan, Tjalaminu Mia and Blaze Kwaymullina (eds), Fremantle Arts Centre Press, North Fremantle, 279–298.

——2007b, 'Kura, yeye, boorda: from the past, today and the future', in *Heartsick for Country: Stories of Love, Spirit and Creation*, Sally Morgan, Tjalaminu Mia and Blaze Kwaymullina (eds), Fremantle Arts Centre Press, North Fremantle, 59–80.

Collard, Len and David Palmer 2006, 'Kura, yeye, boorda, Nyungar wangkiny ngulla koorlangka: a conversation about working with Indigenous young people in the past, present and future', *Youth Studies Australia* 25(4): 25–32.

Gadamer, Hans-Georg 2004, *Truth and Method*, second edition, Sheed and Ward Stagbooks, London.

Garden, Donald S. 1979, *Northam: An Avon Valley History*, Oxford University Press, Melbourne.

Green, Neville 1984, *Broken Spears: Aborigines and Europeans in the Southwest of Australia*, Focus Education Services, Perth.

Grey, George 1841, *Journals of Two Expeditions of Discovery in North-West and Western Australia, During the Years 1837, 1838 and 1839*, T. and W. Boone, London, 2 vols.

Haebich, Anna 1988, *For Their Own Good: Aborigines and Government in the South West of Western Australia 1900–1940*, University of Western Australia Press, Nedlands.

Hallam, Sylvia J. 1979, *Fire and Hearth: A Study of Aboriginal Usage and European Usurpation of South-Western Australia*, Australian Institute of Aboriginal Studies, Canberra.

——1983, 'A view from the other side of the western frontier: or "I met a man who wasn't there …"', *Aboriginal History* 7: 134–156.

——1991, 'Aboriginal women as providers, the 1830s on the Swan River', *Aboriginal History* 15(1): 38–53.

Hammond, Jesse E. 1933, *Winjan's People: The Story of the South-West Australian Aborigines*, Imperial Printing Co., Perth.

Hodson, Sally 1993, 'Nyungars and work: Aboriginal experiences in the rural economy of the Great Southern Region of Western Australia', *Aboriginal History* 17(1): 73–92.

Markey, D.C. 1976, *More of a Symbol than a Success: Foundation Years of the Swan River Colony*, Mount Lawley College of Advanced Education, Perth.

Moore, George Fletcher 1978 [1884], *Diary of Ten Years of an Early Settler in Western Australia*, University of Western Australia Press, Nedlands.

Muecke, Stephen 1997, *No Road (Bitumen all the Way)*, Fremantle Arts Centre Press, South Fremantle.

——2004, *Ancient and Modern: Time, Culture and Indigenous Philosophy*, University of New South Wales Press, Sydney.

Pope, Brian 1993, 'Aboriginal message and mail carriers in South Western Australia in the early and mid-nineteenth century', *Portraits of the South West: Aborigines, Women and the Environment*, Brian de Garis (ed.), University of Western Australia Press, Nedlands, 57–77.

Regan, Paul 2012, 'Hans-Georg Gadamer's philosophical hermeneutics: concepts of reading, understanding and interpretation', *Meta: Research in Hermeneutics, Phenomenology and Practical Philosophy* 4(2): 286–303.

Richards, Ronald 1993, *Murray and Mandurah: A Sequel History of the Old Murray District of Western Australia*. Mandurah City Council, Pinjarra.

Rolls, Mitchell 1998, 'Cultural colonisation: Monica Furlong and the quest for fulfilment', *Australian Feminist Law Journal* 11: 46–64.

Rose, Deborah Bird with Sharon D'Amico, Nancy Daiyi, Kathy Deveraux, Margaret Daiyi, Linda Ford and April Bright 2002, *Country of the Heart: An Indigenous Australian Homeland*, Aboriginal Studies Press, Canberra.

Rose, Deborah Bird 2004, *Reports from a Wild Country: Ethics for Decolonisation*, University of News South Wales Press, Sydney.

Scott, Kim and Hazel Brown 2005, *Kayang & Me*, Fremantle Arts Centre Press, Fremantle.

Walley, T. 1995, 'The good samaritan robin redbreast (demlark): A New Norcia Dreamtime story', in *A Town Like no Other: The Living Tradition of New Norcia*, David Hutchison (ed.), Fremantle Arts Centre Press, South Fremantle, 37.

Wilson, Helen Wood 1981, *Bushman Born*, Artlook Books, Perth.